CREATIVE INTERVIEWING

The Writer's Guide
to Gathering Information
by Asking Questions

2nd Edition

KEN METZLER

University of Oregon

PRENTICE HALL, Englewood Cliffs, New Jersey 07632

METZLER, KEN
    Creative Interviewing : the writer's guide to gathering
information by asking questions / Ken Metzler. -- 2nd ed.
        p.   cm.
Bibliography:
Includes index.
ISBN 0-13-189747-0
    1. Interviewing in journalism.   I. Title.
PN4784.I6M4 1989
070.4'3--dc19
                                              88–9797
                                                 CIP

Editorial/production supervision
    and interior design: Mary Kathryn Leclercq
Cover design: Diane Saxe
Illustrations: Thomas H. Bivins
Manufacturing buyer: Ed O'Dougherty

© 1989, 1977 by Prentice-Hall, Inc.
A Division of Simon & Schuster
Englewood Cliffs, New Jersey 07632

Printed in the United States of America
10 9 8 7 6 5 4 3 2 1

ISBN   0-13-189747-0

Prentice-Hall International (UK) Limited, *London*
Prentice-Hall of Australia Pty. Limited, *Sydney*
Prentice-Hall Canada Inc., *Toronto*
Prentice-Hall Hispanoamericana, S.A., *Mexico*
Prentice-Hall of India Private Limited, *New Delhi*
Prentice-Hall of Japan, Inc., *Tokyo*
Simon & Schuster Asia Pte. Ltd., *Singapore*
Editora Prentice-Hall do Brasil, Ltda., *Rio de Janerio*

For Betty Jane
"Look there—a patch of blue! Things are definitely brightening up!"

Contents

3

THE TEN STAGES OF THE INTERVIEW

4

AN INTERVIEW CASE HISTORY

5

THE CONVERSATIONAL DYNAMICS OF INTERVIEWING

6

BEING INTERVIEWED

11

INTERVIEWING FOR QUOTES AND ANECDOTES 106

12

TELEPHONING, NOTE TAKING, AND TAPING 116

13

SPECIAL PROBLEMS 128

14

THE BROADCAST INTERVIEW 143

Preface

In the preface to the first edition of *Creative Interviewing*, I suggested that a startling discovery had prompted this book. In teaching magazine writing and editing classses at the University of Oregon, I learned that many journalism students possessed a fear bordering on paranoia when asked to *interview* somebody, particularly such exotic characters as fire chiefs, city managers, and ordinary people who had been thrust into extraordinary circumstances that made them noteworthy.

So I started an experimental class to cope with the problem. Eventually I wrote a book, the first edition of *Creative Interviewing*. A dozen years elapsed. The book went through ten printings, and I continued to teach ever-increasing numbers of students in the class, which became a standard course: no longer experimental. I also conducted workshops for professional journalists in such widely diverse locales as Toronto, Omaha, New York, and Tulsa.

During those dozen years I learned a lot about interviewing. In that time I oversaw many interviews, about 7,000 of them, according to my rough calculations. Some I actually witnessed in the classrooms, workshops, and laboratories; others I learned about through classroom discussion, through student papers, and through the students' descriptions of their triumphs and failures.

Failures? In one of those rare and lovely little ironies of academic life, I have learned particularly to reward failure. I don't encourage failure, exactly, but I confess to having given A grades to student interview projects that were abject failures. One can learn more from a magnificent failure than from a modest success. Those interviews where everything goes wrong are wonderful learning experiences. So the student who writes a paper that recaptures the failed interview in detail and explains what may have caused the problem can earn a high grade. The chief benefit of such an exercise is that we *all* learn from the failed interview experience. Indeed, much of the advice in this second edition comes from such experience.

Among the lessons learned is how badly you can screw things up in an interview and still emerge with pretty good information. How does falling down a flight of stairs just before your interview rate as a candidate for failure? As we learn in Chapter 1, such an experience actually seemed to enhance the conversational rapport rather than hampering it.

So into this book have gone the distillations of those dozen years of interviewing experience. Into it have also gone further readings and interviews with professionals.

You'll find this new edition substantially the same as the first, but with several major additions. The book continues to discuss such essentials as identifying the problems of interviewing, showing the stages of the typical interview, and exploring the principles of human conversation on which the interview is based. It continues to suggest ways to plan your interview, to cover a newsbeat, and to conduct a broadcast interview or a personality interview. It continues to draw heavily on research findings in academic fields other than journalism itself. Much of the material has been updated with new examples, although a few old favorites have been retained from the first edition.

Several new chapters have been added, however.

1. An elemental and hypothetical interviewing case history has been added (Chapter 3) because students, in the early stages of their interview classes, seem to need an example on which to pattern their first interviews.

2. Material about *being* interviewed has been expanded into a full chapter. To be asked questions yourself—thus to learn the kinds of approaches and questions to which you can or cannot comfortably respond—is to sharpen your own skills. Students especially learn from failed or clumsy interviews such as the one depicted in Chapter 6.

3. Material has been added on listening and observation (Chapters 9 and 10) because experience with students has suggested that almost nothing in their college programs focuses on these two essentials of information gathering.

4. The first edition's brief discussion of interviewing for quotations and anecdotes has been expanded into a full chapter. I've found that the absence of colorful quotations and illustrative anecdotes is *the* major fault with student-written articles and features. The manuscripts tend to represent academic writing, thus displaying barren snowfields of abstraction rather than the warm enclaves of human experience. In short, they are not much fun. The writing is flat. They are dull largely because students have not learned

how to populate their nonfiction stories with real people. It's an interesting paradox: people are fascinating, yet student-written stories about them often fail to capture the fascination. As Chapter 11 points out, however, certain interview techniques seem to encourage people to talk as they normally would (anecdotally and sometimes colorfully) rather than assuming the facade of stiff and formal—and usually dull—conversation.

5. The first edition's short sections on telephone interviews, note taking, and tape recording have been expanded to a full chapter, largely because they represent the problems most frequently raised in classes and workshops.

In sum, the "startling discoveries" that inspired the first edition continue to accumulate and have found their way into the revised chapters of this second edition. To be a student of the journalistic interview is to become a lifelong learner.

Sources
and Acknowledgments

Information in this book comes largely from the insights gained in teaching university classes and conducting workshops on the subject of journalistic interviewing. Through fifteen years of conducting such sessions, I've kept in close contact with the problems of journalistic interviewing, problems that range from shyness to arrogance. The insights gained from observing about 1,000 students conduct the seven interviews required of each student in the interviewing class have worked their way into every chapter of this text. Four other sources contributed to this book.

1. I have continued through the years to build on work done during a sabbatical leave (1974–1975) in the newsroom of a daily newspaper, the *Honolulu Advertiser*. I interviewed both reporters and news sources on the subject of interviewing and news gathering. I have continued to conduct similar interviews through the years in Oregon, in Washington, D.C., and at numerous points between.

2. Like most journalists, I learned interviewing the hard way, by trial and error and by making just about every mistake possible. My journalistic projects over the years have included interviews for news and feature articles for the *Advertiser* and other newspapers, interviews for magazine articles (*Science Digest, Farm Journal,* and many others), and interviews of residents of my home state for two books, *Confrontation* (1973) and *The Best of Oregon* (1986). Much of what I have learned in thirty-five years of such work has found its way into this text.

3. During the fifteen years of specific concern with the topic of interviewing, I have surveyed the literature of interviewing and related topics. I have prepared an extensive bibliography from a variety of fields, largely to encourage journalists to read more widely about interviewing in fields other than journalism itself. Unfortunately, precious little research has been done in journalistic interviewing, so we are forced to review and adapt principles of interviewing in other fields. Keeping pace with the literature has been aided by the establishment in 1987 of a new academic journal, *Questioning Exchange,* edited by James T. Dillon of the University of California–Riverside and published by Taylor & Francis, London.

4. I've been interviewed myself, many times. Just as students learn from being interviewed, so have I. Part of this experience comes from class projects where students must interview me (usually en masse like a news conference). At one time, when the interviewing class was small and intimate, I had students interview me by phone for the final examination—an experience so terrifying for them (so they informed me) that I finally dropped it as a requirement. Many of the interviews were done by professionals. On one occasion I survived fourteen news media interviews over a two-day period. The sessions focused on a "research" project I had undertaken, a largely tongue-in-cheek quest to find the "lonesomest community" in my home state, Oregon, most of which is sparsely populated. The fourteenth interviewer, a radio reporter, was by far the worst interviewer of the group; he was new on the job and didn't know what to ask. On the phone he confessed his inexperience and suggested that I merely talk for five minutes while he taped my comments. He obtained a splendid interview—largely because I gave my best answers to the best questions asked by the previous thirteen interviewers. Such are the vagaries of creative interviewing—a sample of the kind of insights I have undertaken to provide in this volume.

But I had a good deal of help, so much that I wish I could name every one of the approximately 1,000 students who attended my interviewing classes through the years. Or the hundreds of journalists and interview sources who contributed ideas and insights. Alas, I shall have to settle for a few:

Michael Thoele, newspaper feature writer, who teaches the interviewing seminar at the University of Oregon from time to time.

Karl Nestvold, a faculty colleague, who keeps me posted on broadcast interviewing.

Tom Bivins another faculty colleague for illustrations.

Lisa McCormack, who introduced me to a wide array of prominent Washington, D.C., journalists one memorable evening but who remains herself among the most skilled and resourceful of interviewers covering the nation's capital.

And special thanks to the following persons who have offered comment and criticism at various stages of these two editions: John L. Griffith, Del Brinkman, Al Hester, Kenneth S. Devol, David Rubin, Joe Scanlon, and John F. Dillon.

CHAPTER ONE
Interviewing Problems

> **Q.** What are your views on the future of
> humanity?
> **A.** Why should I care? I have just swallowed a
> cyanide pill. I'll be dead in twenty seconds.
> **Q.** Uh-huh, okay . . . . Now I'd like to ask about
> your hobbies—uh, do you engage in any kind
> of athletic endeavors? . . .

When you think you have an interviewing problem, consider the plight of a young woman named Nora Villagran. She was about to begin her first assignment on her new job as entertainment writer for the San Jose *Mercury News*. Her task: interview the famous folk singer, Joan Baez. Nora put on a fine white dress that morning, complete with hose and high heels, and hurried to her rendezvous with her first entertainment celebrity. A small problem intervened. Nora fell down a flight of steps en route to the interview. She received only minor scratches and bruises, but she was bleeding through her white dress, and her stockings were torn. Now what? Change clothes and repair the damage? No time for that. Cancel the interview? She might not get another chance.

Nora decided to plunge ahead, and she appeared at Joan Baez's doorstep in her disheveled condition, which now included puffy eyes from crying over the likely demise of her new career in journalism.

Joan Baez answered the door in her bare feet. She looked at Nora. "You've either been mugged or been in a car accident—which was it?"

"Neither," said Nora. Her recounting of events led Joan to invite her to use the bathroom to repair the damage. She prepared an ice pack for Nora's swollen ankle.

She suggested that Nora take off her shoes and her torn stockings. They wouldn't have an interview, she said. Rather they'd be, in Joan Baez's words, "just two barefooted women talking."

Just Two Barefooted Women Talking

Recounting the incident months later, Nora concluded that it had been one of her best interviews, one that involved great candor on both sides. What seemed like a disaster turned out precisely the opposite. Nora saw a barefooted celebrity exhibiting an unusual degree of candor—not in spite of the reporter's disheveled appearance but quite possibly because of it.

This is not unusual. Nora, having taken a course in interviewing, had already heard of similar incidents through the class discussions, and she says her decision to go on with the interview drew inspiration from the "spilled coffee" story.

We'd been discussing that story for at least ten years in the interviewing classes I teach at the University of Oregon. It concerns another young woman, Ann Curry, who became a television reporter in Los Angeles. For a class assignment, she interviewed a prominent businesswoman. The conversation, though, failed to develop the candor that Ann had hoped for. She suggested that they repair to a nearby coffee shop. Sitting side by side at a counter, they conversed more amiably now. Then Ann—in a wild gesture to emphasize a point—spilled her coffee. Mortified, she thought she had blown the interview. But, to Ann's astonishment, the woman began talking more candidly. It was almost as though Ann's social gaffe had allowed the woman to drop her own facade of dignity. Suddenly they could become just a couple of women talking.

The story illustrates something unpredictable and ironic about human nature. We can discern at least two truths from the incident.

One suggests that if you want candor—if you want human responses rather than defensive exaggerations and false facades—try revealing a little of yourself in the conversation.

The other is that striving for technical perfection can intrude on candor. Better that you should be just two barefooted women talking. Only through such exercises in candor does the full dimension of the human condition come forth. The best journalists savor the unpredictability of human response, and they pass it along to their audiences when they can.

The spilled coffee story has inspired a tradition of long standing in those interview classes: *Can you top that story?* Several former students have done so. In Florida, reporter Scott Martell showed up at a black-tie occasion wearing blue jeans, ratty tennis shoes, and a smudged T-shirt. He'd dressed for a ride on a fishing boat in pursuit of a story, but bad weather led to a cancellation. The paper reassigned Scott to a furniture store opening instead. Nobody told him it was a formal occasion. Even if someone had, Scott had no time to change clothes. Yet he looks back on it as one of his best interviews. He still wonders why.

WHAT IS YOUR INTERVIEWING PROBLEM?

The stories about Nora, Ann, and Scott seem to suggest that a higher level of candor and truth emerges in the context of "just two barefooted women talking" than amid the strictures of the formal interview. The latter seems to produce the false fronts, defensive exaggerations, and cover-ups that characterize much of what has passed for journalistic interviewing in recent years. The interviews we see on television have become so strained that an authority on oral history interviewing claimed that he'd learned quite a bit about interviewing by watching *Meet the Press*. He studied the reporters' questioning techniques, he said, and then he did just the opposite.

You do indeed sometimes find reporters aloof and hostile—maybe that's how they believe they have to act with celebrities and high-level government officials. But most people respond best to an amiable and friendly approach. Reporters often ask questions in an adversarial manner, yet most studies on questioning technique suggest that the nonjudgmental approach works best to enhance rapport and candor. It shows that you have come not to judge, not to argue, not to destroy, but to listen, to ascertain the facts, to learn. When people discover that you have come not as judge and jury but as a student of human affairs, they become more amiable and candid.

Under such circumstances, the professional interviewer ought to be able to talk with practically anybody about practically anything, to paraphrase the title of a book by TV interviewer Barbara Walters. Name the most despicable of human beings—my candidate would be a rapist or a child molester—and ask yourself: Could you interview this person without displaying your contempt? To the extent that you can answer yes, consider yourself a professional journalistic interviewer. Professionalism in journalism requires not that you win arguments or display moral superiority, but that you learn something from the encounter that you can share with an unseen audience. How can you be sure that you have nothing to learn from a child molester? The insight you gain from such an interview could help others in ways we cannot always predict.

Given what seems to be a reasonably valid truth from the episodes described here, it seems remarkable that so many young journalists claim to have enormous problems in interviewing.

"I just hope that my source will do all the talking," said one young journalism student, a woman, "so that I won't have to ask any questions."

In the almost two decades I have taught classes in interviewing, the technology has changed, but the list of problems has not. Interviewers who now take their notes on tiny lap-top computers still profess inability to cope with a taciturn interviewee (henceforth called respondent in this text). How do you avoid that awkward silence when you can't think of a question to follow an unexpected answer? Do you just go to your next question on the list? That could lead to non sequiturs almost as silly as the one illustrated at the head of this chapter.

Students attending interviewing classes at the University of Oregon have for almost two decades filled out questionnaires identifying their most severe interviewing problems. The exercise seems to bring two results: the problems that inexperienced interviewers can voluntarily identify and the problems they can't. Although fully one-fourth of the nearly 1,000 students have identified their own lack of self-confidence as a major problem, no one to date has suggested that falling down a flight of stairs or clumsily spilling your coffee could somehow become an interviewing problem. The two categories of problems are interesting when compared.

THE OBVIOUS PROBLEMS

First, consider the problems of which young journalists are all too painfully aware, judged by their responses to the survey in the interviewing class.

1. Lack of Self-confidence. Students have many colorful ways of expressing it. "Basically, I am a chicken," said one woman. "I wish I could find a way to avoid breaking out in a cold sweat during an interview," said a man. By whatever label, it remains the number one problem of novice interviewers. A tally of comments over the years reveals that almost a third of the women and twenty percent of the men confess to having some form of the problem. "Most people are, I think, inherently uncomfortable in an interview situation," suggests one student. "Although they are normally quite capable of carrying on a pleasant conversation with others, when it comes to what they consider a 'formal' interview, they tend to become tense and unnatural."

That brings up some interesting questions: Does an interview always have to be "formal"? Or could it be something more equivalent to two barefooted women talking? Does "tense and unnatural" demeanor by the interviewer lead to similar behavior by the respondent? And under which circumstances—tense and unnatural or barefooted women talking—will the most candor and truth likely emerge?

2. Thinking up Questions during the Interview. This is number two on the list of problems perceived by students. A student explains: "Let's say I ask a question, and the answer I get is something totally unexpected—I never know what to say next." Question: Is getting an unexpected answer necessarily bad?

3. *Getting Complete Information.* "I had a wonderful conversation with my source," complained one student reporter, "but when I sat down to write a story, I realized I had nothing new or interesting to write about." Another student had a "first-rate interview" with a young policewoman who worked on a rape crisis team. The conversation with her had been fabulous, he said. But when he reviewed his notes, he realized that he had practically no information about her or her work. He confessed that he'd done most of the talking. He must have been enormously charming, for he had a date with her that very evening. The problem of getting complete information is a real one, and it's also an encouraging sign when students mention it. It shows a certain dissatisfaction with their own work, and it suggests a promise to try harder next time. Question: Are problems 2 and 3 related—that is, could the inability or unwillingness to think up new questions to meet unexpected turns of conversation contribute to a lack of new or interesting things to write about?

4. *Taking Notes.* People who have to write an account of the interview consider taking notes a major problem. This seems surprising, given that college students are experienced note takers. But journalistic note taking is different. First, you must identify and record the major points. That's not easy in informal conversations where people just talk, rather than organizing their thoughts for formal lectures. Second, you must record supporting material and illustrations—colorful quotations, revealing anecdotes, facts, figures—all necessary to support the points. Question: Can you integrate note taking into the conversation? Could you suggest to a respondent, "I love what you said about arms control—will you give me a moment to get that into my notes?" Could such a comment actually enhance the conversational rapport?

5. *Coping with Taciturn or Uncommunicative Respondents.* Students consider this their worst nightmare—you ask all the right questions but receive only short answers or none at all. Question: Does the attitude of the interviewer have anything to do with the response? Would the interviewer who acts as judge and jury likely get more terse responses than the one who listens nonjudgmentally?

6. *Coping with a Respondent Run Amok.* In contrast to problem 5, this one deals with the respondent who babbles on at great length and in excruciating detail. Some do it by nature; others do it to throw the questioner off the track. It's a growing problem, given that public officials and business leaders often take expensive courses in "how to be interviewed" and have learned such techniques as "bridging," which means subtly changing the subject whenever a potentially sensitive question comes up.

These six by no means complete the list of problems perceived by inexperienced journalists. They are merely the most common problems. Among the others are (1) beginning and ending an interview, (2) asking sensitive or potentially embarrassing questions, (3) preparing for an interview, (4) establishing an easy-going rapport with respondents, (5) securing interviews with busy and important people, and (6) formulating, in the words of one student, "the perfect question that will unlock the interviewee and cause him to rattle off enormously candid and heretofore unpublished insights without my having to think up a single additional question."

THE UNSEEN PROBLEMS

The problems that students *don't* perceive may be more important than the ones they do. Indeed, failure to recognize these deeper problems often underlies the problems students do recognize. Nudging a garrulous person back on the interview track, for example, requires that you know what the track is— that is, the purpose of your interview. And failure to understand the purpose of your interview is a common problem. Had you understood the purpose and explained it candidly, your garrulous performer might not have strayed so recklessly. Or, if the conversation did stray, you'd have brought it back on course sooner.

Here, based on almost two decades of watching student interviewers in action, is my list of hidden problems. Knowing about them can make interviews easier right from the start.

1. An Aversion to Asking Questions for Fear of Being Shown up as Ignorant. True learning is accompanied by pain, says the philosopher Aristotle. The painful truth is that human nature dictates a behavior that tends to cover up gaps in knowledge. How many men (men, more than women, I suspect) will drive miles out of their way rather than stop to ask directions to an unknown address? A natural, childlike curiosity seems unfortunately to go out of style as people reach a certain age (high school age, perhaps). Young people consider the asking of questions a little uncool. Too bad. But it has ever been thus, as this Chinese proverb suggests:

He who asks is a fool for five minutes. He who does not is a fool forever.

The Chinese exhibit especially good sense in such matters. The following wisdom emerged from a Chinese fortune cookie:

He who is afraid of asking is ashamed of learning.

2. Failure to Define Clearly and State the Purpose of the Interview. When our interviewing laboratory exercises call for pairing off students to interview one another, this emerges as the number one problem. About half of the respondents in the interview pairs complain that, while they answered questions to the best of their ability, they never really understood why the interviewers asked a certain sequence of questions. As a result they felt slightly uncomfortable: What was it, precisely, that the interviewer wanted to know? Some respondents tried to guess at the purpose. When they guessed wrong, as they usually did, they gave answers that were not useful. In short, they had strayed off the track and didn't know it. How could they know? They were never informed.

3. *A Lack of Enthusiasm and Natural Curiosity about People and the World at Large.* People are not insensitive or unperceptive. They quickly perceive the level of interest a journalist has in a topic under discussion. And when they perceive a lack of interest, they sometimes turn to short, terse answers to avoid the pain of talking to anesthetized ears. Some journalists who lack the requisite enthusiasm and curiosity about people and the wider world may be forever condemned to interviewing politicians and other garrulous zealots who are as insensitive to the niceties of human communication as the journalists are themselves—a fate not undeserved.

4. *Failure to Listen.* Items 3 and 4 are probably related. If you're not interested in the topic, you won't listen, and vice versa. Perhaps the solution is to heed the advice of a famous journalist, A. J. Liebling: "Reporting by and large is being interested in everyone you meet." This problem cannot be dealt with in a single paragraph (see Chapter 9 for a full discussion). For now, just consider the mostly nonverbal ways we *show* that we aren't listening and that we don't really intend to. These include excessive note taking, lack of eye contact, talking too much, slumped body posture, excessive and gratuitous argumentation, absence of follow-up questions, and a wide array of nervous mannerisms, such as drumming fingers or sitting cross-legged and jiggling a foot.

5. *Lack of Preparation.* Who can blame you for being nervous about an interview when you haven't done your homework? How would you know what questions to ask? You would feel as unarmed as a college student who had not bothered to study for an exam. Preparation involves learning what has come before, and this can range from going to the newspaper library to study clips from previous stories to conducting preliminary interviews with people who know your respondent. Preparation also involves giving serious thought to what information you're seeking and what questions might logically draw out that information. Assisted by student interviewers, we once surveyed about 150 public officials on what they perceived to be the interviewing problems of working journalists. Lack of preparation stood at the head of everybody's list. "They literally don't know what they're talking about," said one official.

6. Failure to Probe.   Many inexperienced interviewers think the proper approach calls for asking a set of questions and securing some kind of answer to each one. If you think that's true, you can be replaced by a computer. By contrast, good interviewers know that the best questions in any interview are the ones they didn't know they were going to ask. It's not question one—the one you've prepared—that yields the best answer. The answer to question one leads to question two and so on until you arrive at the heart of the topic. The more you've prepared for the interview, the easier you'll find it to improvise subsequent questions on the spot. It probably doesn't matter that those subsequent questions aren't as nicely rehearsed and phrased as the planned questions. What matters is that you are listening and thinking throughout the interview and asking new questions based on those thoughts.

"I understand that you, and/or, your organization are directly responsible for the recent upsurge (or as some would have it, incline) in the current situation facing the global, economic environment; or, at the very least, partially in favor of inverted trade sanctions against all, or most, of the European Common Market, at least according to my most reliable sources. Would you care to comment?"

7. Vagueness.   College students tend to generalize and intellectualize. Their interviewing and writing thus fail to realize the drama and impact that concrete details could provide. They're forever asking academic kinds of questions, such as this one of a reformed alcoholic: "Do you think alcoholism is a disease?" Such a question prompts the respondent to give an equally abstract and dull answer. Journalists, by contrast, need specifics. They need, as one student suggested, something "interesting and different to write about." A group of students was on a more productive track when asking this question of a reformed alcoholic: "How much alcohol, all told, did you consume over the fifteen years of your alcoholism?" It took a while to make the calculations, but the answer emerged dramatically: nearly 2,000 gallons of wine, beer, and whiskey. The cost of all this? Loss of forty jobs, two wives, eleven wrecked cars, and "a hell of a lot of self-esteem."

8. Careless Appearance.   One young woman complained that she kept getting brush-offs from counselors and doctors in her attempt to conduct interviews for an article on the emotional problems of college women. Someone suggested she dress for the occasions—stop wearing to interviews the tattered blue jeans and faded Stanford sweat shirt that were her campus uniform. She did, and her ability to collect interview data improved dramatically.

9. Convoluted or Overdefined Questions.   In one community a TV reporter became famous for her long questions. A story—likely apocryphal—suggests that when she starts a question the entire press corps exits the news conference, returning minutes later just as she's finishing the question. An interviewer ought to practice confining questions to fifteen to twenty words and depend on follow-up questions if the answer does not yield the appropriate information. (In the TV reporter's defense, follow-up questions are not always possible in news conferences, as they are in individual interviews.)

10. Defining before Seeing.   Some reporters have a tendency to see a story first and then collect only that information that confirms their idea of what the story is about. A Honolulu businessman separates reporters into two categories: the "listeners" and the "dogmatists." The dogmatic reporters, he says, "always put you on the defensive. They seem to have all the answers and they merely want you to confirm what they already have decided. The listener *really* listens. He takes the issue from various angles, gets underneath it and over it and around it. Then he wants to know who else he should talk to about it."

11. Laziness.   Some reporters—possibly the same ones who complain about how boring or taciturn their sources are—expect brilliant, dramatic, highly entertaining answers to dumb, fumbling questions. It happens occasionally, particularly when you encounter respondents sufficiently zealous or egotistical to burst forth no matter what—politicians, maybe, or civic boosters or authors or axe grinders. But, for the most part, reporters have to do their homework and set their goals lest the result become aimless and superficial.

12. Insensitivity. Experienced journalists, more than beginners, suffer from this malady, usually without knowing they have it. Once on the job, journalists soon come to understand that interviewing is little more than talking to people—the sort of thing you do every day, much like bank tellers or investment counselors. Sometimes journalists forget that being interviewed is a once-in-a-lifetime experience for many respondents. These experienced reporters often fail to identify themselves, fail to define the purpose of the interview, and fail to make clear the reason for a sequence of questions.

Given the spectacle of arrogant, aloof, and hostile interviewing seen on televised news conferences and talk shows—not to mention TV drama's depiction of reporters as brash, rude, and obnoxious—it's a wonder that anyone will talk to media representatives at all. That they do so, often eagerly, remains one of the more remarkable circumstances of American journalism, something to be discussed in subsequent chapters.

CHAPTER TWO
Concepts of the Interview

> **Q.** Charlie Remington, famous world traveler and
> bon vivant—you've been to the Arctic and the
> Antarctic, you've been to deepest Africa,
> you've explored the bottom of the ocean,
> you've flown hot-air balloons over the Alps,
> you've dated the world's most glamorous
> women in Paris and New York and Rio, you
> know Nuku'alofa and Pago Pago like the back
> of your hand, and you've even worked the oil
> rigs in Alaska— how's it feel to be one of the
> truly great men-about-the-world, Charlie?
> **A.** Fine.
> **Q.** Uhhhhhhhhhhhh. . . .

Reporters are no better than their sources. No talking reporter ever wrote a good story. Reporting means being interested in everything and everyone. Interviewing represents eighty percent of reporting. Listening—picking up those half-articulated thoughts and subtle nuances of meaning—that's what reporting is all about.

These comments by experienced journalists all seem to point in one direction: the importance of good interviewing. Perhaps you realize this already and are eager to start. But the best interviews are done by the people who understand the dynamics of human conversation, and so a discussion of interviewing principles should be our first concern.

Interviewing, after all, involves more than simple technique: if this problem, then that solution. A computer could do that. Computers, indeed, show great promise for routine kinds of journalistic interviewing to produce standard news stories such as auto accidents or wedding announcements: "fill-in-the-blanks" news writing.

NONJUDGMENTAL DEMEANOR: THE BASIC PRINCIPLE

What makes human communication successful? In 1952, Carl Rogers, famous counseling psychotherapist, and an associate, F. J. Roethlisberger, proposed two theories (Rogers, 1952). The first theory suggests that communication becomes successful when party A convinces party B that what he or she says is true.

The second suggests that communication becomes successful when party B makes it possible for party A to say what he or she really thinks and feels, regardless of whether B believes it's true or not.

Journalistic interviewing works best under the second theory, which serves as the guiding principle for this text. Mike Fancher, executive editor of the *Seattle Times,* has placed the same thought into a journalistic context. He suggests that good interviewers encourage sources to say what they really think and feel, rather than having to think about what they say.

One thing a successful interview is not. It's not a session in which an arrogant, self-righteous interrogator browbeats a hapless respondent. If that's your concept of interviewing, you'll not find much encouragement in these pages. Successful interviewers—assuming factual accuracy, perhaps even truth, is the primary objective of an information-gathering interview—come to listen and understand, not to accuse and judge. A good interviewer tries to ensure that both parties emerge with their self-esteem intact.

HOW JOURNALISTS OBTAIN INFORMATION

Compared to other methods of information gathering, interviews account for eighty to ninety percent of a journalist's research. The other methods are documentary research and observation. Journalists do, indeed, write from documents or use them to prepare for interviews, but the documents tend to supplement the interview, not replace it. The same is true of observation. Observation alone seldom produces a news story, but it's particularly useful in providing touches of description or action. On-camera interviews have a built-

---

*See Bibliography for full citations.

in observational aspect, but the viewer does most of the observation, not the interviewer.

Interviews come in several types. The information-gathering process that we normally think of as the journalistic interview is but one of them. The field includes interviews used for counseling, employment, oral history, opinion surveys, medicine, law enforcement, and any number of business and personal conversations whose purpose is to elicit information. It also includes courtroom cross-examination, even something called the "persuasive" interview, the kind you normally encounter in automobile sales rooms. Most of them have points in common. Indeed, most of our knowledge of journalistic interviews comes from academic areas other than journalism. Precious little research has been done on journalistic interviewing. We draw on such areas as psychology, social science, oral history, and anthropology.

DEFINING THE JOURNALISTIC INTERVIEW

What is a journalistic interview? The typical definition calls it a "conversation between two parties for the purpose of gathering information on behalf of an audience."

The definition describes routine news interviews. The typical pattern of the event-oriented news story prompts the questions asked in the interview. A television reporter calls the state highway patrol office, for example, to inquire about a fatal auto accident. The reporter asks questions based on what information a typical accident story requires, one that begins, "A fatal car crash took the life of a local resident tonight . . . . " The traditional news criteria are the Who, What, When, Where, How, and Why, and the telephone conversation can follow that pattern: *What happened?* (details of how car spun out of control, plunged down a steep bank into the river), *Who was involved?* (source gives names, ages, and addresses of dead and injured), *When?* (tonight about 9), *Where?* (location cited), *How (did it happen)?* (driver lost control on slick, wet pavement), *Why (did it happen)?* (driver had been drinking.)

The reporter may ask a few cleanup questions: Were any citations issued? Are police continuing to investigate? Will charges be filed against the driver? Were any unusual circumstances involved? ("Why, yes, good thing you asked that. Seems that a young passerby dove into the river to rescue a child trapped inside the car. . . . " This new information will add drama to the story.)

THE CREATIVE INTERVIEW

The term *creative* has been added to this book's title to reshape slightly the definition of the journalistic interview. Let it now read: "A two-person conversational *exchange* of information on behalf of an audience to produce a level of intelligence neither participant could produce alone."

Most beginning journalists assume that they start at zero knowledge and, through preparation and questions, learn about a topic or event. As you gain experience, however, you bring a higher level of knowledge to the conversation. A veteran sportswriter probably has more overall knowledge of football than the young quarterback being interviewed. The writer can thus bring a certain historical perspective to the interview—the young quarterback has many of the same passing qualities of a Joe Namath, let's say, and the writer's questions will reflect that perspective.

One veteran sportswriter, Ken Moore, who covers track and running for *Sports Illustrated*, is a runner himself, having placed fourth in the 1972 Olympic marathon run. Moore clearly does not start with zero information about running. He even incorporates running into his interviewing methods, often accompanying such famous runners as Joan Benoit and Henry Rono on their training runs, committing the highlights of the conversation to memory, to be recorded in his notes afterward.

To suggest a further dimension of creative interviewing, imagine an experienced journalist undertaking a book-length biography of a celebrity. Most people, famous or not, tend to exist day by day without much thought about the principles that guide their lives. How much thought have *you* given them? Have you ever written them down or even spoken them? Most of us do not. It is only when our biographer asks questions to elicit those concepts that we begin to see ourselves in a new light. Thus, through creative interviewing the pair arrives at some conclusions about the meaning of the celebrity's life. More about creative personality interviewing will appear in Chapter 17.

A final dimension of creative interviewing centers on use of the imagination in picking the people you interview and in developing the overall plan for asking questions.

To cite some obvious examples, an interview with a mountain climber contains more color and excitement if done on a windy mountain peak than in the television studio. Perhaps you can interview the river rafting enthusiast between scenes of exciting whitewater or the airplane stunt pilot while flying upside down over Pike's Peak. It just takes a little creative imagination and courage.

Similarly, creative interviewing calls for careful selection of persons to interview. When a group of women's magazines agreed to publish articles in support of the Equal Rights Amendment, one of them, *Woman's Day*, decided to focus on just one person: a woman who had changed her mind from being mildly against the ERA to becoming strongly in favor of it. How did the change take place? What incidents contributed to her change of heart? Anyone who has studied the technique of dramatic literature—the characterization, suspense, and irony within a series of incidents that lead to a climax—will recognize the narrative possibilities in interviewing and writing about such a person. They require only that an interviewer search out the details.

So we are talking here about a form of creative writing—the kind of writing that reads like fiction in that it shows life in action. But because we deal with factual reality, we employ methods of creative interviewing to supply the details that will allow us to write factual articles that read like fiction.

Why do we bother? Probably to avoid what one editor, Edward Kosner, of *New York* magazine, calls "mushball journalism." That's journalism that concentrates on facts—perhaps a whole reservoir of facts—but lacks thematic direction, lacks life, lacks dramatic impact. Some of our most memorable literature tells us more about life through storytelling than a thousand purely factual reports ever could. We don't recall the factual details of the Great Depression of the 1930s so much as we remember one family coping with the crises of migrants seeking a new life in California in John Steinbeck's classic novel, *The Grapes of Wrath.*

More about this element of creative interviewing will appear in subsequent chapters, notably Chapters 10, 16, and 17.

Meanwhile, to summarize, creative interviewing involves these points:

1. An *exchange* of ideas and information that creates an intellectual level that neither party could achieve alone.
2. Introduction of novel circumstances into the interview in the choice of respondents, settings, and topics to bring up.
3. A desire to explore and exchange ideas on personal and conceptual matters, such as what makes a celebrity tick.
4. Seeking elements of drama through the interview, such as identifying and portraying a main character confronted with a problem that's resolved after one or more dramatic incidents.

THE CREATIVE QUESTION

The very act of asking a question contains an element of creativity, largely in its implied desire to extend your knowledge from the known into the unknown. Chapter 7 will explore questions in more detail, but for now picture the way a question formulates in your mind. It happens when we reach the limits of our knowledge and want to know more. We know how to drive to Cleveland but not how to find Euclid Avenue, and so we have to ask.

The same principle guides our thinking in journalistic interviewing. That's why we prepare for interviews, so that as we approach a respondent we know what has already been published. We begin to formulate questions that will elicit material that has *not* been published. Clearly, the more we prepare, the further we can extend our knowns. The novice interviewer asks the sailboat skipper why the wind makes the boat go. The prepared interviewer asks the skipper what happens in this era of electronic navigation when the loran receiver is out of commission and you don't have a sextant.

And so it is with most news situations. A building catches on fire—that much we know. We don't know what caused it, so we ask. We don't know if anyone was hurt or how much damage resulted, so we ask. We interview a celebrity whom we've seen constantly on TV and in the movies. But we don't know what she's *really* like in a personal way, so we ask questions to find out. Or we wonder what it would be like to be mobbed by adoring fans wherever you go, so we ask. We ask, that is, assuming we can't find out through pre-interview research. If we discover through research that she hates those adoring fans, then we wonder about other unknowns. What does she do to avoid them? What does she do when she can't avoid them? And when we obtain the answers to those questions, we'll no doubt have additional questions. A creative interviewer, guided by a lively curiosity, never runs out of questions.

Questions, then, help you extend your knowledge into the unknown. That is the principle behind the questioning, creative or otherwise, done to obtain information. The journalistic question takes you from the security of the known into the uncertainties of the unknown. It's a little like stepping off the firm diving board into the unknown depths of the swimming pool.

Some find it frightening. Others find it exhilarating to let their questions draw them into ever-more exotic unknowns and to learn from the answers. The more daring (read: creative) your approach, the more you will learn. Instead of asking the who, what, why of still another traffic accident, you may be asking the what and why of drunk driving, perhaps focusing on a dramatic case history of how a life-style of drunkenness and recklessness led to a fatal traffic collision. Creative approaches, in short, will pull you out of the tired old routine.

COMMON TYPES OF INTERVIEWS

Journalistic interviews vary considerably. One basic division comes between the directive and nondirective interview. The terms come from the psychological counseling field but relate as well to information-gathering inquiries.

In the directive interview, the interviewer asks lots of questions, expecting and usually obtaining short answers.

Q. Did you see the robbery?
A. Yes.
Q. Where were you located when you saw it?
A. Just inside the front door.
Q. Was the robbery done by one person or more than one?
A. Far as I could tell, there was just one.
Q. Male or female?
A. Female, I think . . . it's hard to tell with the mask on.
Q. Did she come through the front door? [And so on.]

The nondirective interview lets the other person do the talking. Thus:

Q. Did you see the robbery?

A. Yes.

Q. Okay, please start at the beginning and tell me what you saw.

A. Well, I was standing just inside the front door, and . . . .

In the second case the interviewer lets the respondent tell the story, whatever can be remembered. At the end, the interviewer may ask a few specific questions for expansion or clarification. In the situation depicted here, the nondirective interview works better; it saves a lot of questions and elicits a more accurate account. In other instances, when you're seeking specific information, the directive interview eliminates useless diversions.

Both have a place in interviewing technique, the directive for specific information, the nondirective for more wide-ranging conversations, as in a personality interview. A variation of the directive interview is the scheduled interview—the type normally used for opinion polls. Here the interviewer operates from a script to interview a variety of people who comprise a carefully selected sample that represents the general population. Here the interviewer asks each respondent the same questions in precisely the same way so that the responses can be tabulated.

Here are some other interview types common to journalism:

Routine Newsgathering. As already described, the reporter seeks the details of an event using the 5 W's and the H. It is used by both print and broadcast personnel who usually take notes and write news articles from the information gathered.

Sound Bites or Actualities. These are broadcast terms, and they refer to the interviews on camera from which perhaps 20 to 60 seconds of the conversation will show on the newscast. The interviewer typically starts by asking the questions that will put the event or situation into understandable context; then, with the camera turned on, re-asks questions that will yield an appropriate sound bite.

Special-purpose Information Gathering. Unlike the routine newsgathering effort, the interviewer here sets a specific and usually narrow purpose and asks only those questions related to the purpose. An example is the person-on-the-street interview in which you ask several people an opinion on some major issue of the day. Magazine writers often narrow their interviews to highly specialized topics, consistent with the specialized nature of magazines. *Working Woman,* for example, might interview office workers on some specific subject such as stress or office politics. Here the interviewers seek to learn from the respondents' experience information that will help readers cope with the problem.

Project Interviews. A variation of the special-purpose interview, the project interview seeks to gather information from a wide variety of sources in order to develop a documentary effort, such as a book, a comprehensive news or magazine article, or a broadcast documentary. To develop a documentary on drug addiction, for example, interviewers may consult a wide variety of sources ranging from junkies on the street to counselors and scientists. Writers and editors then synthesize the many interview fragments to form a coherent statement. The project need not always be grimly serious; these interviews may lead to light features such as "a day at the county fair" or a sidebar on how people are coping with unusually hot weather.

The Extended Broadcast Interview. Here the entire interview runs on the air and the respondent is a "guest." You see these daily in such diverse programs as *Good Morning America* and *Tonight.* More on broadcast interviews will appear in Chapter 14.

The Personality Interview. Some of the broadcast interviews cited above are personality interviews in which some celebrities or otherwise interesting persons talk about themselves. More extensive personality interviews are done by biographers—more soul-searching kinds of interviews designed to produce book-length biographies or detailed magazine profiles. More on this will appear in Chapter 17.

The Exploratory Interview. This is a fishing expedition, conducted to obtain ideas for news stories or to gain one's bearings for a major documentary or similar project. A reporter sits down with the governor to talk of issues facing state government. The governor happens to mention a new project on the drawing boards for a crackdown on drunk drivers on the state highways or maybe talks of the administration's concern for overcrowded prisons or polluted rivers. Any of these could form the basis for a news story, perhaps to be obtained directly from the governor or from other sources. Some journalists call it "coffee cup reporting." It is discussed further in Chapter 15.

The See-It-In-Action Interview. Personal observation combines with the asking of questions to secure details sufficient to develop a nonfiction narrative account of a scene or anecdote. The result is factual writing that reads like fiction. More about this appears in Chapter 10.

CHAPTER THREE
The Ten Stages
of the Interview

Q. General, how long have you been in military
life?

A. If you don't know anything about me, why do
you want to interview me?

The typical interview runs through ten stages. Four of them occur before you even meet your source. The success of the six subsequent stages depends largely on how well you accomplish the first four. The ten steps are:

1. Defining the purpose of the interview
2. Conducting background research
3. Requesting an interview appointment
4. Planning the interview
5. Meeting your respondent; breaking the ice
6. Asking your first questions
7. Establishing an easy rapport
8. Asking the bomb (potentially sensitive questions, if any)
9. Recovering from the bomb, if necessary
10. Ending the interview

Let's examine each stage.

DEFINING THE PURPOSE

What, precisely, do you expect to accomplish through your interview? Why did you select *this* respondent? Lack of clear answers to these questions can turn your interview in a fumbling nonconversation that confuses both parties. Not only must *you* have clear answers, but you must communicate them to the other party. Having the answers will accomplish two things. First, it will make your questions easier. You "never know what to ask," as some beginners assert, because you lack a clear purpose. Your interview drifts frequently off the track because the track has never been defined. Second, your candor about the purpose can sweep away many barriers to communication. Sources tend to be wary of requests for interviews these days. It helps to state precisely what you want and to announce, by your tone of voice as well as your words, that you plan to listen and understand, not confront or accuse. Both parties can use your statement of purpose as a guide to information to be exchanged.

Purposes vary. Let's say you plan to interview the county sheriff. Will you do so to write a news story about a particular crime or an arrest or a jail break? Overcrowding in the jail? Crime trends? A personality profile? Perhaps you are writing a story about the family problems of law enforcement officers, and the sheriff is one of a dozen or so officers you'll interview. Whatever the purpose, you must inform the sheriff. Purposes can change, of course, sometimes because new information has altered the picture.

CONDUCTING BACKGROUND RESEARCH

This step may vary widely. The veteran sportswriter interviewing the young quarterback may have merely to rely on memory or may review clips of previous stories about this or other athletes. The reporter conducting interviews on problem marriages may visit the library to find books or magazine articles on marriage and family topics. The one writing about the jail break may quickly review clips of news stories about previous jail breaks—or about the escapees if their identity is known—in the newspaper or station library. The person writing the personality story about the sheriff may want to interview other persons *about* the sheriff—colleagues, enemies, friends, family—anyone who can provide insight into the personality.

Reporters in a hurry, as often happens in busy news offices, may find that other reporters or editors can offer suggestions about the respondent or about the issue to be discussed. Suppose you've been assigned to interview the undersecretary of agriculture during a stopover at the airport. You have ten minutes to prepare. A quick call to the agricultural extension agent or to the president of your local wheat grower's league can yield enough information on major farm issues to permit a reasonably intelligent interview.

REQUESTING AN INTERVIEW APPOINTMENT

In this stage you call your proposed interviewee to set up an appointment. Before you do, though, keep in mind that no one has an *obligation* to grant you an interview. You may have to do a little subtle (or maybe overt) persuasion.

Every interview contains some negotiation. You may, for example, have established your purpose, but what if your respondent declines to cooperate? Perhaps the sheriff doesn't want to talk about jail conditions, but will willingly discuss child abuse, drunk drivers, or marriage and family life. Or, as often happens with celebrity respondents, you can't even get past a protective secretary. What now?

Two factors may help you. First, if your purpose seems sufficiently compelling, the respondent may readily agree. Or the respondent may agree under certain conditions (the sheriff will discuss family problems but doesn't want to discuss a son who died of a drug overdose). The second helpful element is your sales ability. While people can find lots of reasons not to grant an interview, you'll find just as many reasons to grant one. Consult the list (Chapter 6) and prepare your sales pitch accordingly.

Many objections can be overcome with a compelling statement of purpose when you request your interview. Your own enthusiasm can also help. It's wise to avoid use of the word "interview"—too formal sounding. Professional journalists learn to call it "a quiet chat" or "a discussion" or anything *other* than interview.

Let's say you call a prize-winning high school teacher. "Ms. Johnston, may I interview you on the subject of education?" Your topic is too broad and vague and dull. The term "interview" sounds ominous. Make your purpose more clear, be more enthusiastic, and give a few examples of provocative questions you'd like to ask:

"Ms. Johnston, every so often in my job as reporter I hear of the exciting things going on in your classes—the time you had students acting out Shakespearean roles, for instance, or the time you had your students out searching for the elusive Spencer Butte ghost. It sounds fascinating. But I'm curious. How do you think up these ideas? How do students react? How about parents? What if your students don't believe in ghosts? I'd like to write a feature article about your teaching practices—may I come over some time to hear some answers to these and similar questions?"

Chances are that Ms. Johnston, flattered by your remarks and comfortable with the kinds of questions you say you'll ask, will put up only token protest, if any. She might say she's only one of fifty teachers at the school, and it's embarrassing to be singled out, and besides she's very busy, and—

If you've done your homework—background preparation—you'll have counter arguments at your fingertips—her teaching award has *already* singled her out, her methods should inspire other teachers, it's her chance to clear up misunderstandings that parents may have, you've already talked with other teachers about her and they say she's the most exciting educator since William James, and so forth.

Don't forget the details: time, place, additional details, such as a preliminary rundown on questions you plan to ask or the topics to be covered (she, too, may need to prepare for the interview). Don't list all your questions; just give a preview. Ask if she has any questions about the interview; she might wonder about such things as whether the interview will be on-camera, what she should wear, whether you'd like to attend her class, and so on.

PLANNING THE INTERVIEW

With the interview appointment secured and the background research substantially complete, this stage requires you to think through just how you will conduct the interview. Here's where you cope with that "taciturn" or uncommunicative respondent. Here you also consider the topics to be covered, conversational icebreakers to start the interview, specific questions to be asked, and so forth. Consider, too, the kind of information you want. For a newspaper feature story you may want illustrative anecdotes, a need that will guide some of your questions.

Here, too, you must consider your respondent's personality. You may have to repeat your purpose several times with garrulous respondents lest they get carried away with useless diversions. Or you may guide taciturn respondents onto conversational pathways that cater to their special interests. The prepared interviewer will have researched the respondent sufficiently to know of these special interests—gourmet cooking, let's say. So you plan to talk about cooking before getting down to business.

This important stage of interviewing will be discussed in detail in Chapter 8, but for now remember two points:

First, make your plans consistent with your stated purpose, the one you mentioned when making your appointment. Failing to do so casts suspicions on your motives. If you change your mind about the purpose, let the other person know as soon as possible.

Second, build into your plans the likelihood of unexpected answers and surprising turns in the conversation. Indeed, the better-planned your interview, the greater the chances that the interview will *not* go according to plan. That's good. The well-prepared interviewer does not seek answers that merely confirm what is already known. The interviewer seeks to explore *new* territory. To recognize something new, you have to know what's old. The sudden fresh insight, the new twists, the new pathways explored, the unexpected turns, the recalling of new illustrative anecdotes—all these are the golden nuggets of interviewing. They come more easily to the interviewer who has planned for them.

Breaking the ice

MEETING YOUR RESPONDENT: BREAKING THE ICE

Custom dictates that strangers, meeting for the first time, test the conversational waters with icebreaking techniques born of social convention. "Hello, how are you? Nasty weather outside. Have you ever seen such cold weather? By the way, we have a mutual friend— your old college buddy, Jim Duncan, says hello." And so forth. You should prepare icebreakers uniquely suited to your respondent. If you're interviewing a lawyer, scan the headlines for interesting court cases that you can talk about ("What do you think of the Supreme Court decision on . . . ?"). Keen observation of the respondent's surroundings will yield on-the-spot possibilities ("I love the view from your window—it must be quite an inspiration. . . . Your wall posters of outdoor scenes are superb—they remind me of my vacation in Colorado . . . . That's an impressive golfing trophy, Mr. Big; is it true that you once considered professional golf?").

The small talk has vital importance. It is the first bond of human communication and trust. Use of small talk identifies the conversation as a human one, not a mechanical Q–A format. You have to play this early stage by instinct to some degree. Some busy respondents want to get right down to business and resent wasting time on small talk. Others seem to need the sense of trust and security that can be built up only through the inclusion of such seemingly trivial but important discussion.

The other person will take these moments to size you up, too, and decide whether your role will be that of trusted confidant or meddlesome outsider. One authority suggests that what happens in the first four minutes of a meeting between strangers largely determines what happens henceforth (Zunin and Zunin, 1972).

This early conversation should exude a friendly, amiable tone. Small jokes help, depending on how you read the respondent's human qualities—and maybe also how you read your own ability to make small jokes. The more laughter that occurs at this stage, the more that will follow, even in the more serious aspects of the conversation. Laughter lubricates conversation.

ASKING YOUR FIRST QUESTIONS

You can guide the opening small talk into business talk in an easy transition. In interviewing the prize-winning teacher, for instance, you talk of a mutual friend, Jane Doe, with whom you have discussed teaching techniques. The transition can be as casual as this:

Q. Your friend, Jane Doe, says hello—says she hopes to see you on the ski slopes next winter.
A. I wish I had time—winter's my worst time grading papers.
Q. Funny you should mention that—one of my questions had to do with grading students' papers. Jane says you spend a *lot* of time on each student's paper . . . .

Suddenly you're into the topic of the interview. This would be a time to pause to explain again why you've come and what you hope to obtain from the conversation. Some respondents may have paid close attention to what you said when you originally made the appointment; they may even have rehearsed a few answers. Others will have forgotten. In either case, the explanation must remain essentially the same as you said originally, unless you've changed your mind. If this is the case, you must explain your new tack. Then you return to your transition: "Now what were you saying about grading student's papers?" More about first questions will appear in Chapter 7.

ESTABLISHING AN EASY RAPPORT

If you've accomplished properly the first six stages this seventh should follow naturally. The conversation should settle into an easy conversational rapport, something akin to the two barefooted women talking noted in Chapter 1. The more informal the conversation, the more you will learn. The more you listen and respond to what the source says, the more you will learn. And the more you show your curiosity and your preparation by the questions you ask, the more you will learn.

When things go wrong, chances are an earlier stage has been neglected: perhaps you didn't explain your purpose sufficiently or you failed, despite your best intentions, to convince your respondent of the importance of your mission. But you may find it amazing, as I have occasionally, how a bad start can bumble along and still somehow reach that mellow stage of easy rapport.

The prime example in my experience came during a period when I had been interviewing public officials about their relationships with the news media and, most particularly, their reactions to reporters' interviewing techniques. I had an appointment with a city manager. In preparing for that interview, I called his community relations assistant to find out more about him—the kinds of issues and problems that concerned him at the moment and anything she could tell me about his attitudes toward the news media. Strictly a routine procedure; I'd done it before dozens of times.

But she'd never heard of anything so outrageous, she said testily. Who was I to be asking *her* these kinds of questions? She hinted darkly that I must have some ulterior motive for asking questions about her boss. Just what kind of dirt was I looking for?

I realized then that I hadn't bothered to explain precisely who I was and what I wanted. I assumed that a community relations person wouldn't require much explanation. I had told her merely that I planned to interview her boss tomorrow about media relations—so how would she describe his attitudes toward newspapers and TV? In short, I did the very thing I tell student interviewers not to do. (Don't start asking questions until you've thoroughly discussed purpose.)

Her reaction bewildered and angered me (mistake 2—interviewers should keep their cool), and I would have slammed down the telephone except for one problem. Being a little slow-witted, I couldn't think of a perfect squelch with which to end the conversation. While I toyed with some sarcastic remark about the low quality of public employees these days (which would have been mistake 3), a remarkable thing happened.

She began to talk in more mellow tones. I don't know why. It may have happened in response to my moments of silence. While she berated my bad interviewing techniques, I remained silent, trying to think of that devastating final retort. I never found it. She, meanwhile, may have misread the silence as showing more patience and self-control than really existed.

Whatever the reasons, I finally managed to blurt out my purpose in detail, and the conversation began anew. We got along fine from then on. In fact, we grew sufficiently curious about each other to make a date to meet for coffee a day or two later. It might have been the start of a fine romance had we not already been married to other spouses.

The story illustrates at least three important points about conversational rapport.

1. Interviewers must not neglect to explain purpose.
2. Conversational rapport often emerges under the worst of circumstances if your motives are sincere and you keep your personal emotions under control. Telephones are fine instruments for hiding emotions, incidentally; had my conversation taken place in person, she probably would have read anger and frustration in my silence rather than patience. (On the other hand, in a personal conversation she might have read more sincerity in my opening demeanor than she picked up on the telephone.)
3. The stage of easy rapport forms the heart of any interview. Without it, you can ask many fine questions and get little more than stilted answers by respondents who have not quite come to trust you. With rapport you can bumble around like the fictional TV detective, Columbo, and still receive candid, sincere answers.

It's less technique than personal sincerity. That may sound naive, but it's true. As noted in Chapter 2, when respondents perceive that you have come not to judge but to listen and to understand, they tend to relax and just be themselves.

ASKING THE BOMB

The term *bomb* means a possibly sensitive or threatening question. It doesn't mean that as an act of aggression you drop explosions into the conversation to destroy the rapport of stage 7. Rather, it means that care in handling sensitive questions will prevent an emotional reaction. This is discussed further in Chapter 13. For now, let an example explain the problem.

As you plan an interview, you'll realize that some questions will be easy and pleasant to answer and others will not. The prize-winning teacher who answers so willingly your questions about why students really love and learn eagerly from her methods may balk at answering questions about the delegation of parents who visited the school board protesting her teaching methods. Yet she may tell *you*—if rapport has been established in stage 7—because you're the sensitive interviewer who has come to understand, not the mean-spirited journalist out to impale a victim.

RECOVERING FROM THE BOMB

If stage 8 has been sensitively handled, little rapport need be lost. Sometimes a little human reassurance can help at this point ("The personal problems you mention could have happened to anyone"). Rarely do embarrassing questions kill an interview if the original rapport has been good. If rapport has been shaky in the first place and the embarrassing questions destroy the little remaining rapport, you'll at least appreciate the fact that they were the last questions you planned to ask.

CONCLUDING THE INTERVIEW

Beginning interviewers sometimes find it hard to break away gracefully from a conversation that has gone well. Try following these steps to end your interview.

1. Stop the interview on time unless further time has been granted. Make another appointment if you must talk further.
2. Signal your intent to close, perhaps by reexamining your notes to see if you've covered everything you came for. Be frank: "I see time is just about out; may I take a moment to review my notes?"
3. Ask if the respondent has any "final thoughts," anything to add to what has been said. You may get answers to questions you didn't think to ask but probably should have.
4. Ask for any documents mentioned in the interview; sources often mention reports, letters, and other materials they're willing to loan you.
5. Leave the door open by asking if you may call back if further questions come up.
6. Say goodbye—"and thanks a lot for your help."
7. Watch for the afterglow. This is an extension of the good rapport. Some of the best comments come as you are standing at the door saying goodbye. Now the respondent, relaxing after the "ordeal," will offer some of the most interesting insights and quotable remarks. Listen carefully (pulling out a notebook at this point would destroy the mood) and write down the comments after leaving. Some may question the ethics of using such candid material in a story. Reporters who are not basically meanspirited seem to have little trouble separating the confidences not intended for publication from the usable material.

CHAPTER FOUR
An Interview Case History

Q. Charlie Rockne, you're one of the most macho
    men known to professional football. I'm
    curious to know about your
    hobbies—mountain climbing, perhaps? Or
    wild horses? Wild women?
A. Naw, none of that raucous stuff for me.
    Actually I'm into crocheting.
Q. Well, nothing of interest there. Let's go on to
    talk about your pet peeves . . . .

Many veteran journalists say they learned interviewing largely by trial and
error. Young reporters, those lucky enough to work in busy newsrooms, often
confess to having learned by eavesdropping on telephone conversations of
more experienced reporters at nearby desks. The case history in this chapter
may be the closest thing to eavesdropping possible in a text. Here you see the
interviewing principles cited thus far applied to a hypothetical model interview based on actual experience.

The model illustrates several principles already discussed:

1. Anatomy. The model contains most of the ten stages of the interview.
But this is a short telephone interview rather than the extended face-to-face
interview contemplated in Chapter 3. So the conversation contains no

Is there anything particularly fascinating about you, Mr. Aldridge?"

"bombs" (potentially threatening or embarrassing questions); indeed, most routine news interviews don't contain bombs.

2. Rapport. The principle of working toward a harmonious personal relationship shows up in the dialogue, largely through the reporter's advance preparation, through her enthusiasm for the topic, and through her informal telephone demeanor and her encouragement with comments such as "that's interesting." It's easy and enjoyable to talk with a reporter who has bothered to learn a little about your topic and has a way of drawing you out in a non-threatening manner.

3. Creativity. The principle of "creative" interviewing shows in the reporter's attempt to bring something fresh to her story. It shows in the way she uses her imagination to develop questions based on what she already knows about the person and the topic.

Reporters say that once you have done a few interviews, you lose most of your intimidation about approaching sources. You are on the phone much of your working day, talking to sources. You often conduct routine interviews on the telephone itself. If you have any qualms about telephone interviews, you quickly dismiss them. Some reporters do three-quarters or more of their work by phone, finding it the most efficient way to do business.

In this case history, we'll suppose that a newspaper reporter— call her Betsy Shaw—learns that a local historian is planning to give a speech tomorrow night at the monthly meeting of a local civic organization. The historian, Clarissa McGee, has spent a lifetime studying the folklore of the sea, and on this occasion she will speak on lighthouses. And that is about all the information Betsy Shaw has to go on, but both she and her editors agree that the local newspaper (it could be a local TV or radio station) should obtain additional details and run a brief item so that citizens interested in attending the session might learn about it.

So, as an example of a typical, routine news interview, let's follow the reporter through the steps leading to the publication of a small news item about the speech.

DEFINING THE PURPOSE

An experienced reporter more or less subconsciously develops a purpose for the interview, a purpose largely governed by the kind of story planned. Clearly, a 150-word advance requires less information, and consequently a shorter interview, than, say, a major personality feature or an ambitious documentary about lighthouses. Betsy knows that her purpose is strictly routine: to produce a short news article that calls attention to the speech. Such a story will require the speech's title, its time and place, the identity of the civic agency sponsoring the talk, perhaps a little background on the speaker, and perhaps a brief example or two of the content of the speech—just enough to give a clear preview so that people can decide if they'd like to attend. So the purpose is uncomplicated: *to gather enough factual information to write an advance on Clarissa McGee's speech.*

BACKGROUND RESEARCH

Who is Clarissa McGee? Betsy's next step is to consult the newspaper library, which contains clippings of previously published items indexed by name and topic. Many newspapers have computerized files, and Betsy can obtain information on previous stories almost at the touch of a button. More precisely, Betsy will enter key words or names; if she entered *both* "Clarissa McGee" and "Lighthouses," the computer would list the headlines and dates of articles in which the two terms appear. Betsy could then call up on her screen any articles in which McGee has previously talked about lighthouses. If the file contains stories about lighthouses or McGee or both, Betsy could soon have a dozen or more pertinent stories at her fingertips. If she tapped into a *national* file of previously published material, such as Dialog or Nexis to name a couple of the better-known ones, she'd probably be overwhelmed with the amount of material available on her topic.

For our purposes, we'll keep things simple. From the local newspaper files, Betsy learns that McGee is a retired high school history teacher, that she has traveled widely (especially to lighthouse locales in the United States), that she has written a book, *Lore of the Sea,* that she occasionally speaks to historical groups around the country, most recently in Kansas City, about the many ghosts who presumably haunt the seacoasts around the world. From another set of files—stories about lighthouses unrelated to McGee's work—Betsy learns that the United States once had as many as 1,400 lighthouses serving as navigational beacons for seafarers, but that the number has dwindled to a mere 750, of which perhaps only 400 are still operating. Armed with such information, the reporter proceeds to her next step.

PLANNING THE INTERVIEW

Because her purpose is a simple one, Betsy will not make an appointment for a face-to-face interview. She could, however, envision writing a major feature story about McGee, noting with some interest that the file contains no such story from the past. But that would be another story, perhaps some time in the future. She will conduct this interview by phone. With so brief a story as this, the planning is simple. Betsy will ask the questions necessary to establish the who, what, where, and when of the forthcoming event, perhaps even the "how" (will she show slides or video tapes?).

An innovative reporter, Betsy will also try to learn something a little out of the ordinary—a Fascinating Fact or insight, or maybe something paradoxical or controversial—that could lift the story out of the routine announcement category. At least she planned to try; she might not succeed. She toyed with questions that might ferret out such an exception to the routine. She ran through what she already knew from her background research and tried to develop questions that projected from the known into the unknown.

Thus Betsy let her professional imagination wander. Lighthouses are declining in number; will they eventually all disappear? Is anything being done to save them? What's replacing them—electronic innovations? She also noted that McGee had spoken about ghosts of the sea; do ghosts frequent lighthouses, too? McGee has traveled widely; how many of the 750 standing lighthouses has she seen? Has she developed favorites among them? What's her candidate for the most interesting lighthouse or the most precarious or loneliest locale? Betsy's professional curiosity even extends to McGee herself. She's devoted a lifetime researching the sea. What got her started? What maintained her interest? Nothing in the files about that, Betsy noted.

The reporter will maintain this kind of professional curiosity throughout the interview itself. Thus the answer to a prepared question will lead to another question. If McGee proposes a certain lighthouse as her candidate for "most interesting," then Betsy will ask for a description of the lighthouse and more details about why it's interesting.

Even as she thought through some of the possible areas she might explore with the lighthouse historian, Betsy began to envision the kind of story she might write. She could always write the routine story, of course, one that begins, "Clarissa McGee, noted historian and authority on lore of the sea, will speak on [insert topic or title] tomorrow night at 7 . . . . "

That would be a perfectly acceptable way of handling so brief and routine a story, but Betsy hoped for more—the Fascinating Fact or insight—something that would *touch* the readers, make them curious or interested. In her mind she began to develop a crude sketch of the story she'd like to write—perhaps something like this:

> You probably didn't know [Fascinating Fact] about the nation's 750 standing lighthouses. You might not even know [Fascinating Fact 2].
> Tomorrow night at 7, Clarissa McGee, local authority on lighthouses and sea lore, will discuss why [Fascinating Fact 1] is among the strangest mysteries of the lighthouses that guide seafarers along [insert number] miles of U.S. seacoast....

Yes, it seems a little fanciful, but Betsy tries to place a touch of creativity into every interview. She *expects* to find a Fascinating Fact or two. She frequently gets what she expects: the proverbial self-fulfilling prophesy.

Such are the rewards of the creative interview. That's why Betsy does preliminary background research and why she takes a minute or two (more for a longer or more complex interview) to think through some possible questions or routes of inquiry. Betsy never writes out her questions, but she does jot down a few words to remind her of items she plans to cover. Thus a word like "decline" will remind her to ask about the dwindling numbers of lighthouses, "save" reminds her to ask about attempts to preserve them, and "ghosts" reminds her to ask whether any lighthouses are haunted. Betsy writes a list of areas she plans to cover in the conversation.

1. Details [who, what, where, etc.]
2. Decline
3. Save?
4. Replace?
5. Ghosts
6. Loneliest/most precarious
7. McGee's start

Some reporters might write more elaborate questions, but Betsy prefers to jot down areas of inquiry and improvise the questions themselves on the spot. She'd like to keep the conversation informal and perhaps even a little rambling. Too much precision, too much formality and organization tend to intimidate people. An experienced professional, Betsy knows that she may not cover *all* of those topics in detail. She may not cover some at all. She very likely will cover topics she could not have envisioned at this preliminary stage.

She will remain alert for whole new lines of inquiry based on what is discussed in the interview itself—areas that just drop out of the conversation. The best reporters adapt quickly to new information, and they don't mind improvising their questions on the spot, even at the risk of sounding a little clumsy. For a creative interview is not a straight line of Q's and A's, but a winding conversational pathway in which a professional observer and a knowledgeable source compare ideas.

ON THE PHONE

The interview depicted here is a simplified version of a face-to-face interview. Phone interviews contain fewer ice-breaking social amenities. They are more businesslike. They require a reporter to be prompt and clear about the purpose of the call. People get so many "junk" calls that they become wary of strangers. Note how Betsy strives to make clear immediately that her proposed article will serve the respondent's purpose as well as her own, a good procedure whenever possible. Another important telephone procedure is to respond to what the respondent says, perhaps by another question or, in the event of a long answer, by a grunt or an "uh-huh." Through the interview, the reporter will take notes, perhaps on a typewriter or VDT, perhaps by hand, depending on personal preference.

A. Hello?

Q. Hi. Is this Clarissa McGee?

A. Yes.

Q. Well, hello. I've just been reading about you and your work with lighthouses and the lore of the sea. My name is Betsy Shaw, and I'm a reporter for the *News-Tribune*. I've just learned of the talk you're giving tomorrow night, and I'm planning to write a short article for today's paper about it that I hope will enlarge your audience. Before I can write that article, though, I have a few questions—would you mind talking with me for a few minutes on the phone so that I can get the information I need? [Note the ego reinforcement: *I've been reading about you...hope to enlarge your audience....*]

A. I'd be glad to help you any way I can.

Q. Thank you. I trust I'm not interrupting anything?

A. No, things are perfectly calm at my house.

Q. Good. This will be a brief story citing the time and place and topic of your speech, and I also hope to include some little touch of fascinating folklore about lighthouses—maybe something about ghosts in the lighthouses or something.... I understand that some of them are haunted—

A. All of them are.

Q. Really?

A. Well, I won't swear to it, but I've yet to visit a lighthouse, and I've visited a lot of them, where I couldn't find a local person to tell me some kind of fanciful story about a ghost that frequents the place. Lighthouses are such legendary and romantic places, you know, so picturesque and all.

Q. Uh-huh—

A. Well, it's hard to imagine such a legendary scene and not find a ghost story attached to it. Quite a few have *more* than one ghost.

Q. That's interesting. I read somewhere that there are about 750 lighthouses still standing in the United States—I wonder how many of those *you've* visited in your travels?

A. Close to 300 I think. I've missed quite a few.

Q. I want to get back to ask you about some of those 300 and especially about the ones that are haunted, but I do have a few more-or-less routine questions I have to ask, especially about your speech.

By announcing the interview's purpose as including more than routine information—some fascinating folklore—the reporter is well on her way toward finding that extra touch that may lift the story beyond the routine. Stating a clear and perhaps provocative purpose helps to guide the source's thinking. The extra minutes involved in scanning clips of previous articles and thinking through your questions can pay high dividends. Here we have a fortunate situation—both interviewer and respondent are interested in getting information to the public. A perceptive respondent will quickly sense the reporter's attempt to bring something special to her story and will try to help.

Q. First, I need to know the title of your talk, when and where it will take place, and also the name of the civic group that is sponsoring it.

A. It's at 7 o'clock tomorrow night in the Rose Room of the Downtowner Hotel. It's sponsored by the River City Historical Society, and it's open to the general public. I'm calling it "The Case of the Disappearing Lighthouse and Other Tragedies of the Sea," and it will be illustrated by slides.

Q. Sounds like interesting material . . . give me just a moment to get all this in my notes . . . is this a case history of a particular lighthouse disappearing?

A. Well, the talk is about the sad state of our lighthouses, how they are falling into disrepair. We have only half as many as we once had, and we are losing lighthouses at the rate of several a year.

Q. What's happening to them?

A. They're being decommissioned and left to disintegrate. I do have several specific examples that I will be talking about.

Q. Well, I think it would be fun to include a tantalizing tidbit about a specific lighthouse in my story—maybe as a kind of come-on.

A. Okay, without giving away all my best stories, I can say that I'll be talking about such things as the lonely lighthouse keeper who amused himself by writing notes about the idyllic life on his little island. He put them in bottles and cast them into the sea, thinking that they'd be discovered by beautiful Polynesian maidens who would write to return his greeting.

Q. Great story! Where did this happen?

A. Tillamook Rock, off the coast of Oregon. And the irony of that is Tillamook Rock is one of the most hellish places on earth with great seas sweeping over the rock in the winter. Or maybe you'd like to know about the lighthouse at Egg Rock, Maine, where the keeper went ashore to get groceries and didn't return for four days because of a storm. His wife kept the light going and wrote in the log, "Keeper was drunk ashore all the time."

Q. Another good story! You'll sprinkle your speech with stories like those?

A. Yes, and now that you mention it, I'll try to throw in a ghost story or two.

Q. You seem to have a lot of enthusiasm for the topic—I'm curious to know how you undertook the sea and lighthouses as an area of interest.

A. I think it's because of a deprived childhood.

Q. Deprived childhood?

A. I just think it's human nature to spend one's adult years making up for some childhood deprivation—I mean, what do you think? The hungry kid dreams of big meals and eventually takes up gourmet cooking as an adult. The lonely kid seeks out crowds as an adult or the scrawny kid too small for athletics becomes a sportswriter. In my case, I grew up on the plains of Kansas and never saw the sea until I was twenty-three years old. So naturally I thrived on sea lore as a child, read every book on the sea, read *Moby Dick* thirteen times, saw every sea movie until eventually my blood turned to seawater. I remember the first time I saw the ocean. It was on a trip to California and we went to the beach at Santa Monica, and I confess that I was a little disappointed. The Pacific just didn't look all that big. I mean it didn't *look* any bigger or rougher than Lake Michigan! I don't know what I expected—mountainous waves crashing against the shore; I mean, I expected to be thrilled, *terrified*, even.

Q. And you weren't—

A. Well, not at Santa Monica. There were times, however, when I was working on a fishing boat in the Gulf of Alaska—

Q. You worked on a *fishing boat*?

A. As a teacher I had my summers free, you see, and . . . .

Asking personal questions can have a strange effect on an interview, particularly when the conversation turns to childhood memories. As Studs Terkel has suggested, personal and ordinary conversation—along with talk of childhood—tends to open the sluice gates of dammed up hurts and dreams (Terkel 1967, 1974). So the above dialogue is by no means exceptional.

Perhaps we can leave the interview at this stage and not belabor the points. The interview will proceed more or less methodically through the planned topics (perhaps rearranging and skipping and adding as the conversation progresses). We have thus seen the interview through six stages: defining purpose, background research, planning, meeting, getting to business, and easy rapport stages. The appointment request for a face-to-face session is not part of a telephone interview, of course, and the bomb and recovery stages are not appropriate for this routine interview. That leaves the problem of concluding the interview.

Q. Clarissa, I think I have more than enough for the story I plan to write—may I just take a moment to check a few things with you? First, am I correct in assuming that the main thrust of your speech is the decline and deterioration of lighthouses around the country? [As often happens, reporter and source are on a first-name basis now.]

A. Yes, together with the attempts of citizens and groups to restore and preserve them.

Q. I see. You'll talk about what's happening to the surviving lights?

A. Yes, some have been taken over by civic groups for restoration, some have been purchased by private citizens—a few have even been converted into small inns.

Q. How interesting! I'll make a note of that. Can you think of anything else that belongs in the story? . . . keeping in mind that this is going to be a pretty short story . . . .

A. I suspect you have more than enough.

Q. Okay. I do want to check some minor details—I have your name spelled [spells out names], and your address is . . . . [The details may seem minor but they're essential to avoid error; it takes only a moment to double check names, ages, addresses, titles, and similar details.] And one final point—may I call you back if, in the middle of writing this, a question occurs to me that I should have asked but forgot?

A. Of course.

Q. Great! Goodbye, and thanks a lot.

SOME POINTS TO REMEMBER

The model interview described in this chapter is a typical example rather than the perfect interview. No doubt one can find fault with the interviewer's tendency to allow some comments to stand without further follow-up questions. But no doubt she has more than enough to write 150 words. But who knows? Perhaps her editors will agree that the story is worth more than 150 words or that she should write a feature story about McGee at some future time.

Out of the sample interview dialogue, in any event, come additional points. Here are some worth noting.

1. Interviews work best when the reporter has prepared and thought through a few preliminary questions.

2. You'll secure a more productive interview when you envision the ideal form a story might take and look for the kind of information that will help to produce that story. Make sure, though, that you do this *objectively*. Do it in terms of story technique rather than content. For example, you surely would *never* interview a college woman to confirm a preconceived notion that she is an empty-headed fluff in search of a husband, right? Or a college man to confirm a preconceived notion that he's a macho chauvinist? That would be the antithesis of the creative interview, which requires that you keep an open mind.

3. Interviewers should communicate fully. Tell your source what you need for the kind of story you envision, a fascinating fact, perhaps, or examples. Don't keep secrets.

4. Accuracy is vital. Double-check your understanding of concepts, such as the central theme of the forthcoming speech.

5. Small details are important, such as double-checking names and addresses.

6. Ideas for future stories often emerge from these conversations. Perhaps the speech should be covered or a story written about Clarissa McGee and her lifelong romance with the sea.

7. Note taking is important, and it helps to report that you are taking notes to explain any delays in your response or in your next question. Note taking is covered in Chapter 12.

8. Repeating a few words from something a speaker said earlier can encourage further discussion, as in the reporter's comment, "Deprived childhood?"

CHAPTER FIVE
The Conversational Dynamics of Interviewing

> **Q.** Okay, Dogbreath, up against the wall! Answer
> my questions or I'll break your arm!
> **A.** I just love it when you officers talk tough like
> that—and so does my lawyer.

You'll probably think of hundreds of ways *not* to conduct an interview if you stay in journalism long enough. Logically, they ought to include spilling your coffee, falling down a flight of stairs, or showing up at a black-tie occasion in T-shirt and blue jeans. Yet the discussion in Chapter 1 suggests that each of these incidents not only failed to dampen the conversational spirit of the interview, but may even have enhanced it. You wonder why.

People tend to open up to sincerity and to nonthreatening approaches. When they perceive sincerity, they often forgive such wayward gaffes as spilled coffee. Conversely, they build strong defenses against psychological or physical pain. The tough television cop who thinks he can obtain information by threatening physical punishment has not bothered to study human nature—or the law. Such incidents make good theater, as do the hostile interviews on television news.

Actual police methods differ sharply from the "shove 'em up against the wall and shake your fist" technique of TV drama. Such violence is both illegal and unnecessary. Perhaps if reporters had to read Miranda warnings ("Any-

"As a reporter, I should warn you that anything you say can, and will, be used against you in my story."

thing you say can be used against you"), they, too, would adopt more gentle and concerned approaches. The key to asking questions is building a friendly rapport between the two parties to the interview. Without rapport, you can ask a hundred clever questions and still fail. With good rapport, you may not need questions at all; you can conduct the session with little more than a clear explanation of your purpose followed by empathic listening. People do pick up subtle signals. Some can read an expressive face like a TV monitor, and when they perceive sincere interest, they respond to it. They quickly perceive insincerity and deceit, too, and they respond appropriately—they clam up or they resort to defensive exaggerations.

So the essence of interviewing is rapport, which means a harmonious relationship with the other person. The journalist who would conduct interviews with all manner of people, from kings to felons, must become a student of human nature. Courses in psychology can help. So can tolerance for the wide diversity in other people's points of view. So can common sense. Imagine yourself interviewing the child molester or rapist mentioned in an earlier chapter. Ask yourself, "Why do I want to interview this person?" If you merely want to exhibit your hate or your moral superiority, don't bother. Suppose, on the other hand, that you really want to know what he's like, how he feels about women, children, sex, the world around him, or what causes him to harm other people. An article or broadcast documentary covering such questions might well contribute to society's understanding of a major problem.

When you decide that you really want the answers, you may feel the hate drain away, replaced by an almost eerie brand of professional curiosity. That's the mark of a fine interviewer, one who can establish conversational rapport with just about anybody.

So you need to learn something about people, especially about what happens when two people get together to talk. Unfortunately, not much research has been done specifically on journalistic interviewing, an astonishing fact when you consider that a multibillion dollar industry relies on journalists who obtain information largely through interviews. Can you imagine any other industry so poorly informed about the source of its raw material? Agriculture, petroleum, forestry—all are supported by full-time research laboratories. In journalism, little has changed since the late A. J. Liebling, long-time press critic for *The New Yorker*, remarked in 1948 that the American press reminded him of a "gigantic, super-modern fish cannery, a hundred floors high, capitalized at eleven billion dollars, and with tens of thousands of workers standing ready at the canning machine, but relying for its raw material on an inadequate number of handline fishermen in leaky rowboats."

In the forty years since then, little systematic research has evolved to help those wayward fishermen accomplish their task. Research in other academic areas—psychology, sociology, and anthropology, in particular—has proved helpful to journalistic interviewers, however. So we turn to them for most of the research evidence that underlie the principles in this text.

SOME RESEARCH FINDINGS

The first—and still the best—effort to draw on research data from other areas to fill the void in journalism is that of professors Eugene J. Webb and Jerry R. Salancik. In 1966 they published a study entitled *The Interview, or The Only Wheel in Town*. The title itself suggests a primary conclusion they drew from their review of research studies in sociology, psychology, and other disciplines in search of material adaptable to journalistic interviewing. "The only wheel in town" refers to a gambler's lament that a roulette wheel is crooked. Then why play it? "Because it's the only wheel in town."

Journalistic interviewing presents the same problem, the authors concluded. It's as warped as a crooked roulette wheel, but it's the only game in town. To illustrate the problem, they cited numerous studies from survey research interviewing—the kind intended to determine how people plan to vote in the next election or to identify people's opinions on issues. One classic example (Rice, 1929) compared the findings of two interviewers who were attempting to learn why a group of welfare applicants had ended up as skid road derelicts. What had caused their downfall? Overindulgence in liquor was the finding of one interviewer. Social conditions over which they had little control was the finding of the other. How strange it seemed that two interviewers could come up with such divergent results. But Rice explained it logically enough. The first interviewer was a prohibitionist. The other was a socialist. In short, their interviews produced an uncanny reflection of their own beliefs. They got the answers they wanted—answers that matched their own way of looking at the world. Rice called it "contagious bias": a tendency of interviewers to telegraph their own views.

This and similar studies suggest that attitudes of interviewers can influence answers. All of us unconsciously transmit our attitudes about certain questions, particularly those about which we feel strongly. The most blatant example is the "leading question"—one that suggests the expected answer ("Isn't it true that liquor was a primary cause of your present situation?"). Sad to say, reporters often do ask questions that way.

But even using a rigid phrasing of questions—as is usually the case in poll interviews—questioners can subtly transmit opinions that can influence the answers. Indeed, most interviewing subtly delivers rewards and punishments—such encouragements as "Yes, I see," "Uh-huh," "Okay," or such nonverbal cues as smiles, nods, eye contact, leaning forward in one's chair. The punishments include absence of eye contact, frowns, distractions, shaking of the head, and so forth.

So powerful is this subtle stimulus that a legendary story suggests that a professor who paced while lecturing was nonverbally cued to deliver his lecture motionlessly in a corner of the lecture hall. By prearrangement, students gave positive cues when he paced toward the corner (smiles, nods, rapt attention, alert posture) and negative cues when he paced away (frowns, averting eye contact, dropping things, shuffling papers, whispering to each other, and similar signs of inattention).

Such nonverbal communication serves as part of the "exchange" of information that helps to form the definition of the creative interview. It cannot be otherwise. Say authors Webb and Salancik:

> For our purposes, "exchanging information" is an essential notion. An interview is not just a set of questions and answers. By the character of his question, accompanying gestures, the clothes he wears and a thousand other elements, the reporter communicates to his source clues as to what kind of man the reporter is, how he views his source, and what he thinks about the source's replies. A titanic amount of information pours toward the source, and it heavily influences both the amount and tenor of the information he sends back.

The tendency of journalistic interviews to show biases in the direction of the reporter's own way of looking at the world is but one of several conclusions reached through an examination of the literature assembled by Webb and Salancik.

Another conclusion suggests that interviewers tend to play different roles in different interview situations. They can be therapists to the beleaguered. They are saviors to the downcast. They are shoulders to cry on for the troubled. They are pipelines to power and influence for social climbers and promoters. At the very least, they can be a boost to sagging egos—most people, after all, enjoy being interviewed, another not-so-surprising finding.

The role playing contains another dimension, however. Journalists clearly behave differently in situations that can range from interviewing a bereaved family to interviewing a celebrity on tour to promote a newly released movie or book. Public officials and business executives are, unfortunately, considered fair game for rude, arrogant, or adversarial techniques, as though the reporter who asks the most obnoxious questions is somehow closer to truth. The opposite is often the case, but, again, theatrics—something a drama professor calls "news theater"—may be the primary goal of such behavior, not an unbiased attempt to assemble the facts.

Role playing, as described by Webb and Salancik, also suggests that the status of the reporter's medium defines the reporter's role. Clearly, reporters representing media that have great power and influence—broadcast networks, national wire services, *The New York Times*, major news magazines—can play their roles more confidently than those from lesser media.

Even granting the influence factor as a fact of journalistic life, the evidence clearly suggests that journalistic seekers after truth might better avoid arrogance or hostility in their pursuits. The authors refute a reporting textbook that says reporters should "inspire confidence and even awe by directness in speech."

"Now it might do the reporter's ego a great deal of good to have someone stand in awe before him," they write, "but what confident, direct speech does for the completeness and accuracy of the information this cocky interviewer extracts is open to question. The evidence and idea of role suggest less attention to creating an impression of omnipotence would be advisable."

To be sure, considerable literature has accumulated in the decades since "the Only Wheel" emerged. A more recent survey of literature (Dillon, 1986) confirms most of what "Wheel" proclaimed earlier. J. T. Dillon of the University of California–Riverside consulted the literature on "questioning" from sources ranging from teacher classroom practices to interrogation of criminal suspects. Although this work was not specifically directed at journalists, Dillon has found still more studies that dramatize the fragile nature of the interview as an instrument of truth seeking.

Synthesizing the literature on questioning, Dillon identifies three elements in the questioning process: (1) assumptions, (2) the questions themselves, and (3) the answers. All three are fraught with the risk of interviewer bias and inaccuracy.

The *assumptions* typically include the belief that the respondent has the answers and that any factual basis for the question is accurate. Such is not always the case. For example, the proverbial question, "Have you stopped beating your spouse?" logically *assumes* that such beatings have occurred in the past. Unless that assumption is correct, it's merely a loaded or trick question, unanswerable except to deny the assumption.

Studies of the *questions* have tended to confirm the Webb–Salancik thesis of the crooked wheel of interviewer bias. One study (Loftus, 1987) suggested care in choices of words used in question phraseology. Interviewers asked accident witnesses, "How fast were the cars going when they *contacted/hit/smashed*?" The word choice made a vast difference. The estimates ran systematically higher with each choice of word: averaging 31 miles per hour when the cars merely "contacted," but almost a third faster—41 miles per hour—when they "smashed."

Other studies suggest that accuracy can suffer when the interviewer applies too much pressure for answers. When sources are encouraged to tell what they know in their own words, the results are invariably more accurate but less complete than when responding to specific questions. So the question, "Tell me what you remember of the accident" will achieve higher accuracy than a series of specific questions, which too often introduce error: "Where was the yellow car when the driver lost control? . . . How close was the other car?"

Literature dealing with *answers* is even more revealing. The term "response" better describes what happens after a question is asked, because many of the reactions are not answers at all. The nonanswers range from evasions to "stonewalling." A report entitled "How not to answer a question" (Weiser, 1975) suggests that responses to so simple a question as "How old are you?" can extend from "selective ambiguity" ("Don't worry, they'll let me into the bar") to direct refusal ("I'd rather not answer that"), and may even include sly diversions ("Oh, no! I think I left my headlights on").

Responses can change with circumstances, as suggested in a study (Getzels, 1954) that envisioned three different situations calling for answers to the question, "How do you like meeting strangers?" A person who is actually nervous with strangers answers, "I enjoy meeting them," to an employment interviewer, "depends on the stranger," to an opinion pollster, and "strangers make me feel nervous and inferior" to a therapist.

The solution to such nonanswer responses and the associated problems? *Listen to answers,* suggests Dillon. "The practical importance of listening to answers should be obvious, yet practitioners seem to be preoccupied with asking their questions and thinking up the next one to ask."

THE PLACE OF THE GENTLE QUESTION

Additional searches through the literature of questioning, interviewing, personal communication, and similar topics suggests, among other things, that gentle, listening, empathic interviewing works best. Not much evidence supports the idea that interviewing arrogance somehow helps in the discovery of truth, and much evidence suggests the contrary. Courtroom cross-examination may be an exception to the rule, but here the purpose tends more toward befuddling unfriendly witnesses than discovering truth.

The literature suggests that in fields other than journalism interviewers are more sensitive to nonverbal communication today, and more committed to empathic, gentle techniques, including careful, nonjudgmental listening. Even the literature of law enforcement interviewing or interrogation eschews rough techniques and emphasizes kindness, tact, empathy, and honesty (Buckwalter 1983). One book on police methods bears the title, *The Gentle Art of Interviewing and Interrogation* (Royal and Schutt, 1976). "Gentle" art? The impact of numerous court cases has accounted for the change, especially the Miranda case, which resulted in the requirement that officers warn suspects that they have a right to have a lawyer present during questioning and that they need not answer any questions. How does an officer interview a suspect after such a warning? Gently, tactfully, empathically, and logically, because courts have overturned convictions based on evidence or confessions obtained through deceit, coersion, or strong-arm methods. "Any interviewers who have need of such methods are certainly sadistic, uninformed, and incompetent," say Royal and Schutt.

"Taking an adversarial stance," says another author, Buckwalter, "is inviting the suspect to hurl defiance at your attempts to overcome him . . . . The 'hatchet-man' interrogator is a failure. He has never learned how to gently but persistently probe for the facts, or how to lead the suspect to reveal himself and his doings. Any suspect will resent an abusive or antagonistic approach."

NONVERBAL COMMUNICATION

All of us read people quite a bit. Research evidence suggests that we read their actions as containing a greater accuracy than their words whenever the two seem in conflict. Television interviews have a distinct advantage in this regard, because what is said nonverbally is as important as the words, often more so. An obvious case would be sarcasm. "I had a wonderful time on my blind date," says a college woman. You might take that at face value reading them here, but you'd realize the falsity of the words if said in person or on TV, accompanied by an appropriate sneer, rolling of the eyes, and the hollow sound of the words.

A creative interviewer uses nonverbal communication in two ways. The first is an awareness that your own dress, mannerisms, body posture, eye contact, fidgeting, and similar behavior do communicate interest and careful listening (or the lack of them). So you take care that you are not communicating an unintended message that could hamper the conversational rapport.

Second is the wealth of information to be obtained through careful observation of nonverbal behavior. It provides clues—often subtle, sometimes dramatic—to what the respondent is thinking. The perceptive interviewer can find meaning in so subtle a sign as a frown, a shrug of the shoulder, a wisp of a smile, the raising or lowering of the voice. Given a choice between following up a sly little chuckle in response to a question and the long-winded verbal comment, the interviewer may well follow up the chuckle.

> Q. That was a marvelous comment, Ms. Celebrity, but I couldn't help noticing the sly little chuckle that preceded it. So naturally I'm wondering what the chuckle means.

Nonverbal communication comes in several categories.

Paralanguage. The grunts and noises we make in response to comments—the "Umms," "Uh-huhs," and "Mmmmms"—are called paralanguage, and the numerous studies of their effect leave no doubt that they contribute to the rapport. People speak longer when they hear those kinds of responses, as they do in response to smiles, nods of the head, and so forth.

Voice. Our tone of voice carries subtle but effective meanings, including the sarcasm mentioned earlier. Albert Mehrabian (1972) has developed experiments that suggest that when words come into conflict with the tone of voice or with facial expression, the more believable aspect of the communication comes through the tone of voice and the face. What do you make, for example of a smiling face and a voice that says amiably, "So far as I'm concerned, you're the worst student I've ever had"?

Eyes. That the eyes speak volumes is suggested by the folklore on the subject, ranging from language terms ("shifty eyes") to proverbs ("reproof on her lips but a smile in her eyes"). Various research studies suggest that eye contact does enhance response, and that, among white persons at least, people tend to look at the other person more while listening than while talking. One interesting study suggests that the speakers who gaze upon the other person most of the time while speaking were judged to be friendly, self-confident, natural, mature, and sincere. The study used film clips and asked viewers to evaluate the people who looked at them while speaking compared with those who seldom looked at them. The nonlookers were judged cold, pessimistic, defensive, evasive, and immature (Klick, 1968). Other studies have suggested similar results. For interviewers the lesson is clear: Eye contact is important, more so probably in listening than in speaking, given that most interviewers listen more than they talk.

Kinesics. Numerous research studies have suggested that we move our bodies in countless ways to communicate—the ways ranging from a speaker's pounding the table to emphasize a point to subtle changes in eye contact. An alert interviewer can read such signs—most people have sufficient conversational skills to do so—but other signs are not so easily deciphered. The notion that you can tell whether a member of the opposite sex is "available" through delivery of subtle nonverbal signs does not seem well grounded in scientific research. A study once asked a group of people to act out six emotional messages through nonverbal methods. As a video camera rolled, the admittedly amateur actors tried to project anger, fear, seductivity, indifference, happiness, and sadness. When audiences viewing the tapes tried to determine which emotion was which, they usually misperceived four of the six. They perceived one young woman as "seductive" in every one of her six mood transmissions and another woman as "angry" in all six of hers (Beier 1974).

So much for accurately decoding nonverbal signals. They are nearly impossible to judge out of context, and for the interviewer they merely provide hints to be probed for detail.

The interviewer nonetheless must take care to project appropriate nonverbal signals that show attention to the conversation. Research generally acknowledges that attention and interest show through alert body posture, eye contact, leaning slightly forward in one's chair, facing the other person squarely, nods of the head—even, as you are evaluating what is being said, stroking your chin or nose.

Inattention or disagreement frequently shows in leaning back or slumping in the chair, lack of eye contact, shakes of the head, or fidgeting nervously with an object (a pencil, perhaps) or with your hair, beard, or clothes. Sometimes you project messages that you don't intend—you lean back in your chair not to show inattention, for example, but to signal a change of pace, perhaps a more informal and relaxed line of questioning. Or you avoid eye contact because you are reflecting on something just said. Often verbal reinforcement can help here, your contemplative mood accompanied by a remark such as "You said something a moment ago that interests me" (and you either tell what it is or you ask for another moment or two to think it through).

Proxemics.   Edward T. Hall, an anthropologist, has defined four levels of distance between human pairs as they converse in everyday life: *intimate, personal, social,* and *public* distances. They range from touching at the intimate distance to about twelve feet and beyond for public distance. The typical interview tends to range from the far side of personal distance (eighteen inches to four feet) to the near side of social distance (four to twelve feet). Clearly, as Hall suggests, the distance varies with the type of activity taking place, from the intimacies of lovemaking on the close side to public events where two-way communication is difficult or impossible. The closer people are together, the more personal the conversation.

The implications for journalistic interviews should be obvious here. The closer you can get to your respondent, the more personal the conversation is likely to be. And vice versa.

As Hall points out, people put up barriers when others approach uncomfortably close. We all retain a bubble of private space, to be invaded only by selected intimates, and we move to preserve that bubble with others. People

Some interviewees try to put obstacles between you and themselves.

indulge in various "barrier behaviors" when others approach too close, either by moving back to preserve the bubble or by putting up barrier objects, a book or purse on the table between the two parties, for example. Or they may fold their arms in front of their chest, clutch a book to their chest, or cough, scratch, or avoid eye contact (the "elevator syndrome": it's okay to touch in a packed elevator but not to stare).

By the same token, an interviewer coming into a respondent's office can quickly perceive some probable touches of character. Does the bureaucrat hide behind a giant desk/fortress with the visitors' chairs strategically placed directly across? You're being kept at arm's length by the formality of it all. That person demands a large space bubble and probably has the status to enforce it. One of my students encountered not only the giant desk/fortress, but noticed to his discomfort that the legs of the guests' chairs had been shortened so that visitors sat slightly lower than the host—who apparently had learned to win through intimidation.

Enlightened design has called for offices that resemble living rooms, a desk at one side, a sofa and coffee table arrangement on the other side. Some democratically inclined executives use an office with a circular table so that no one sits at the "head" of the table.

Visiting interviewers cannot always dictate the interview arrangements. Given a choice, you should always opt for the most informal arrangements— the coffee table or the round table instead of the big desk, or around the corner of the desk instead of directly across, or possibly moving to a conference room devoid of defensive paraphernalia.

If it's important to defuse the symbolic defense mechanisms in the respondent's office, it's equally important to ensure that you don't bring in defense symbols of your own. Taking notes on a big yellow tablet or clipboard—and holding it directly between yourself and the respondent—is in itself a defense symbol, rather like a shield and sword. Keep the notepad off to one side if possible, perhaps balancing it on your knee. Also keep the tape recorder out of the line of sight between you.

And avoid microphone swordplay in broadcast interviews. A student once witnessed a TV reporter doing a standup interview with the late Idaho Senator Frank Church. Most of the time the interviewer kept the microphone in a neutral position between them. But when Church evaded her question, she thrust the microphone in his face, even forcing him to step back on one occasion. Yet neither party seemed conscious of the microphone dynamics that were occurring (Laine, 1976).

ESSENTIALS OF DYADIC COMMUNICATION

From these and other studies of interviewing, three conclusions emerge.

1. Almost all evidence about interviewing—and most notably from sources dealing with investigative techniques—suggests that communication flows most freely in an atmosphere of sincerity and trust, and generally under informal circumstances.
2. Communication flows most freely when the goal is not to win a victory but to learn the truth—"truth" defined as factual reality.
3. Evidence assembled by Webb–Salancik and subsequent studies all make clear that the interview is a fragile and wayward means of learning factual reality, so fragile and wayward that most scientific methods of information gathering—polls, opinion surveys, and the like—simply could not survive the crude methods of interviewing utilized by journalists. This is not to condemn all journalistic interviewing, but merely to suggest that more attention needs to be paid to eliminating hostility, adversarial approaches, and personal biases from journalistic questioning.

For it seems that a cruel irony intrudes whenever one attempts to transfer appropriate principles of interviewing to journalism, particularly to that journalism commonly seen in daily newspapers and broadcast news. The irony, simply, is this: Often the worst interviewers get the best stories.

The point is not lost on public officials, business executives, and politicians, the typical "victims" of bad interviewing technique. A public official in Honolulu expressed it when he remarked that "if you want a *lot* of publicity, the best way to get it is to prohibit reporters from attending your meetings. Conversely, if you want something ignored, particularly something unfavorable, then call a news conference. It will be a one-day story and quickly forgotten." The public saw dramatic evidence of this concept in 1987. When several candidates for public office fell by the wayside as a result of public disclosures of past indiscretions, there came a rash of confessions by those still in the running. Jesse Jackson admitted that he was an illegitimate child and that his wife was two months pregnant when they married. Even patriarchal Senator Claiborne Pell, then 68, admitted that he had puffed on a marijuana joint one time years earlier but had not enjoyed the experience. Such confessions defuse the potential media bombshells because they remove the intrigue and the mystery of discovery.

The problem—many journalists do not consider it a problem, actually—reflects certain time-honored elements of news and literature, such as conflict, adventure, personality, and mystery.

A classic example of how confrontation reporting tends to puff up minor stories into major editorial conflagrations is the case of a reporter's "tough questions" to a homicide detective in Honolulu. The officer was investigating the death of a woman. He brusquely replied "I don't know" to most of the questions, not because he didn't know but because he didn't trust the reporter to be discreet. A splendid mystery thus emerged in the paper: "Police today were puzzled by the mystery death of a woman last night . . . ."The chagrined cop, completing what had been a routine case of wife murder, learned two lessons. He learned to trust reporters even less. And he learned to use henceforth the phrase, "I cannot comment on that aspect of the investigation at this time." If his patience was running thin, he simply said, "No comment."

Bad interviewing, in short, tends to produce a literary striptease rather than naked truth. It is a variation of news theater. If the arrogant interviewer can put the errant bureaucrat in a defensive position—thus forcing the proverbial cover-up—then a splendid mystery can run for days or weeks with commensurate attention from the public. If the warm, sensitive interviewer can persuade the official to tell all—it usually is beneficial to do so—then it's a minor one-day story, probably not even worth page one, and quickly forgotten.

Unfortunately, some journalistic interviewers take the adversarial relationship with government so seriously that each interview becomes a verbal chess game. Attempts by a reporter to convince the reluctant bureaucrat to reveal all for the ultimate salutary benefit is perceived by both parties as a win-or-lose situation in the verbal chess game. Reluctant to lose the game, the official simply tries to cover up the truth, sometimes winning a temporary battle in the personal war with the reporter, often ultimately losing the overall communications war.

CHAPTER SIX
Being Interviewed

Q. Coach, you've just blown another one—so how's it feel to lose twenty-three games in a row?

A. Well, I—

Q. Coach, you can level with me! You're really at a dead end; isn't that true?

A. Why do you say—

Q. Coach, you've had an illustrious career—the big time, the pros. You've been a winner all your life. But now you're all washed up—isn't that true?

A. I—

Q. Coach, talk to me! How's it gonna look in the headlines—"Coach refuses to discuss losing streak"?

What's it like to *be* interviewed? "It's like playing Russian roulette," says an experienced radio-newspaper journalist, Melody Ward Leslie. Several student journalists had interviewed her for class assignments through the years at the University of Oregon. Each one made her nervous, she said. "You never know what question's going to get you."

A curious change often overtakes interviewers when someone turns the tables on them. *They* suddenly become the apprehensive respondents squirming under a ruthless cross-examination. The late Alfred Kinsey of sex research fame once explained to a reporter how he knew, when questioning a person about intimate sexual details, whether he was receiving a truthful answer. "Very simple," replied Kinsey. "I look them straight in the eye. I lean forward. I ask questions rapidly, one right after the other. I keep staring them in the eye. Naturally, if they falter, I can tell they are lying." The reporter tried the same technique on Kinsey.

"Now look here," Kinsey sputtered, "that's not fair. I just don't like what you are doing!" (Hohenberg, 1978).

The *Washington Post's* Sally Quinn suffered a similar experience when interviewed by the news corps after she flopped as co-anchor of a morning news show. The ensuing bad publicity caused interviewers to dislike her even before they met her, she claimed.

"They would come on very hostile, I mean, really vicious," she explained. "They'd sort of attack me with the first question—what makes you think you're so hot, sweetheart? My reaction was to close up immediately. They weren't going to get anything out of me at all." [(*MORE*), July 1975.]

Such painful experiences can make you a better interviewer. One example is Charlayne Hunter-Gault, the award-winning journalist who worked for *The New York Times* before joining PBS's *MacNeil/Lehrer NewsHour*. As the first black to integrate the University of Georgia in 1961, she suffered numerous indignities at the hands of both students and reporters. One reporter arrived too late to film an angry crowd protesting her presence on the campus. So he pulled his own mob together and filmed *that* as the riot he'd missed.

The experiences made her a sensitive, caring kind of reporter with a strong interest in people. "I'm a person, and I try to see beyond the labels put on people," she says. (*Dial*, February 1987.)

WHY BE INTERVIEWED AT ALL?

If the journalistic interview represents such a painful experience, then why do people submit to it? Perhaps because there's only one thing worse than being interviewed, and that's not being interviewed. So consider why people will agree to media interviews. Keep the reasons at your fingertips so that when you encounter reluctant sources you can use the reasons as persuasive arguments in favor of doing the interview. Consider, too, the reasons people do *not* want to be interviewed. Then, when you request an interview, prepare a case that will enhance the positive and minimize the negative. The more you're convinced that being interviewed is a worthwhile and enjoyable experience, the more effectively you can persuade others.

Here are the most common reasons for participating in media interviews:

1. An opportunity to obtain recognition and publicity.
2. An opportunity to tell your side of an issue or controversy.
3. An opportunity to educate the public on some issue about which you feel strongly: there's a little educator (or propagandist) in all of us.
4. An opportunity to clarify a position or eliminate misunderstanding.
5. An opportunity to influence or impress others.
6. A novel experience, ego inflating; friends call to say they saw you on TV.
7. A touch of immortality, words frozen into print.
8. Sympathy with a purpose or cause—enough sympathy to override the pain (for example, parents of a teen suicide victim willingly discuss the case to prevent others from repeating their mistakes).

Here are some standard reasons *not* to grant interviews:

1. Distrust of interviewer's motives: "He's just looking for dirt," or "She wants to make a lot of money off someone else's pain."
2. Lack of time.
3. Lack of interest in discussing subject.
4. Source wants to avoid publicity or minimize it.
5. Lack of knowledge of subject.
6. Lack of confidence in interviewer's ability to handle complexities of subject.
7. Snobbery: interviewer's medium lacks sufficient prestige.
8. Fear or anxiety (especially for televised interviews or talk shows where inarticulate or nontheatrical respondents can't match the wit of a Johnny Carson).
9. Lack of sympathy with purpose of interview.
10. Resentment at past media injustices, such as a media hatchet job, misquotations, or perhaps a critical editorial by the interviewer's newspaper.
11. Interview burnout. Celebrities sometimes say "enough." In 1987, James Meredith, in 1962 the first black to integrate the University of Mississippi, announced that having given scores of media interviews over the previous 25 years—all for free—he was now charging at least $2,000 to talk with the media.

THE WAYWARD INTERVIEW: A CASE HISTORY

Good interviewers make the process look easy. The best of them have a way of putting you at ease. They listen carefully, they seem interested, and they ask good follow-up questions. Most respondents emerge from such a conversation feeling good about themselves and their opportunity for self-expression.

Nothing is more instructive, on the other hand, than being interviewed by an inexperienced person. Classroom exercises in our interviewing seminar—a simple pairing of students with instructions to one to obtain certain kinds of specific information from the other—illustrate the point. By being interviewed, students learn the importance of clearly stating the purpose at the start. "I thought you wanted to know my political views *in general*," said one student respondent in class discussion after the interview. "If you only wanted to know how I planned to vote in the next election, why didn't you just *say* so?" A typical reaction.

When classroom interview respondents heard vague and convoluted questions, they learned to sharpen their own questions. When they experienced frustration in the frequent interruptions, they learned to hold their own tongues and become better listeners. One young woman described her experience in a post-interview discussion: "I decided to relax and see what kinds of questions would be asked to bring me out. They were never asked. They bounced all around, and I felt that the real Sharon Johnson never got a chance to come out."

Let's examine more closely one such problem interview. A graduate student in our interviewing seminar, Margaret Laine, had worked as an epidemiologist for the health department in Oklahoma City. She investigated cases of venereal disease in order to prevent its spread. The job required extensive interviewing under difficult circumstances—not all people willingly reveal their sexual activities—to determine the identity of sexual contacts. The job also required fieldwork, which often took her to the worst districts of the city to locate some vaguely described person who had been identified as the sexual contact. She then encouraged the person to visit a clinic for examination and possible treatment.

Margaret Laine seemed the ideal interview respondent, a personable and articulate young woman whose work sounded interesting, even exciting in its more hazardous activities. She'd been interviewed before by Oklahoma newspaper reporters writing feature stories about her work.

We sent her out of the classroom so that out of her hearing we could set a purpose and structure for the interview. We decided to ask her to describe the interview techniques she used in her investigative work. We believed that we could learn a lot about interviewing under difficult circumstances from her description of her experiences. We thought she'd provide a few tips and ideas for students if they ever got into similar situations involving reluctant respondents. We knew that she'd undergone intensive interview training for her work. We knew also that she'd used interviews in seeking to identify the sexual contacts of infected persons. In short, we imagined that she could enlighten us about interviewing under less-than-ideal conditions and perhaps even entertain us with an interesting experience or two to illustrate her points. All we had to do was ask.

A young man in the class volunteered to start the interview. When Margaret reentered the room, she did not know the purpose we'd established. She sat in a chair across a conference table from the interviewer. About a dozen other students sat around the table as observers. We turned on a tape recorder.

Here is the verbatim transcript. The Q-numbers serve as reference points for the interview analysis that follows.

Q1. I'd like to ask you some questions about your job as a VD investigator in Oklahoma City.

A. Okay.

Q2. Okay, I think I'd like to start out not by trying necessarily to pin you down in your own experience, but in some of your impressions of the most successful techniques you used for getting the information you wanted—

A. You mean—

Q3. Ah, your contacts that, ah, or other contacts that you found that were the, ah . . . [four to five seconds of silence] . . . when you go out and meet someone, you ran into someone we'll say was kind of hard to talk to—

A. Uh-huh—

Q4. —what did you find worked most successfully in getting through to them—

A. Okay, I—

Q5. —in terms of loosening them up to the point where they'd, you know, be willing to go along with whatever it is you wanted them to do?

A. Are you talking about the regular interviews with someone who has venereal disease, or are you talking about—

Q6. Right.

A. —trying to find someone in the field?

Q7. Well, we understood that you went out and contacted people . . . or did you have a number coming in—

A. Uh—

Q8. —volunteers—

A. Okay. Well, it's a combination of both, and two highly different situations. Some people came into the clinic with VD, and anybody who came into the clinic, we talked to them while they were at the clinic. That was the formal interviewing situation. Going out in the field was to find people who had been exposed to VD and to get them into the clinic. It was not an interviewing situation, more a finding situation.

Q9. How did you get word on them?

A. From the people that came into the clinic or from private hospitals or private doctors or from laboratories.

Q10. When you went out, would you pick a particular time of day you thought would be most successful, I mean, you probably wouldn't go out at night—

A. Yeah, you'd go at night sometimes. Of course lots of people would be home at night that weren't home during the day.

Q11. Uh-huh.

 A. Ah . . . [silence] . . . .

Q12. So the time of day wouldn't have much to do with it—when you were going out?

 A. Well, it had a *lot* to do with it when you're going out. It varied with each case.

Q13. Did you work all hours?

 A. Yeah, you pretty much had your own hours. Your job was to do the job, and sometimes it was done before five, and sometimes you just went swimming and you did it at night. It just depends on who you were looking for and when. We worked every morning.

Q14. Can you give me some idea of what would happen during an initial contact, say, someone who's not particularly glad to see you?

 A. [Chuckles.] That's kind of a hard question to answer because, ah, many, many different things would happen. If you kind of narrow it down to—

Q15. Sort of type of person?

 A. Yeah, type of person, or someone who's angry or someone who's crying or someone who is belligerent, you know; I don't know exactly what you're looking for.

Q16. Let's say someone who is belligerent . . . older than you, who is belligerent. Male.

 A. Okay, that I've gone out to look for?

Q17. Uh-huh.

 A. And . . . okay, let me think if I can remember an instance like that . . . there were lots of them, of course, ah . . . the way you handle it, of course, just depends on the situation . . .okay . . . in this one particular instance, I went out in the country . . . [She tells, with great animation and gesturing, how she'd visited a woman on the front porch of a dilapidated shack in rural Oklahoma. The husband was there, too, so Margaret couldn't discuss the possibility of VD infection in his presence, so she alluded vaguely about the need for an "examination." The husband rose up and said threateningly, "Best be gittin' off my land before I get my gun." As Margaret beat a hasty retreat, she heard three shots, one of which shattered a window of her car. "I don't know if he was shooting to hit me or just to scare me, but I wasn't gonna hang around to find out." Clearly, a most entertaining story that elicited much laughter and response from the students around the table. At this point, Margaret was no longer talking with the interviewer; she was playing to the crowd from which she received such gratifying response.]

Q18. Have any of you ever been shot?

 A. And killed, you mean?

Q19. Well, I'd just settle for wounded.

    A. Not in Oklahoma. One guy got beat up, but nobody actually got wounded.

Q20. . . . [Silence]. . . .

The interview ended at that point, the interviewer apparently emptied of his pool of questions. Other students asked a few questions, none of them related to what we'd established as the purpose of the interview. Margaret seemed willing to entertain the class with accounts of her dramatic adventures, but it was time to analyze the interview. Everyone present, including the courageous young man who volunteered to start the interview, agreed that it was a fumbling, unsuccessful venture—in short, a splendid learning experience.

And so what lessons are to be drawn here? Most are reinforcements of points made in earlier chapters of this book. Although one can learn interviewing principles from a book, putting them into practice is not easy. That much granted, let us cite six problems with this interview.

1. Absence of purpose. First, the purpose was never clear, perhaps not even to the interviewer. It certainly was not clear to the respondent. A careful rereading of the transcript reveals that the two started on different wavelengths and continued to misread each other throughout. Margaret confirmed this afterward; she really hadn't understood what we wanted. She had perceived the purpose to be something like "my experiences as a VD investigator in Oklahoma City." Newspaper writers who had interviewed her before usually had that purpose in mind. As people gain experience in being interviewed, they usually presume a purpose if none emerges in the preliminary discussion. At no time, she said, did she become aware that we sought to elicit *interviewing* experiences that might help the other students on a practical level.

So the fumbling can disappear when both parties clearly understand the purpose. How do you explain the purpose? Imagine this replay of the interview's beginning:

    Q. I'd like to ask you some questions about your job as a VD investigator in Oklahoma City.

    A. Okay.

    Q. Let me explain precisely what we're looking for. I know from the discussion we had in your absence that you used interviewing quite a bit in your job, even took intensive training in interviewing. I think you'd have a lot of ideas and experiences that would prove helpful in our own interviews—particularly the kinds of interviews where people might not want to talk with you or might not want to reveal intimate details of their sex lives. Perhaps you could tell us a few of the basic problems, particularly the ones you think are pertinent to journalistic interviewing, and explain how they're handled. And, of course, I'd be delighted if you could illustrate the problems with examples from your experiences. [And now a question that should always be asked at this point.] *Do you understand what I want, and do you have any questions before we start?*

A. [How might Margaret have replied to that explanation? Most people say, "Sure, let's get started." Sometimes one asks for minor clarifications. Often a respondent will quickly assemble a mental list of the "basic problems" called for in the introductory explanation and will respond with a remark like "I think the biggest problem is . . . . "]

Q. Okay, I think a good starting point might be for you to explain just how you use interviews in your work, and maybe tell me some of the major problems as you go along.

A. [Conjecture suggests that she probably will launch into an explanation similar to the answer to Q-8. If so, more specific follow-up questions could be asked: "Would you describe that formal interviewing situation in the clinic—just what happens there? Are people reluctant to discuss their sexual activities? What are some of the topics about which they might become uneasy or reluctant or belligerent? How would you handle such situations? Do you think your techniques would work for a TV reporter or newspaper writer? Can you give me an example—a kind of case history?" And so forth.]

Absence of a clearly stated purpose heads the list of errors in just about every failed interview, and this was no exception. In contrast, the other problems seem less severe, though they represent a certain contributory negligence.

2. Absence of icebreakers. The interviewer was probably nervous, a common occurrence when performing in front of a group of potential critics. But did he consider the respondent's nervousness? A little preliminary human communication at the start might have relaxed both parties: "Hello, how are you? Wasn't that a terrible exam the professor gave last week? I suppose with all your interviewing experience, you probably got an A"—and so forth. Note how the last remark could logically lead to the heart of the interview ("Speaking of those Oklahoma interviews . . . ").

3. Absence of careful listening. Question 12 suggests lack of listening, possibly a desperation remark just to keep the conversation going. More important, the interviewer continues to misread the respondent's perception of the interview's purpose.

4. Absence of ego reinforcement. As is typical in interviews done by beginners, he didn't seem to respond to her responses. If someone tells a blockbuster like the "best be gittin' off my land" story, the dynamics of human communication suggest that she be rewarded. She was, by laughter from the entire class, but that merely took the conversation out of his hands. Some logical responses could be: "What a *terrific* story—got any more like that?" She might have others, including some more closely related to journalistic interviewing technique. But can the interview be salvaged at this point? Of course. It needs only to review the purpose, perhaps with a remark such as this: "I *love* that story. May I take a moment to explain what I hope to get out of our conversation?"

5. *Absence of enthusiasm.* To cite a subtle point, the dialogue reveals a distinct lack of interviewer enthusiasm for the subject. He probably didn't intend to project that attitude. The classroom setting and the barriers that mounted through the misunderstanding of purpose seemed to put the interview on a stiff and formal plane—almost the opposite of the barefooted-women technique and certainly the antithesis of a creative interview. They seem to have one another at arm's length. Most experienced interviewers try to get closer. Some have learned to carry enthusiasm to the point of not-so-subtle flattery. Flattery seldom fails to enhance the interview rapport: "What an *incredible* set of adventures you must have had on that job! Have you considered writing a novel? . . . Where can I get your book?"

On the other hand, it's unflattering to have run out of questions at Q-20. It suggests that she's not terribly interesting or worthwhile. People tend to clam up when they're not appreciated. The problem plagues interviewers who have prepared written questions and can't seem to continue the conversation after asking the last one on the list. A skilled interviewer, by contrast, listens carefully to the answers and develops new questions on the spot. The "gittin' off the land" story could surely prompt a dozen follow-up questions: "Did you learn anything about interviewing [or about people] from that experience? . . . [If not] What were some of the experiences on the job that taught you the most about interviewing? . . . Have you learned any techniques to sense danger before you get into trouble?"

6. *Absence of organization.* The interview lacks organization, a problem enhanced by the unclear purpose. Some questions seem to be almost random shots in the dark. We as readers know what should have been the purpose and can therefore see a slight relevance, but Margaret is entirely in the dark, and as a result the rest of us are deprived of Margaret Laine's wisdom in providing useful ideas about interviewing under difficult conditions. We'll never know. She was never asked.

This kind of exploratory interviewing resembles walking into a black cave with an armload of unlighted candles. Each candle represents a question to be ignited by the answer, which then sheds light on a tiny part of the cave. One question leads to another, and eventually a whole section of the cave becomes visible. A well-organized set of questions, especially the ones prompted by earlier answers, can systematically lead to a visible reality, to truth. Too often interviewers light random candles anywhere and everywhere so that only random fragments of reality become known. Most times, fragmented reality is no better than abject darkness.

CHAPTER SEVEN
Questions

Q. Princess, if it's not too personal, can you tell
   me why you never married? Are you just not
   interested in men, or what?

A. *Not interested?* I'll have you know that I've had
   no fewer than thirty-three lovers in the past
   twenty years!

Q. Ah .... [blushes]

A. So! You didn't expect such candor, I see. It
   seems they didn't teach you in journalism
   school to cope with real life!

Samuel Johnson, the great eighteenth-century English writer, insisted that
curiosity is one of the permanent and certain characteristics of a vigorous
mind. Nowhere is this more evident than in the journalistic interview. Here
the vigorous mind, eager to seek out the essence of any subject under discussion, uses the question as the conduit to a richer, more rewarding intellectual
life—or at least to get the details of an event for the six o'clock news.

   This means the human curiosity behind the specific question is a more
powerful force than any individual question can be. Sources tend to respond
more to what they perceive to be the curiosity than to the question itself. Still,
the way you ask is important.

PHRASE YOUR QUESTIONS CLEARLY

"How do you feel about the upturn in the 'stock' market?"

Questions should be short, unbiased, and clear. Examine this dialogue between a reporter and a weather forecaster.

Q. Is it going to rain tomorrow?

A. No.

Q. So we'll have good weather?

A. Depends what you mean by "good."

Q. Sunny?

A. No.

Q. What, then?

A. Snow.

Q. Well, why didn't you say so?

A. You didn't ask.

A clumsy dialogue. By asking about rain, the reporter closed out all other possibilities. Had the reporter asked, "What's your prediction for tomorrow's weather?" the answer would have been easy: snow. It may be that the forecaster was playing games by literally answering the questions asked (instead of the questions *meant*), but the lesson remains clear: ask what you really mean. Many bureaucrats take advantage of that kind of verbal fuzziness to evade your questions.

So make them clear and direct. If the point seems obvious, you need only to listen to the way people ask questions in everyday conversation. Note, for example, how they display personal biases through their questions. "I don't feel well," says Jim, and his friend, Bill, responds, "Is that because you drank too much last night?" Bill is not asking a question; he's expressing a subtle opinion about Jim's drinking. A more objective question would have been, "What's wrong?" or "How come you don't feel well?"

People often ask convoluted, overdefined questions. A college student once asked a police officer who visited the class:

Q. Sergeant, have you ever had to use your gun, I mean, more than just target practice, like, for example, shooting at a fleeing robber, or maybe a hostage situation, or maybe like so many police officers I've read about, you've never actually used your gun in anger, so to speak, and then again maybe . . . .

The student seemed unable to let loose of the question. What's wrong with making it simple? Use follow-up questions if the answer is not sufficiently detailed.

Q. Sergeant, have you ever had to fire your gun? [Note the change from "use" to "fire" to avoid ambiguity.]

OPEN VERSUS CLOSED QUESTIONS

Questions come in two broad categories: open and closed. Open questions are general and allow plenty of leeway for the answer. Closed questions are specific and call for a specific answer.

Examples of the open question:

"What can you tell me about yourself?"

"Miss Manley, after seven broken marriages, what have you concluded about the institution of marriage?"

"Mr. President, how can we keep inflation in check while at the same time providing full employment?"

Examples of closed questions:

"Governor, do you plan to veto the legislature's tax-increase package?"

"Sergeant, what type of weapon was used to kill the victim?"

"Admiral, where will the battle fleet be sent next?"

As the examples suggest, both types have their place in the journalistic interview. Sometimes inexperienced interviewers jump too quickly into the closed question. A reporter approaches a witness to an auto accident and asks, "Was the driver of the green car drunk?" Not only does the question suggest a bias, but it calls for a conclusion that the witness is not able to make. Even if the driver was staggering as though drunk, other explanations are possible, an injury perhaps. A more objective question would be, "What did you see?"

Some questions straddle the two categories: "Senator Fogg, I understand you had a big argument with the president last night over foreign aid. What happened?" Is that open or closed? Perhaps more closed than open, but a little of both.

SEQUENCING OF QUESTIONS: THE FUNNEL

Journalistic questions usually come in sequence, either from specific to general or from general to specific. Comments that emerge from general questions will logically lead to a request for details. The reverse is also true. The interviewer, hearing a source cite several specifics, will then search for a generalization or principle that suggests what the specifics mean. Here are hypothetical examples of both. First, the general to specific, sometimes called the funnel. Note how the closed questions follow the open.

Q. Coach Meyers, as your football team moves into the first game of the season, do you see any major problems ahead?

A. I'd say injuries are gonna slow us down quite a bit in the first week or two.

Q. Oh, you've had some injuries among your players?

A. You bet.

Q. Who?

A. Well, Charlie Rice for one. He's the guy we'd originally planned to start at quarterback.

Q. Rice is out? What happened to him?

A. Sprained an ankle in practice yesterday . . . .

The reporter will ferret out the additional specifics about what happened to this and other members of the team. A specific-to-general sequence (the reverse funnel) looks like this:

Q. Coach Meyers, I notice Charlie Rice is on crutches—what happened?

A. [Gives details.]

Q. How is his absence going to affect your opening game next week?

A. It's gonna slow us down quite a bit the first week or two...[and so forth].

OPENING QUESTIONS

Many journalists consider an interview's first questions "throwaways," intended merely to get the interview under way. And so they are. Yet they do help to start the interview on the right track. Imagine the television interview where an articulate but nervous guest stumbles over the first question, something unexpected or loaded perhaps. This proves so embarrassing that the guest never recovers. Better to throw away an initial innocuous question or two than to throw away an entire interview. Opening questions come in two categories, icebreakers and first moves.

Icebreakers

Earlier we suggested some icebreaking comments upon first meeting your respondent: commenting on personal effects or the office scene or reviewing mutual acquaintances or topics in which you share an interest such as fishing or art. Here are some additional thoughts.

1. Prepare your openers. If the source is a business manager, a quick reading of the *Wall Street Journal* can yield enough material to serve as the topic of a preliminary conversation. Read an art magazine before interviewing an artist, a law enforcement magazine before talking to the police chief. Learn the issues in which *they* have an interest. This becomes easier with experience. If you're talking to a lawyer, the fact that you once interviewed, say, a U.S. Supreme Court Justice, gives you an opener (but one to be used deftly lest it appear arrogant).

2. Use the respondent's name. Most people like to hear their names pronounced properly. One reporter succeeded in interviewing an infamous British wife murderer where others failed. His name was Sleighter, and most called it Slay-ter. The successful reporter had learned the correct pronunciation: Slick-ter.

3. Use subtle provocations: good-natured kidding or banter. Human nature dictates that conversation goes better with laughter and amiable repartee as lubricants. Some people put fun and sparkle into the conversations, and they receive the same in return. Think of the quotable remarks that fun and sparkle can inspire. Some amiable journalists seem to be able to get away with anything. A male journalist tells a feminist that he likes her legs; a female journalist tells the macho football coach that she "hates" the cowboy hat he wears to games—but both do so in an obviously jocular manner.

What happens if your provocation misfires and your source becomes angry? You slug it out and/or apologize, thus clearing the air. You achieve a mutual understanding, and the interview proceeds, often with no loss of rapport, sometimes with a gain. It's one of those tiny human ironies that defy simple explanations, a little like gaining rapport by clumsily spilling your coffee. Perhaps it has to do with revealing vulnerability. You tried a corny wisecrack and it fell flat. You thereby gain a touch of human sympathy. Maybe. Journalists who read people—their sense of humor or lack of it— perform best in these conversational subtleties.

First Moves

These are your first serious questions, though they need not be grimly serious. They might even drop logically from the amiable icebreaker repartee that preceded it. A certain logic resides in the woman interviewer suggesting to the football coach that her wisecrack about the cowboy hat leads to the topic of her interview—a feature story, let's suppose, about the demeanor of coaches during games. Her observations have suggested that coaches pace and curse and kick the water bucket—well, is the cowboy hat part of the act, too?

Whatever the first moves, they should have four qualities.

1. They should be easy to answer, particularly for a broadcast interview. Indeed, they should be questions you're pretty sure the respondent will relish answering.
2. They should reinforce the respondent's self-esteem. Save touchy questions for later.
3. They should demonstrate that the interviewer has prepared for the conversation.
4. They should follow logically from the interviewer's announced statement of purpose.

FILTER QUESTIONS

Filter questions establish a respondent's qualifications to answer subsequent questions. You arrive at the scene of a tragedy and ask "what happened?" You're told lots of details, only to learn that the person answering didn't really see it. You're receiving second-hand information that the "witness" has picked up from others. A simple filter question—"Where were you when the tornado struck?"—would have avoided the wasted effort.

A filter question proves useful whenever you're interviewing a person with unknown credentials. For a story about runaway kids, you approach a police officer you don't know personally. So you ask a filter question: "Sergeant, how much experience have you had dealing with runaway kids?"

Filter questions enhance conversational rapport with highly qualified sources and weaken it with poorly qualified. Questions that qualify you as an authority reinforce your ego. Those that expose a lack of knowledge can be humiliating. Remember, though, that celebrated people resent questions that advance preparation could easily answer. Don't ask Sally Field if she's had much acting experience.

PROBE (FOLLOW-UP) QUESTIONS

The probe represents the heart of the interview. It encourages the source to explain or elaborate on something already said. Probes range from silence to repeating something just said. Imagine the response to the hypothetical dialogue at the head of this chapter. The reporter has asked about the princess's unmarried status, and she replies that she's had thirty-three lovers in twenty years. The interviewer blushes and doesn't know what to say next. Blushing *is* a probe of sorts, a nonverbal response that encourages further comment, not a helpful comment in this instance. Here are the typical kinds of probes designed to encourage elaboration.

1. Passive probe. "Hmmmm . . . I see . . . ." It's probably accompanied by a deadpan expression. This kind of passiveness suggests that the interviewer is prepared to listen further.

2. Responsive. "Really! . . . How interesting! . . ." Probably accompanied by more animated facial expression—nod, smile, eye contact, raised eyebrow—no doubt these should be practiced in front of a mirror before any public debut. Avoid judgmental responses: "What a fickle woman you are!"

3. Mirroring. Mirroring means repeating pertinent examples of the source's own words. It's used effectively by counseling interviewers working with psychologically troubled patients. "Thirty-three lovers . . ." followed by a pause tends to encourage elaboration as the respondent hastens to supply the missing details.

4. Silent. A "silent" response might seem like no response at all and thus an ineffective probe. Experience suggests otherwise. An expectant kind of silence, accompanied by the appropriate nonverbal signals, asks the speaker to continue. Often silence is useful in allowing the speaker time to collect her thoughts, perhaps think through the kind of elaboration that should follow.

5. Developing. "Tell me more about the men in your life . . . . Why so many? . . . Are you bragging or complaining? . . . Tell me about the best and worst of them . . . . Whom do you have in mind for number thirty-four?"

6. Clarifying. "That's one and a half lovers a year, on the average; do you have affairs in sequence or concurrently? . . . Do these men know about each other?"

7. Diverging. "And yet you claim to be in the forefront of the feminist movement—do you see any conflict in that? . . . Do you also know men merely as friends?"

8. Changing. "I'd like to move along now to another topic if you don't mind—tell me about your interest in Renoir paintings." (This assumes you have no interest in pursuing the topic.)

Perhaps it's less important to learn the various types of probes than to let your curiosity guide you toward the heart of the subject under discussion. The best probe may be the question, "Why?" It's also the best question to ask when you can't think of any other. "Why? Why do you say that?" Even the most outrageous comments— especially the most outrageous—should be followed by that question. (See Conceptually Defining Questions, later in this chapter.)

FACTUAL QUESTIONS: THE 5 W'S

Use of the *Who, What, Where, When, Why,* and *How* has already been described (Chapter 2) as a means of obtaining information for the event-oriented news story, such as a story on the train wreck or the governor's veto of the capital punishment bill. *Who?* (the governor), *What?* (vetoed the tax bill), and so on. Five of the six questions allow you to form a sense of the story's dimensions. One of them—the *Why*—is something of an intellectual renegade, to be discussed in a later section of this chapter. Note, meanwhile, that your questioning may focus more on one of the elements than the others. The governor's reasons for veto of the tax bill deserve more attention than the details of how and when. But you can imagine other circumstances that will cause you to focus on, say, the *how* (how burglars cleverly tunneled their way into the bank vault) or the *when* (just minutes before the scheduled execution the prisoner received a pardon).

The five W's and H are particularly valuable to lay a foundation of knowledge before you can proceed with more complex questions. You encounter a group of people picketing at City Hall. The event seems worthy of an item on the six o'clock news, but you haven't the faintest idea what it's all about. What now? You put your Five W's to work. *Who's* in charge? When you find this person you ask foundation-laying questions. *What's* going on? *Who* are these people, and *Why* are they here? And so on.

CONCEPTUALLY DEFINING QUESTIONS

You use a conceptually defining question to seek out the underlying causes or principles behind any event or situation. Sometimes it is a one-word question: *Why?* At least that's how you try to discover the conceptual principles involved in any situation. Sounds simple. The question, however, implies trying to understand the answer, and *that* can be complex indeed. Not only is the answer possibly complicated, but you're never sure it's true. Truth comes at many levels. So do coverups. The real reason behind any commentary may lie deep below successive layers of political, sociological, economic, or even psychological complexities. You are tinkering with the fundamentals of human motivation, the stuff novelists and therapists deal with every day. Who can say the real reason behind the prison riot or the deterioration of a city's downtown core?

To understand the problem, consider a personal example. You ask your neighbor, Mr. Jones, why he bought the new Oldsmobile. "Because I like Oldsmobiles better than Buicks," he replies. True enough. You can settle for that superficial answer, or you can peel away successive psychological layers to get somewhere close to reality: Perhaps he is a timid man who hopes through the purchase of a powerful and expensive car to gain self-confidence, the admiration of friends and neighbors, and the respect of his family. Jones may deny such a motivation should you ask, and who's to say he's wrong? He was merely trying to keep up with the neighbors, he says.

Understanding the conceptual underpinnings beneath the superficial events is less a matter of questioning technique than a complex pattern of learning and understanding. Tracking down concepts sometimes requires dogged pursuit; thus:

Q. Governor, why did you veto the capital punishment bill?
A. Because it was a bad bill.
Q. What was bad about it?
A. Everything!
Q. Well, what would be an example of one bad element?
A. In the first place, it's in conflict with the state constitution.
Q. How so? [And so on, until you get to the heart of the governor's attitudes about capital punishment and her reasons for the veto.]

One pattern for this conceptual level of interviewing has been suggested by Gilleland (1971). It's called *GOSS*, an acronym for four stages of questioning.

Goals
Obstacle
Solutions
Start

GOSS draws on the principle that most of life—that of bureaucratic agencies as well as humans—involves reaching for goals, not all of them within grasp. If you ask about goals and get realistic answers, then you already have some notion of concepts behind a respondent's actions or commentary. You invariably find obstacles blocking access to those goals. But possible solutions exist, either in fact or in theory. The final S suggests that understanding concepts comes more easily if you return to the beginning of any event or situation. How (and why) did it all begin?

You can apply GOSS to interviews ranging from simple news event queries to full-fledged biographical profiles. The governor's goals upon entering office can be discussed by journalists at any stage. ("Governor, what are you trying to accomplish in the field of prison reform? What kinds of problems or obstacles stand in the way? How have you worked—or will you—to remove those obstacles? How did your interest in prison reform begin?")

You could add two letters to GOSS, at least for the type of interview requiring conceptual depth.

E for Evaluation
Y for "Why"

That makes it GOSSEY, still an easily remembered pattern. Evaluation suggests asking a source for a kind of historical overview of the subject under discussion: "Governor, please tell me how you evaluate the controversy between you and the legislature over prison reform—where do we stand and where are we going?" And the Y for Why is just a reminder to press for a complete understanding: Why does the governor feel so strongly about capital punishment or prison reform?

The GOSS pattern, like any attempt to reduce human relations to simple formulas, is fraught with peril. It works almost too well. It can be a crutch for lazy interviewers who don't do their homework.

NUMBER QUESTIONS

How many? By what percentage has population increased over the last decade? Answers to number questions give a sense of definition and precision to the topic under discussion. Vague is dull; specifics can be interesting, even dramatic when used properly. Numbers and statistics seem to dominate sports reporting—the .314 batting average, the coach's won–lost–tied record. Other people accumulate statistical records, too, though the numbers may not be so easily accessible as they are in sports, business, the economy, and the census. Yet a mountain climber could be asked to total his lifetime record of 122 peaks climbed, 383 glacier traverses, or whatever. One reporter, interviewing a call girl, was astonished to find that she kept statistical records on her clients, who averaged forty-one years old with forty percent of them white, middle-class businessmen. She'd even separated them into twelve categories, including "freaks," "lovers," and "those wanting talk and sex therapy."

Such detail is concrete and dramatic and accessible to the interviewer who asks. You may want to carry a small hand calculator when you ask number questions. A reformed alcoholic, for instance, used a reporter's calculator to determine that he'd consumed an estimated 2,000 gallons of booze during his bout with alcoholism. He figured that he'd consumed two bottles of wine or a six-pack of beer every day for fifteen years.

The questions used to discover such drama are simple. How many? How many miles did the retiring postman walk during his forty-year career? To make it truly dramatic, you can use comparisons. He walked 120,000 miles, a distance equal to almost five times around the world at the equator.

REFLECTIVE QUESTIONS

Reflective questions are not really questions, but comments on some point the interviewer would like to see addressed. They are largely conjectural comments, usually delivered in a casual and ego-reinforcing manner.

"You seem to enjoy teaching, Ms. Johnston."

"I notice, Senator, that you chuckle every time I bring up the subject of the federal budget deficit."

"I have a hunch, Ms. Celebrity, that your fan mail must include a lot of oddball items such as proposals of marriage or requests for money."

Such comments are more conversational and less threatening. They allow the respondent to chose the direction of the reply. You frequently receive a counterpoint reply along these lines:

Q. You seem to enjoy teaching, Ms. Johnston.

A. Oh, I do—at least eighty-nine point three percent of the time.

Q. I see—the other, uh, ten point seven percent sounds ominously troublesome.

A. Well, it's just that when you try harder to make sure your students learn what they ought to know, you put more pressure both on your students and on yourself. You run the risk of misunderstanding, and pretty soon delegations of parents come to see the principal. That part I don't enjoy.

Q. But apparently those delegations have not weakened your resolve— [and so on].

Not all such comments must massage the ego, of course. Negative comments, preferably attributed to someone else, can encourage lively responses.

Q. Some students tell me that they avoid your classes because you're so demanding.

A. Yes, and some teachers resent the fact that the very best students register for my advanced English classes, but I want to point out that I also teach remedial English . . . .

CREATIVE QUESTIONS

The creative question has already been defined as one that emerges when you tread forward beyond the limits of present knowledge. You form questions based on what you already know about the topic through documentary research, previous interviews, and general knowledge. Where, you ask, might the trail lead once you have left the known? You devise questions to find out. To illustrate, you see the star quarterback on crutches (the known aspect), and so you call the football coach to find out what happened and what implications it might have for next week's game (the unknown).

That definition confirmed, let us acknowledge that some reporters are more creative than others in devising questions. Their minds are adept at sifting through conversational minutiae for bits of information that seem to combine into new and possibly novel revelations. Some of the pieces are not even verbal.

Why, for example, does the senator avoid your eyes whenever you ask her about foreign policy? She won't talk about military problems except to ramble almost incoherently about arms buildup and American fleet movements. And last week a newspaper quoted her as saying, "I have more questions than answers about American foreign policy." How does *that* fit in? As these and similar items accumulate in an interviewer's mind, they may form a pattern, a possible meaning to explain all the fragments. You form a hypothesis—a possible explanation—and drop it into the conversation.

Q. Senator, several things you've said today suggest that you may be considering a sharp departure from your support of the president's foreign policy, particularly with regard to military buildup.

A. Good heavens! How did you reach *that* conclusion? [A typical reaction.]

Q. Just things you said.

A. Well, you're right! How perceptive! Yes, it's true; I feel the president is deviating from his previously announced policy . . . .

If she denies your hypothesis, you've lost nothing. Perhaps you will have gained some other explanation for the pattern of reactions that puzzles you. But when a respondent confirms such a creative hypothesis, the conversation spirals upward with renewed energy. That's because the respondent may be viewing you with new respect, seeing you as the brilliant and perceptive observer that you truly are.

This further definition of the creative question is really an extension of the previous definition. The interviewer supplies a more detailed and perceptive array of clues to develop a question based on the kind of trifling details that the legendary Sherlock Holmes could enjoy. That's creative interviewing at its finest.

LEADING AND LOADED QUESTIONS

Journalists may find limited use for these two final question types. Although they have tarnished reputations, they can add spirit and drama to some kinds of interviews, particularly live broadcast interviews.

Leading Questions

As noted, the leading question telegraphs its expected answer: "You really do love sunsets, don't you?" Should such a question be used in a journalistic interview? Generally no, not if you want candid and truthful answers or unless, in a live broadcast interview, you want to shake up a lethargic respondent with questions calculated to achieve a lively response. Imagine this question asked of a city official who has dedicated his life to developing parks and playgrounds: "Mr. Mayor, don't you really think the city would benefit if some of those parks were converted into business properties? I mean, think of the tax income and the economic benefits to the city." The interviewer doesn't think for a minute that the provocative question will mislead the mayor into saying yes; it may, however, stimulate a spirited response.

Loaded Questions

If the leading question can stimulate spirited response, the loaded question poses an even greater provocation. "Mr. Mayor, isn't there something almost criminally wrong with city government when police officers harass citizens almost to the point of brutality, when taxes run sky-high, when the firefighters take thirty minutes to get to a fire?" Questions like that suggest the reason many officials and business executives attend workshops on how to be interviewed. The questions and responses represent "news theater" more than information gathering.

CHAPTER EIGHT
Planning Your Interview

Q. Senator, if you were conducting this interview,
   what questions would you ask?

A. I think I'd ask myself, "Why am I so poorly
   prepared as to make an idiot of myself before
   thousands of viewers?"

A well-planned interview contains an organizational pattern similar to that of a well-executed news or feature story. In news writing you usually write from the bottom line forward—that is, the most important element first and additional details in more or less descending order of importance. The fact that the king died of a heart attack ranks higher than details of the funeral arrangements.

So it is with the interview. Most news interviews open with attempts to discover the essence of a situation or event: What happened and why? Once you understand that essence, you can flesh out the details. You might even begin an interview with the newly elected governor by asking about the "most important issues facing state government this year." Your planned questions would next move on to less important matters.

Other interviews unfold like a feature story: an opening anecdote (light-hearted icebreaking conversation), a statement of theme (conceptual discussion related to interview's purpose), and then point-by-point elaboration of the theme (covering the points you wish to ask about). Highly focused or thematic interviews unfold this way. You interview a reformed drug addict, Jane Doe, let's say, for a narrow purpose—to develop a magazine article that will help high school teachers and counselors identify symptoms of drug addiction among students. So you direct your questions narrowly to discover those symptoms.

Finally, some interviews work best in chronology. You ask a person who has witnessed a street shooting to "start at the beginning and tell me what happened." Or ask an author, "When did the idea of writing a novel about business ethics first occur to you?" Some interviews unfold almost like a novel, building up through one dramatic discovery after another to reach some climactic revelation.

So the basic organizational patterns for interviewing are (1) inverted pyramid—important matters first, and (2) thematic organization, and (3) chronology. Avoid the hit-and-miss style of interviewing that often characterizes the work of amateurs.

Planning an interview usually involves these seven steps:

1. Defining your purpose
2. Requesting the interview
3. Conducting preinterview research
4. Assessing your source's character and interests
5. Developing specific areas of inquiry
6. Anticipating answers
7. Developing a game plan

PLANNING STARTS WITH PURPOSE

The role of purpose as the key toward conducting fruitful interviews has been emphasized in earlier chapters. It's also the key to planning. But how do you arrive at purpose? It's easy for some news stories. A major hotel fire breaks out, and your interviewing purpose is to get as much detail as you can for the morning edition or the six o'clock news. You ask questions of fire officials and witnesses, guided largely by the needs of an inverted pyramid type of news story, using the five W's along with GOSS, particularly the OSS leading to the obvious G of extinguishing the fire.

Other purposes are more refined and sophisticated. Jon Franklin, a Pulitzer Prize-winning feature writer, looks for story ideas in which the facts resemble the plot line of a work of fiction (Franklin, 1986). Such a plot line, complete with such fiction elements as character, action, tension, and resolution, requires a vastly different interview plan.

The principle, then, is to know precisely what you're looking for. The writer who seeks to include *action* in a feature story will, through interviewing, gather accounts of things happening. They may be melodramatic happenings, such as a firefighter rescuing a child from a precarious perch atop a burning building. Or they could be more internal, such as a narrative account of an executive making a difficult career decision.

For the sake of discussion, let's examine a hypothetical interview with just such an executive, perhaps for a major magazine article or story for the People or Business section of a newspaper. Let's call her Elizabeth Morgan, the chief executive officer of XYZ Corporation, an electronics manufacturing firm that employs 3,000.Purpose starts with asking yourself, why do you want to interview Elizabeth Morgan? Consider some possibilities.

You're a newspaper business editor, and you want to assess the growth of electronics manufacturing in your locality. Morgan is one of a dozen or more executives you'll interview.

You're a feature writer for the People section, and you want to explore how she combines motherhood and career.

You're a reporter and want to investigate rumors of possible work force reductions in the wake of an economic recession.

You're on the staff of *Executive Woman*, a hypothetical magazine edited specifically for women in management positions. You want to write an article about her struggle against odds to reach the top of the corporate ladder in essentially a man's world. Hers is an exemplary story that will inspire your readers.

Such reasons seldom come from nowhere. Rather they grow from small seeds, sometimes a chance remark. The editor of *Executive Woman* goes to a luncheon meeting of business executives and hears talk about the "remarkable turnaround" of XYZ Corporation, once headed for bankruptcy—"until they got that woman in there." And because the editor's job is finding inspirational stories useful to women in management, she immediately takes an interest. "Who is that woman?" she asks, and the editorial game is afoot. The editor learns that Elizabeth Morgan coped with alcoholism, divorce, vicious company politics, bad managerial decisions—"made every mistake in the book"—but somehow learned from her mistakes to emerge as a dark-horse candidate for chief executive officer in a directors meeting two years ago. And she straightened out not only the company but also her personal life. So goes the talk.

From such tenuous beginnings, articles emerge. The idea of an article on Morgan intrigues the editors of *Executive Woman*. What kind of article? Here is where planning becomes essential. You must have a purpose that will serve your readers and that Morgan might logically agree to. The more specific the purpose, the better. That is, an article entitled "Everything you wanted to know about Elizabeth Morgan" has the appeal of a wet dishrag. "Elizabeth Morgan's Struggle to Reach the Corporate Top against Great Odds in a Male-Dominated Field" has more possibilities. Because they circulate to specialized audiences, magazines focus on a precise and compelling theme. They seek out articles that directly affect their readers with advice they can immediately put to use. Based on what we know so far about Elizabeth Morgan, the interview purpose may likely emerge along these lines: What specific things has Elizabeth Morgan learned about management (on both personal and corporate levels) that will help other women learn from her experience, from her mistakes? Imagine a title on the magazine's cover:

"A Corporate Executive Confesses—XYZ's Elizabeth Morgan's Ten Worst Managerial Mistakes and How to Avoid Them."

Magazine articles tend not only to focus sharply on a narrow topic, but the best ones contain what one expert calls "paradox" (Hubbard, 1982). Paradox means things are not what they seem; they defy common-sense expectations. You don't expect an executive to reach the top after all those mistakes, yet here she is. Executives read it because she is the voice of experience sharing insights from which others might learn. This approach is common to magazines, but don't dismiss it as a possibility for a newspaper feature.

REQUESTING AN APPOINTMENT

Will Elizabeth Morgan buy such a purpose? Why should she "confess" anything? Don't make the mistake of self-censorship. More good ideas are killed by timid journalists afraid to propose a provocative project than by uncooperative respondents.

"Sometimes you get your best material when you pose obvious and bizarre questions," suggests a *Washington Times* writer, Lisa McCormack. She once called several famous people—Richard Nixon, G. Gordon Liddy, Gerald Ford, to name a few—to ask them their secret "Walter Mitty fantasy." To the surprise of just about everyone except Lisa McCormack, they talked freely about their fantasies. Gerald Ford imagined himself as a famous baseball player; Liddy saw himself as a World War II fighter pilot. McCormack wasn't surprised to get so many enthusiastic answers from such busy and important people (Liddy called back twice to expand on his answer and Nixon wrote a personal note). It was a provocative and intriguing question. It was also one that secretaries and aides—the gatekeepers that reporters must get past to reach important people—found so fascinating that they themselves wanted to learn the answer. The celebrities themselves were curious about others' fantasies, particularly Richard Nixon's. The former president saw himself performing great music: conducting a symphony orchestra or playing a pipe organ in a great cathedral (*Washington Times*, April 16, 1986).

Some of the VIPs asked McCormack to cite her own fantasy. The tradeoff aided the conversation, especially when she confessed an elaborate fantasy of being a fiftyish, tough-but-soft-hearted "big white mama" who runs a New Orleans jazz joint.

The experience suggests that journalists with unique or sharply focused ideas should not hesitate to try. So in the interview with Morgan, we'll identify ten major managerial mistakes and tell the readers why each mistake is important and how it might be avoided. We will, that is, if she agrees to the proposed purpose.

Requesting an interview appointment requires both advance planning and preliminary preparation. Background reading and preliminary discussions with other business executives can help identify the typical mistakes of managers, both men and women. In this instance, we are interested primarily in those unique to women. Books such as *The Managerial Woman* (Hennig and Jardim, 1977) and *Games Mother Never Taught You* (Harragan, 1977) can help. From the latter you learn that corporate life largely follows the teamwork and organizational structure of athletics and the military. Failure to understand this can contribute to mistakes among women managers.

In short, when you call Morgan for an appointment, you must be prepared to talk knowledgeably about the subject and to answer questions. You can almost anticipate an objection, for instance, to the word "confession." Yet, the confession is a popular article type among magazine editors, being primarily a case history, or a series of mini case histories, that reads like a short story and contains a worthwhile lesson. But because the term calls forth visions of sex, sin, and criminal activities, you may meet some resistance.

Consider the request from her perspective, however. Why would Elizabeth Morgan grant a request that she make a public confession of her past mistakes—mistakes that quite possibly will include references to such past tragedies as her alcoholism and her divorce?

A complex set of perceptions runs through her mind. Foremost is the prestige of the magazine. If Morgan holds it in high regard—and if she identifies with other women managers portrayed in previous issues—she may find the prospect rather exciting. She'll be in excellent company with the Katharine Grahams and Elizabeth Doles already portrayed in the magazine. Second, the editors speak her language. As former managerial women themselves (the only kind of editors the publisher will hire), they talk business with the same expertise as the veteran sportswriter interviewing the young quarterback. Such an interview will truly be an *exchange* of ideas and information. Morgan is perceptive enough to run a multimillion-dollar corporation; she's also perceptive enough to take note of the way the magazine handles delicate information. Yes, the editors demand a lot of intimate information, but they handle it responsibly and discreetly. Yes, that means she'd probably have to talk about the divorce and alcoholism, but they're both in the past now, and the prestige of being featured in the magazine will do more to enhance her career than anything she can think of at the moment. It is one thing to "confess" in the *National Enquirer*, quite another in *Executive Woman*. The magazine is upbeat. It stands on her side— that is, it sincerely wants women to succeed in management. The editors dedicate every word toward that purpose—a noble one to say the least. So Morgan may decide to cooperate with a project that will demand a lot, but also yield great benefit by enhancing a cause with which both she and the editors agree.

That would be the ideal. In short, success in securing such an interview depends largely on the reputation of the medium and of the writer conducting the interview. Those with lesser reputations may have to settle for more superficial purposes.

Planning your request involves six steps.

1. By phone, letter, or personal visit, you will outline your project and why you think it's worthwhile. If she's important enough to be protected by secretaries and assistants, you may need to make your pitch first to a subordinate.
2. You will suggest reasons why she should agree to it— such as education of the public, helping people achieve, helping women to avoid managerial mistakes. Ego strokes can help, so you suggest that lots of important people are talking about XYZ's remarkable recovery from the brink of bankruptcy. Managers desperately need her visionary ideas on how to avoid pitfalls. She has been singled out by other executives as uniquely qualified to discuss the points you have in mind.
3. You will anticipate possible objections and develop arguments to overcome them. You negotiate the objections you can't overcome.

4. You are prepared to engage in preliminary discussion about the topic. "What kinds of mistakes are you talking about?" she may ask. You suggest a few mistakes you've gained from reading and from conversations with managers. "I'm looking for the kinds of mistakes and problems that are unique to women," you say. "For instance, Betty Harragan, in her *Games Mother Never Taught You*, says women don't recognize many of the subtle points about corporate teamwork and structure that men have gained through military service and athletic competition." (Respondents often wish to debate such a point right on the phone— "That's an old-fashioned concept," Morgan says, "a great deal has changed in corporate life since Harragan's book"—and suddenly you both realize that the interview is a *go*, with only the details to be worked out.)

5. You will arrange time and place and any special conditions. (May a tape recorder be used? May you bring a photographer? May you interview members of her staff or family beforehand?)

6. You offer any points that you may want her to think about prior to the interview. "I hope that together we can identify ten mistakes for the story, but we might want to start with twenty and narrow it down to the best ten." Or, "I hope the article will contain anecdotal examples from your own experience, so I'll be asking for examples as we talk."

DO YOUR HOMEWORK

The whole story of interviewing, suggests author Richard Meryman, "is homework." When he worked for the weekly *Life*, Meryman specialized in personality portraits of celebrities such as Elizabeth Taylor and Hubert Humphrey. *Life* once published an article about his interviewing techniques, and his remarks should inspire all serious journalistic interviewers.

> "I keep telling myself that the perfect interview is a perfect set of questions. The older I get, the more time I spend in advance on that list." Meryman does preliminary interviews with people close to his subject, asking and asking questions until "I start hearing things twice." In addition, he reads whatever is already available on the subject, "all the time writing down questions and working out their phrasing." This groundwork averages out to about five hours for every one hour actually spent interviewing the subject.
>
> A few days before meeting with his subject, Meryman becomes absorbed with his condition, in the manner of boxers and decathlon champions. "I don't touch any alcohol at all for about three days before an interview. I try to get a great deal of sleep. I don't eat starch or sugar. I spend the whole day or at least half the day before in bed. I eat steak for breakfast. Basically, I'm clearing my mind, getting my reflexes and attention as high as I can get them," because, as Meryman explains, "the important thing in an interview is not the first answer to a question on a particular topic. That answer should give you the clue to a second question on the subject, and that will lead to a third—and so on until you get to the nub. That's why I train, so that as the person is talking I am supersensitive to those half-articulated hints which clue me into follow-up questions."[*]

[*]Editor's Note, *Life* Magazine, July 7, 1972. © Time, Inc. Reprinted by permission.

Perhaps not all media can afford to keep you in bed for a working day. But don't lose sight of the point: Interview planning must include preparation, even physical conditioning. Here are two typical areas of research for a major interview.

Documents

Consult the news library for previously published articles on Elizabeth Morgan or her business firm or the topic of management, particularly women in management. Go to your local library and consult an index of library holdings on the related subjects and at least skim the books you find. Books such as Harragan's *Games Mother Never Taught You* (1977) and Dowling's *The Cinderella Complex* (1981) can help you form your own list of typical managerial mistakes and problems common to women managers. They will thus help you talk knowledgeably about the topic. Consult national newspaper indexes particularly those produced by *The New York Times, Wall Street Journal, Washington Post*, and other major newspapers. In *The Wall Street Journal*, for example, you'll find a useful special report, "The Corporate Woman" (March 24, 1986), filled with accounts of the problems and concerns of women in management, particularly the "glass ceiling": the invisible barrier that seems to prevent women from reaching the top in corporate management.

A subsequent book, *Breaking the Glass Ceiling* (Morrison,White, and Van Velson, 1987), elaborates on that theme. Consult magazine indexes such as the *Magazine Index, Reader's Guide to Periodical Literature,* or *Business Periodicals Index.*

Most libraries contain other research indexes that you can use, depending on your needs. If Elizabeth Morgan is prominent, you may find accounts of her in *Current Biography* or *Biography Index.* The community relations department probably has information on both her and XYZ Corporation. General reading in business magazines such as *Savvy* (a magazine for women in managerial positions) is essential.

Basically, you're looking for information that will help you plan the interview, develop your questions, and better inform yourself about the issues of management of a large business firm. Reference books cited here are by no means a complete list. Serious interviewers should have a copy of a book about library research methods, such as Kessler and McDonald's *Uncovering the News* (1987).

Meanwhile, you can produce your own documents. Let's say you are delivering a speech to a group of women in management—not an uncommon experience for an editor of a magazine on management. Passing out slips of blank paper on which you ask each member of the audience to list her "worst managerial mistake" can yield surprisingly effective responses. An audience of fifty may submit twenty or thirty different mistakes and also suggest some of the more common ones. If fifteen of them list a particular problem, you'll have achieved a useful insight to bring to the interview.

Talking to Others

Preliminary interviews with those acquainted with your person can be useful in countless ways. You can start with informal conversations around the office with any reporters who have interviewed Morgan in the past. You may gain good advice on how to approach her and what subjects she might prefer to talk about or to avoid. Business competitors, even enemies, can provide worthwhile insights and information. Colleagues and family members can often provide personal asides. Obviously, you must exercise caution in approaching friends, family, and colleagues whose loyalty is to her, not you. Talk to them only after she has agreed to the interview. They will check with her before they agree to talk with you. If she has come to trust you, so will they.

ASSESSING CHARACTER AND INTERESTS

Some interviewers appear blessed by luck—they seem to have a knack for getting people to open up to them. Most of them make their own luck. People once marveled how Theodore Roosevelt became such a brilliant conversationalist, equally at home with cowboys and diplomats. Simple. Roosevelt sat up late the night before reading up on subjects he knew would interest his visitor (Carnegie, 1936).

A famous interviewer of World War I compared interviewing to "salesmanship." Isaac F. Marcosson, who interviewed such figures as Theodore Roosevelt and General John J. Pershing, said he always made it a point to learn all he could about a person before the interview. "This is precisely what any good salesman would do."

All celebrated people have an interest, such as yachting, art, great books—"and with that interest you can disarm prejudice and even sterilize opposition to your purpose," he wrote. Interviews must be pitched on a "separate and distinct plane. Some silent men must be swept irresistibly into conversation on the high tide of talk. You take the initiative. Then too there is the type who begins to speak the moment you see him. All you have to do is to guide the current of words" (Marcosson, 1919).

So knowing that Morgan sails yachts and adores the work of impressionist artists can assist your preparation. If Theodore Roosevelt could spend the time reading up on subjects prior to the arrival of an important visitor, surely journalists can do likewise. So you spend an evening on art and yachting.

PREPARING AREAS OF INQUIRY

Precisely what is it that you want to ask? In this case you have but one question, "What are those ten worst mistakes women managers make?" You have a focus so precise that both interviewer and source can follow it easily. But you'll prepare questions, or at least topics of inquiry, to help identify those problem areas.

1. Naivete. Is it true that women often don't understand the rules of men's corporate gamesmanship? If so, what can be done?
2. Absence of career goals or plans; do women plan less for the future than men?
3. Insufficient assertiveness?
4. Tough negotiating ability—women at a disadvantage? Or *advantage* perhaps? (Better listening ability? Less threatening?)
5. Drinking; are office expectations different for women?
6. Power—how do women get it and use it?
7. Gentle persuasion, do women use it more than men?
8. Problems of taking criticism too seriously? . . . and so on.

ANTICIPATING ANSWERS

Suppose you ask Morgan a question on the subject of drinking among women managers: "On the subject of drinking, Betty Harragan discusses the difference in expectations between male and female executives. She says men can get smashed at the office party and people hardly notice, whereas if a woman does the same thing it's a corporate scandal forever more. I'd be interested in knowing whether you have noticed these kinds of expectations."

How will Morgan answer your question about drinking? She has about five options.

1. Agree (more or less) that expectations are different
2. Disagree (more or less)
3. Provide some other perception about drinking
4. Decline comment or dismiss drinking as unimportant
5. Bridge to another topic

For each option, you can think through your next step. If she agrees or provides another perception, then you'll probe for reasons and anecdotal examples that illustrate the problem. She may even volunteer her personal problems with alcohol as an example, particularly if she has confidence in your ability to handle discreetly such delicate information. You'll probe for the lessons she learned from the experience and the advice she has for others.

If she disagrees, you'll probe a little. What specifically does she disagree with? Is she suggesting that business executives don't drink? That she herself has not seen the problem? (Will you confront her at this point with evidence of her own drinking? Probably not, unless you expect this to be the last subject covered in the interview.) That the problem exists but is not worthy of the ten worst mistakes?

If she dismisses it as unimportant, then you can agree to drop it or you can discuss its importance after you've settled on your list of ten worst problems.

If she bridges to another subject, you can bridge her right back to drinking so that she responds in one of the other categories. Stay alert for bridges and ignore them only if the original question seems too unimportant to pursue.

It's always useful to put yourself in the other person's place and think how, were the circumstances reversed, *you* might answer some of your questions. How, for example, would you answer a question about drinking, particularly if you had had a bout with alcoholism in your past? The only way you'd talk about your own personal drinking problem, you may decide, is if you're convinced that it would be truly helpful to others. Anyone proposing to ask about drinking had better make a serious sales pitch about why it's necessary and how the matter would be handled. Thus your planning includes preparation for a persuasive argument on the subject.

THE GAME PLAN

Eventually, the elements of the interview will settle themselves into some kind of organizational pattern, a master plan. As you piece it all together, certain questions will emerge.

Will you insist that she "confess" her own mistakes or will you ask her to speak more generally about problems, some of which she has personally experienced, some of which she hasn't?

Will you seek personal anecdotes? If so, you'll ask questions calculated to elicit anecdotes, such as coming in with several anecdotes of your own to prime the pump.

Will you rely entirely on *her* list of ten mistakes or will you negotiate? If she gives you a list of mistakes, and it seems to miss certain points you consider important, what then?

Will your article contain an introduction giving Morgan's background and qualifications for commenting? If so, you'll ask for any background information that you cannot obtain from published sources.

Eventually it all comes together into some kind of master game plan, perhaps something like this one, which follows the "thematic" organization of interviewing as described early in this chapter.

1. Start with icebreaking conversation about artists Van Gogh and Gauguin and yachting in the Caribbean.
2. When the time seems right, move into the theme of the interview, starting with a full explanation of purpose and what you hope to achieve.
3. Discuss the issue conceptually at first: Why do women executives need this advice? What does she perceive to be the differences, if any, in the management styles of men and women?
4. If appropriate, open with some of your own suggestions about managerial mistakes. Or hear hers first if she seems eager to present them.
5. Discuss anecdotal experiences in relation to each major problem; come prepared with stories gained from reading and previous interviews.
6. Stress the need for the lesson to be learned from each experience. Come prepared with possible examples of lessons others have learned as a means of stimulating discussion.
7. Ask any final questions you haven't already covered, such as biographical information if unavailable elsewhere. (This could come anywhere in the interview, depending on circumstances. If the person is not well known—little biographical information is available elsewhere—it will probably come early in the interview because of your need to know the person's background as context for the questions to follow. In Morgan's case, most biographical details will be known through preinterview research, though a few missing details may need to be explored.)
8. Once you have settled on the final "ten worst," seek some overall conceptual statement, perhaps a quotable comment that sums it all up. Although you discussed this earlier, you probably will find it useful here, too, at the end when both parties know precisely what those ten mistakes are. Summarizing kinds of comments often come naturally at this stage as the interview is winding down.

KEEP YOUR PLANS FLEXIBLE

Sometimes interviewers can benefit from the advice that philosopher–educator William James gave to teachers: Know your subject thoroughly and then trust to luck. Knowing your subject thoroughly permits you to follow down new conversational pathways you could not have envisioned in the planning stage. A certain spontaneity—the off-the-wall answer, the unexpected response—contributes to a more robust and insightful interview that can enhance your article.

But it means frequent departures from your game plan. Suppose you have ten basic questions, and the answer to question 1 happens to include a partial answer to question 4. Do you insist on returning to question 1 or do you follow through with 4? There's no good answer other than to suggest that the more the interview follows the pattern of normal human conversation—with all its stops and turns and erratic patterns—the better. If your source is enthusiastically discussing question 4, why not let her continue rather than dampen the enthusiasm? You can return to question 1 later. Your organizational pattern will make it easier to keep track of where the interview is going and what missing pieces must be covered eventually.

In such wayward conversations, however, you must serve as guide. Use of transitional phrases helps keep the organizational pattern on track. "I think we've covered the problems of alcoholism sufficiently, so unless you have a final thought why don't we move along to the subject of power and how managers use it."

You then stay with power until you have what you want—unless the conversation takes another erratic spin into another subject, from point 1 to point 7, for example. If you decide to pursue point 7 and get back to point 1 later, some kind of transitional remark will help. "Your comment on assertiveness among women is a point I had on my list of questions. Let's talk more about it now, but I do want to get back to power later on."

Transitions flow more smoothly if you utilize the respondent's words. "Something you said earlier—about your having to learn to be less thin-skinned in response to criticism—reminds me that I want to talk about that." If you are about to ask something personal, such as whether *she* ever became emotional over criticism, using her words to introduce the subject makes it seem less harsh. It's as though she herself had brought it up. In a sense, she did. Such a transition also shows that you're listening. Nothing encourages conversation and personal candor more than good listening.

CHAPTER NINE
Learning to Listen

Q. Tell me about listening.
A. Ah, listening. Listening is the one area of
   human activity where it makes sense to be a
   little selfish. Imagine! The more you take from
   a speaker through listening, the more that
   speaker will give.*
Q. Huh?

Journalistic interviewers are not equal. Some get more than others. They do it not by clever questions. Quite the opposite. They get more information by asking fewer questions and listening more intensely. Two kinds of listening are involved.

The first kind of listening occurs when you know precisely what kinds of details you want out of an interview. If you want quotable quotes or anecdotes, you must listen for them and recognize them when they occur. Sources don't say, "Here's an anecdote for your lead"; they just talk. It's up to you to distinguish the quotable kernels from the chaff.

People don't often encounter the second kind of listening. Here you listen with the entire self, the eyes and the body as well as the ears. You listen from the other person's point of view, listen not to judge but to understand,

*Paraphrasing Nichols and Stevens (1957).

listen for what is not said as well as what is said. That kind of listening is so rare that we make little jokes about its absence. A *Reader's Digest* anecdote portrays a hostess setting out to test how well people listen. She urged people to try one of her canapes. "I've filled them with strychnine," she said. "Lovely," they said. "I must have your recipe." (Margaret Lane, "Are You Really Listening?" November 1980.)

Listening is a major trait of a good interviewer

AGGRESSIVE LISTENING

Listening is not a passive activity. "Aggressive listening" may indeed seem a contradiction in terms. But, in truth, you have to work hard to catch the meaning of what the other person is saying, and you have to encourage that person by the way you react, both verbally and nonverbally.

Research evidence suggests that adults spend more time listening than in any other communications activity. An early study (Rankin, 1926) calculated that people spend forty-two percent of their communications time listening (versus thirty-two percent speaking, fifteen percent reading, eleven percent writing). By 1975, when another researcher updated the study, the time spent listening had risen to fifty-five percent (Werner, 1975; reported in Wolvin and Coakley, 1985). Yet schools pay scant attention to listening as an academic topic, and even academic research on the subject remains sparse.

The key to listening appears to be the speed at which the human mind processes information. We speak at roughly 125 words a minute, but the mind can absorb material at three or four times that rate. But the mind can do only one thing at a time. It can dart in and out of the conversation, retrieving pertinent bits and pieces of previous conversations, comparing a speaker's ideas with other ideas, and contemplating follow-up questions to be asked. Or it can take totally irrelevant excursions.

How people use that gap between the mind's activity and the speaker's pace distinguishes the listeners from the nonlisteners. The best listeners, according to one authority (Nichols and Stevens, 1957), tend to think ahead of the speaker, sometimes arriving at the point before the speaker does.

The best listeners hold other attributes in common, according to studies that compared the listening habits of the best and worst listeners, as measured by tests of their ability to remember material presented to them orally. The best listeners used the extra mental processing time to think about what was being said. They periodically reviewed what the speaker had said and what they imagined would be said next. They weighed the speaker's comments against other evidence. And they listened between the lines for ideas and attitudes hinted at but not expressed directly.

The worst listeners tended to listen for facts, sometimes trying to memorize them without much regard to their meaning. They were often distracted by little things, the noise of a passing vehicle, perhaps, or by some personal quality possessed by the speaker—too ugly, too attractive, squeaky voice, or whatever. Often the poor listeners were distracted by a single emotion-laden word that derailed their attentiveness to an irrelevant line of thought. Often the worst listeners dismissed the topic or the speaker as boring.

Both Rogers (1952) and Lee (1952) have proposed an experiment in which (at a meeting, say) no one can speak unless he or she has summarized the previous speaker's thoughts to that person's satisfaction. "If you try, you will discover it is one of the most difficult things you have ever tried to do," said Rogers. Lee found in meetings where it was tried that utter confusion reigned for a time, but then something remarkable happened. Garrulous people tried to make their points more succinct, and timid people found the courage to speak up when they found others were actually listening.

Listening also takes courage. It extracts at least two prices. The first price is the risk of having your ideas changed. What you learn by listening to others can change your life. "Such listening requires a kind of courage that few of us have ever mustered," suggest Nichols and Stevens. "Whenever we listen thoroughly to another person's ideas, we open ourselves up to the possibility that some of our ideas are wrong."

It's hard to be a good listener and to be narrowly self-righteous at the same time. Good listeners, as evidenced by the reaction of students who have taken interviewing classes, find a whole new world opening up to them, the timid finding the courage to go out and meet new people, the arrogant finding the courage to venture out from their fortresses to learn and appreciate other points of view.

The second price is the risk of involvement. So powerful a tool is listening that we find ourselves getting involved with the people to whom we listen. Studs Terkel explained that in the haste of interviewing the working people who comprised his best-selling *Working* he sometimes neglected certain social amenities. A Brooklyn fireman invited him for dinner and Terkel mumbled something about having to hustle to another appointment. "You runnin' off like that?" the fireman said. "Here we been talkin' all afternoon. It won't sound nice. This guy, Studs, comes to the house, gets my life on tape, and says 'I gotta go.'" Terkel stayed. "Looking back," he wrote, "how could I have been so insensitive?" (Terkel, 1974.)

HOW TO BE A PROFESSIONAL LISTENER

The following suggestions can help you develop listening skills. Part of the skills development comes in recognizing common pitfalls. Another part comes in recognizing precisely what you should be listening for.

Get Ready to Listen

This relates to the question, What, precisely, do you listen *for*? The advance preparation discussed in earlier chapters is part of getting ready. A carefully planned interview will make it clear just what you want out of the interview, and thus you can identify the points and the supporting material for which you should listen.

Another part of getting ready is the physical aspect discussed by Richard Meryman; fatigue or the mental cloudiness induced by alcohol or drugs will hamper your ability to listen, and so Meryman suggests a physical kind of training for important interviews.

Not so obvious is the need to recognize and eliminate the emotional filters that often block our listening ability. We are talking here about the topics that, sometimes without our hardly realizing why, make our blood boil or turn cold. Such words as *home, mother, patriotism, sex, abortion, Communist, Republican, Democrat,* contain a certain emotional content for individuals. Mention of "home" triggers such strong emotions that, instead of listening to what the speaker is saying about home, we are suddenly picturing mentally a beloved or hated childhood experience.

Everyone has a set of such words. The words accumulate through life's experience, and they change over time. "Evolution" and "hippie" contain less emotional content than they once did; "yuppie" and "AIDS" are more current at this writing. If you faced up to these emotional land mines—perhaps by writing them down—you'd not let them interfere.

Avoid Prejudging People

This has been discussed earlier (Chapters 2 and 5), with the suggestion that if you've come to interview a convicted child molester you ought at least to show respect and appreciation for the answers you receive, particularly if they are candid answers to sensitive questions. You don't have to like the person you are interviewing. But as long as the conversation produces information, you are on the right track. No doubt if your tone and attitude are judgmental—the child molester is a rotten and unworthy person—the attitude will be quickly perceived and lead either to defensive hyperbole or to clamming up altogether.

The child molester is so extreme an example that the point may be lost. You can easily envision an article or broadcast documentary on child molestation and imagine how interviews with both molesters and victims can contribute to the drama and public understanding of the topic. But what about the respondent who is a bore?

Judging a person a bore is the surest way toward a self-fulfilling prophecy. So what if the football coach has uttered the same cliches for forty years? Perhaps the journalists have been asking cliche questions. A listening and thinking reporter may be able to overcome that. Some suggestions for doing so are offered in Chapter 13, but the major suggestion at this point is to avoid stereotyping people in the first place. Even if you have interviewed a person repeatedly and received the same tired old answers, you should remain optimistic. You may not be able to change the other person, but you can change you—the interview purposes you pursue, the questions you ask, and especially the acuteness and perception of your listening. Maybe the reason some people are boring is that they have superficial personality characteristics that cause others not to listen to them. They're ugly or shy or they stutter. A professional interviewer works around these problems and listens for what is being said, not the manner of presentation.

Listen for Major Points

Listening to conversation is not like listening to a prepared speech. A good speaker generally has a theme supported by two or more major points, with each point supported by facts, illustrative examples, and anecdotes. Good speakers often identify their main points, alerting their audience by such remarks as, "My next point is . . . ." Interviews, unfortunately, often ramble the way conversations do. That's not necessarily bad as a means of achieving conversational rapport, but along the way both parties to the conversation must identify the conceptual elements—the points—of what is being said. The interview that focuses on points, such as the ten worst managerial mistakes cited in Chapter 8, will have an easier time of it because both parties have set out to identify those ten points. In a less specific interview, the points might not emerge so readily. Sometimes it helps to ask a garrulous talker what's the point. Do it in a nonthreatening way: "As I understand it, your point is . . ." or "Are you saying that . . . ?" or "Forgive me, but I'm not sure I perceive the point you're making." Sometimes you will discover that the speaker has no point. Or you yourself may ultimately define the points, either during the interview or later when writing an article based on the interview.

Listen for Supporting Evidence

Once you understand the point and perhaps how it connects with the main theme of a person's conversation, you can seek supporting evidence. Suppose, as an example, you are interviewing a VIP about the hidden perils of celebrity status. Sally Celebrity says, "The worst part is venturing out in public." That's her point, now what evidence can she produce to support it? If she doesn't volunteer it, you ask for it. She has signed umpteen thousand autographs. She can't do so common a thing as go to the market for groceries without being besieged by fans. Just try having lunch at a major restaurant. Drunks accost her at the table. Women stare at her in the ladies room. People are forever wanting her to pose for a Polaroid picture with Aunt Suzie, and, why, just the other day—and she launches into an anecdote involving a particularly obnoxious fan. These represent the supporting evidence.

Evaluate What Is Being Said

Open-minded tolerance and nonjudgmental listening do not mean unquestioning naivete. If you have prepared for the interview, you'll know when something said in the conversation doesn't equate with what you have learned elsewhere. Asking about the possible discrepancy shows not only that you're listening, but that you're thinking. The combination is hard to beat—a prepared interviewer who also thinks, doing so by examining comments, weighing, comparing, evaluating, and devising new questions on the spot.

Often you will think through several remarks, putting them together in novel ways, maybe to test a hypothesis as defined in the creative question (see Chapter 7) or perhaps merely to clarify comments that seem at odds.

Listen for What Is Not Said or What Is Only Half-articulated

Listening with the third ear is the theme of a classic work by Theodor Reik, who published a book by that name in 1952. People communicate in various ways, often by nonverbal means. You ask a woman a question about her future and she blushes or smiles or raises an eyebrow ever so slightly. You suspect you may have hit upon a question that has more than routine significance to her. The signal doesn't tell you what the significance is, only that you might profitably ask further questions, even if only, "Why do you smile when I ask that?"

Similarly, people's word choices are clues to deeper meanings. An interviewer sensitive to words may well pick up on a phrase such as "As a public administrator, you are subjected to questions that defy explanation...."

Subjected? What an interesting choice of words. What does it mean? That's precisely what you must ask. Doing so will turn up interesting responses, possibly even nonboring responses.

Offer Encouragement and Direction

Interviewers should ask questions. If this seems obvious, apparently it isn't to a lot of interviewing students who tend to state agenda topics and then, with no further comment or follow-up questions, simply sit back deadpan and take notes on what is said, like a stenographer. When the monologue has ended on topic 1, the interviewer announces topic 2 and the monologue begins anew. Such interviews aren't much fun. A listening interviewer will not only smile, nod, frown, say "uh-huh," and so forth, but will direct the conversation with probe questions. Ask Sally Celebrity if she's devised ways of coping with the autograph seekers, such as trying to circulate incognito or going in disguise or denying she's really Ms. Celebrity. (And, by chance, does she feel downhearted if she goes out in public and no one pays any attention to her?)

Show That You're Listening

As mentioned earlier (Chapter 5), when people aren't listening, they're obvious about it, often through distracting mannerisms such as averted eye contact, fondling a pencil, tapping or bouncing a foot, and so on. All these show preoccupation with concerns unrelated to the conversation. The reverse is sometimes true. Deadpan or glassy-eyed expressions are often the giveaway. Excessive note taking—trying to get *everything* down—gets in the way of listening (more about that in Chapter 12).

Men often use body posture to demonstrate nonlistening attitudes. The extreme instance in my experience came in a classroom exercise where students were paired off to interview one another. A young man interviewed a young woman while slumped down in his chair, his feet up on a window ledge. His head rested lower than his feet, and from this supine position he conducted his interview. When, in subsequent class discussion, she commented on his "strange posture" as being a little too informal, he confessed that he was only vaguely aware of his posture in his attempt to keep the session casual. The preoccupation with keeping things casual no doubt hampered the listening. The problem is not confined to students. When I mentioned this bizarre posture in a workshop attended by newspaper professionals, a business writer confessed to the sudden realization that he, too, had indulged in sloppy posture almost as bad.

Showing that you're listening means avoiding all the pitfalls cited here. It means utilizing the subtle and mostly nonverbal signs that facilitate communication covered in Chapter 5, such as alert body posture, eye contact, smiles, nods, and paralanguage responses such as Uh-huh or Mmmmm.

How to be too casual while interviewing

Dress for Listening

What has dress to do with listening? Years ago, college students asked that question frequently. The answer then, as now when the question is less frequent, is that in theory dress wouldn't seem to make a bit of difference. But in practice it makes a world of difference. People often dress to tell the world something about themselves. Other people perceive that message. Visiting the plush office of a bank president while wearing faded jeans and tattered sweatshirt will probably result in disaster. Your mode of dress suggests that you've come to make a statement, not to listen. True, that might not be your conscious intent, but that's the way the president perceives it—unless you can offer a reasonable explanation as Scott Martell did the time he showed up for a black-tie store opening wearing blue jeans (Chapter 1).

So it's best to dress in a way that does not call attention to yourself. Don't wear a tattered sweatshirt to the banker's office, but don't wear a cocktail dress to interview migrant farm laborers in the field. On the other hand, don't go to ridiculous extremes trying to fit in.

CHAPTER TEN
Journalistic Observation

Q. So, Champ, you've been in the boxing ring
with some of the great prize fighters of all
time— so what's it like to get creamed by
someone like Sugar Ray Leonard?

A. Stand up, fella, and I'll show ya.

One problem with interviews is that they are largely words. If you trust the adage that actions speak louder than words, then observing and reporting action can bring you closer to truth. Journalists sometimes call this "showing" rather than merely "telling."

To illustrate, imagine asking people what they would do if they drove down a street and saw a young woman in distress? They'd stop and assist her, of course. When a woman tested that hypothesis years ago by having herself hogtied to a telephone pole in San Francisco, she may have come closer to truth. No fewer than 110 cars passed by before someone stopped to help.

So journalists use observation to supplement what they can learn through documents and interviewing. It is not new. A century ago the irrepressible Nellie Bly, pen name for a reporter named Elizabeth Cochrane, feigned insanity to get herself admitted to a New York insane asylum. In vivid detail she wrote articles for Joseph Pulitzer's *New York World* about the wretched conditions she observed in the asylum, thus leading the way for countless similar projects by later generations of journalists. In 1889, Bly became a legend when the *World* sent her on a mission to see if she could circle the globe in less time than that envisioned in Jules Verne's fictional account, *Around the World in Eighty Days*. By trains, ships, sampans, and horseback, Bly made it in 72 days.

Such activities subsequently acquired an academic name, "participant observation," which means the researcher takes part in the activities being described. If you want to write about hobos, become one yourself, get to know them, and live as they live, as sociologist Nels Anderson did in a classic and pioneering study (Anderson, 1923). The hobo days are by no means past. In 1983, a *Sacramento Bee* editor chanced to talk with an aging hobo who said things had changed; the ancient art of hoboing had been taken over by a "bunch of greenhorns." The editor assigned reporter Dale Maharidge and photographer Michael Williams to the story, and they promptly hopped a freight to Oregon. They became so enthralled with the project that they not only produced an award-winning series for the *Bee*, but they became "professional hobos" for a year, producing a book on the topic.

Like interviewing itself, most of what we know about methods of systematic observation comes from academic areas, notably anthropology and sociology. They speak of "field methods," combining interviews with systematic methods of observation, in a variety of exotic locales ranging from the villages of Samoa in Margaret Mead's classic *Coming of Age in Samoa* (1928) to street gangs in Boston depicted in William F. Whyte's *Street Corner Society* (1943). A more recent example is Elijah Anderson's adventures in a south Chicago tavern frequented by ghetto blacks, depicted in his book, *A Place on the Corner* (1978). From such experiences have come numerous books on the methods of field research, such as Whyte's *Learning from the Field* (1984), Spradley's *Participant Observation* (1980), and Wax's *Doing Fieldwork* (1971).

For the journalist, observation offers an opportunity to exercise all the senses. What you experience—not only what you see, hear, feel, taste, and smell, but also what you feel inside, your emotional response—can produce high drama. If all goes well, the views and activities of the observer and the observed will coalesce into a vivid and substantial commentary about the topic.

Clearly, this adds a new depth and vitality to the journalistic interview. But it is by no means confined to participant observation. Print journalists can improve their reporting techniques by learning to provide descriptive touches from almost any interview. Television interviewers can enhance TV's already formidable advantage in showing whatever topic is being talked about.

THE NEW RESEARCH REQUIREMENTS OF LITERARY JOURNALISM

Print reporters have witnessed a recent trend toward "literary news writing," which to one observer represents no less than the death of a contradiction in terms. "Literary news writing," says R. Thomas Berner, "is the marriage of depth reporting and literary techniques in newspaper writing. Among those techniques are narration and scene, summary and process, point of view, drama, chronological organization, rhythm, imagery, foreshadowing, metaphor, irony, dialogue, overall organization (beginning, middle, end)—all girded by good reporting" (Berner, 1986).

Such writing places a special burden on the journalist's reporting methods, particularly interviewing and observation. Examine the kinds of articles that win prizes, for instance. The Pulitzer Prize committee began awarding prizes for feature writing in 1979, giving the first to a *Baltimore Evening Sun* science writer, Jon Franklin. His "Terrifying Journey through Tunnels of the Brain" was a suspenseful, tragic account of a brain operation. Pulitzers awarded for features since then—including one (later returned) to the ill-fated Janet Cooke of the *Washington Post*—have recognized dramatic accounts that read like fiction stories.

The story by Janet Cooke was indeed fiction, an account of an eight-year-old heroin addict named Jimmy. The article was eventually exposed as a hoax: Jimmy simply didn't exist. All of the intricate details about him, even the "cherubic expression on his small, round face," came out of the writer's imagination. But that fact merely dramatizes the enormous pressures on writers to produce dramatic nonfiction. Eventually, their ability to interview and observe may catch up with their ambition to become literary news writers.

And that is where observation comes in. Everything said about interviewing—especially about having a well-defined purpose and knowing precisely what you're looking for—applies to observation. If you are going to observe people in action as a means of developing narration, scene, even dialogue, then you'd better know when pertinent activities occur and get them into your notes. Knowing what's relevant and useful in literary journalism could require a whole course of study in short story writing. Take tension, for example. It means suspense, the fuel that keeps the reader going, wondering what happens next. How did the operation on Mrs. Kelly's brain turn out in Jon Franklin's prize-winning account? You have to read to the end of the story to find out. And to keep the reader in suspense, the writer has to provide details that march relentlessly toward the climactic resolution.

Among such details will be tense scenes. One of them in Franklin's story shows the surgeon's probe pressing through a tunnel in the brain, nudging up against an aneurysm, a ballooned-out section of artery resembling, in Franklin's words, "a tire about to burst, a balloon ready to burst, a time bomb the size of a pea." The time bomb must be defused before the surgeon's probe can pass on to reach a brain tumor farther along the tunnel. Franklin shows the probe nudging gently against the aneurysm and quotes a nurse: "Sometimes you touch one and blooey, the wolf's at the door."

THREE TYPES OF JOURNALISTIC OBSERVATION

Three types of observation are normally part of the interviewer's techniques.

Nonparticipant Observation

This might be called the first level of observation, and it is something journalists do, or should do, routinely. The sportswriter covering a basketball game, the drama critic attending a play, the political reporter viewing a debate in Congress—all are examples of a "spectator" kind of reporting common to much news coverage.

Think of nonparticipant observation as "going along for the ride." It means sitting in on the action. It can be more than a city council meeting, however. You ride with the teenagers in a car cruising Main Street on a Saturday night for a story on teen society. You stand by in the hospital emergency room to witness the handling of victims of Saturday night traffic accidents. Or you accompany a long-haul truck driver on a trip across America.

In nonparticipant observation, journalists make clear their identity and their purpose. The line between the participant and nonparticipant turns hazy at times. The operative factor is whether you actually *do* the things the other participants do. In the emergency room, you clearly won't participate in any of the medical activities, but you might be asked to comfort a screaming patient or a frightened child. When you do that, you become a participant observer.

Participant Observation

Here the journalist takes part in the activity being described. In 1963, feminist author Gloria Steinem obtained a job as a Playboy Bunny in the early days of the Playboy phenomenon so that she might write a magazine article about the experience (*Show*, May–June 1963). John Howard Griffin, a white man, darkened his skin so that he could pass as a black. He wrote a moving account (*Black Like Me*, 1961) about travels through the South as a black man. The work helped to usher in the civil rights era of the 1960s. In Honolulu, reporter Mike Keller spent five days in the state penitentiary to write a series of articles for the *Advertiser*. In Portland, Oregon, reporter Jann Mitchell lived for three days as a skid road denizen, begging for money, sleeping in flop houses, and on one occasion even eating a half-finished sandwich retrieved from a garbage can. She was hungry, and hunger can turn a passive participant into an eager one, it seems.

Some journalists have made participant observation a literary trademark. George Plimpton is widely known for ventures into professional

"So, tell me, do you find this exhausting or what?"

athletics. He once trained with the Detroit Lions and actually served as quarterback for five plays in an exhibition game, all of it depicted in his book, *Paper Lion.* Others have had participation thrust upon them, ready or not. It was a wasp sting on the leg that prompted Oregon reporter Lisa Strycker to research and write a story about an unusually heavy infestation of wasps in her community one summer. That, too, is participant observation.

Sometimes reporters keep their identity secret, as in Nellie Bly's encounter at the insane asylum or Griffin's travels as a black man in the South. It could not have been otherwise in those cases where it was important that people behave as they normally would. In other instances, such as Plimpton's *Paper Lion* adventure, the participants know of the reporter's identity. That knowledge gives the reporter certain advantages: With no deception involved, you're free to circulate freely and to ask questions. People often seek you out to offer suggestions and insights when they know your identity.

The secret-identity type of project poses difficult questions. Are you a good enough actor to fake insanity, for example? It's not so easy in today's era of sophisticated psychiatry. Is it really worth the time and trouble? And if someone confided in you thinking you were a fellow patient—only to find the comments quoted later in the paper—are you being fair? More on ethics later.

Unobtrusive Observation

This is a quiet mouse-in-the-corner type of observation, often accompanied by some numerical tallies. College students do it frequently in their classes, it seems. When members of an interviewing class undertook to query students about what they thought about while sitting through "dull" classroom lectures at the University of Oregon, the answers astonished them. They expected to hear confessions of students daydreaming anything from erotic fantasies to vacation plans, and in part that's what they found. They did not expect to find that students spent vast amounts of time engaging in precisely the same kind of unobtrusive observation that professionals use.

They prepared tally sheets and counted such things as the number of times various professors uttered cliches in their lectures. Each time a professor uttered a term like "viable alternative" or "in my judgment," one student tallied it on his chart. The all-time winner was the phrase, "In the final analysis." Another student reported that a teaching assistant in English had used the term "you know" no fewer than seventy times in a fifty-minute lecture.

Professional observers use the same technique, as described by the leading book on the subject (Webb, 1981). It's known academically as "nonreactive measurement," so called because the techniques of observation do not affect the behavior of the people under observation.

So it is with social scientists. In a classic study in 1922, for example, researcher H. T. Moore spent several weeks strolling up New York's Broadway and recording any fragments of conversation he could overhear. Among 174 fragments, Moore found "talk of the opposite sex" in eight percent of the man-to-man conversations and forty-four percent of the woman-to-woman conversations.

The differences between the genders has been the subject of observation ever since. In 1981, a study reported differences observed in speech patterns between the sexes: women ask more questions, and men interrupt more often, particularly when talking with women. Other studies have shown that women are more inclined to look people in the eye when listening. One observer found that when crossing the street men strayed outside the painted crosswalk lines more than women did (twenty-three percent versus ten percent).

We know from such studies (all reported in Webb, 1981) that college students are more inclined to wear clothes that identify their school affiliation after the football team has won a game.

Auto honking studies have shown that drivers are less likely to honk at pickup trucks carrying a rifle in the rear window. Male drivers are more inclined to honk in hot weather than cold, except when a "sexily attired female" has crossed the street in front of them.

Even classroom seating has been observed. Students who participate the most and get the best grades tend to sit in the front and center of the room, while the poorer students sit on the sides and in the back.

Journalists have done similar projects. In Oregon a woman reporter stalled her car along a country roadway and feigned a flat tire to see what kinds of people would stop to offer assistance. Men dressed in suits and ties whizzed past her; the men who stopped to help wore casual clothes and drove dusty pickup trucks.

Journalists often do this on a purely informal basis. Careful listeners will note the approximate number of times a person in conversation will make a particular reference. "Every time Jones uses a metaphor, it comes out airplanes," a journalist remarked of a colleague one time—an example of an informal kind of unobtrusive observation. Although it lacks the precision of an actual tally, it does show an acute listening ability, thus demonstrating the difference between the perceptive journalist and the hack.

WHAT TO OBSERVE

We've already noted that targets of journalistic observation are formed by your needs as a news writer or storyteller. Given that authors' requirements vary—dull writers require less detail than exciting writers—a system of observation can help. If you want to write something dramatic, you can use what the Greek philosopher, Aristotle, identified as the four elements of dramatic literature—tension, unity, action, and irony.

Tension has already been defined as suspense, and unity means that your story ought to hang together on the basis of a theme—a central point you want to make through what you write. Action means showing one or more characters doing something. And irony has two possible meanings, one, an unanticipated outcome of events, and, two, a meaning opposite of the intended meaning, that is, a meaning humorously or poignantly reversed from the intended meaning.

Irony is a powerful element of dramatic literature and not well understood. If your teacher writes on a paper, "You have mispelled too many words in this paper," that is irony (definition 2), made so by the erroneous spelling of "misspelled." The classic example in drama is the play where a husband praises his wife's virtue while we, the audience, know that even as the husband speaks the wife's lover hides beneath her bed. An example of irony's definition 1 is the spilled-coffee story where the reporter ironically gets a better interview for having committed a social gaffe.

Those points in mind, what, precisely, do you look for in the three observation methods cited in this chapter?

In a word, *detail,* massive amounts of it, preferably organized in a way that clarifies the significance of the detail. It is the same as a "creative question." As you gather details, you see patterns and trends emerging, and you explore them further and develop a tentative hypothesis about their meaning. If, for example, you watch a classroom teacher berate a student for lateness on Monday, explode in response to a student's "stupid question" on Tuesday, and angrily fling an eraser at a sleeping student on Wednesday, you might wonder what Thursday will bring. When Thursday and Friday bring similar spats with students, you may have come upon a noteworthy character trait, one that deserves a hypothesis as to its meaning.

Observation comes in four categories that help to capture the essence of dramatic nonfiction writing. Much of the tension, action, irony, and unity can be observed in more or less systematic procedures using the acronym SCAM.[*] If, as Shakespeare suggests, all the world is a stage and all the men and women merely players, it follows that writing about reality can benefit from the elements used in playwriting. Here they are:

1. Scene or setting
2. Character
3. Action
4. Meaning

These elements resemble the journalist's traditional news elements: Where and When (setting), Who (character), What and How (action), and Why (meaning).

Setting

Although the age of long, flowery description is past, all but the most routine news stories benefit from descriptive touches that give your readers a firm sense of place. You may even seek out for your interviews (television especially) places that have special meaning. Backstage, perhaps, for your profile of the famous play director. On the Los Angeles freeway for your documentary on traffic problems. In the control tower for your article on air traffic problems around busy airports. You may switch scenes, on the freeway for one segment of your traffic story, at police headquarters for another, even in a hospital emergency room or the morgue if the article pertains to traffic accidents.

Whatever the scene, your eyes should take systematic note of what you see, starting with the overall scene—like a crowd shot at the football stadium—then focusing on individual items, like a closeup shot of one or two of the football fans.

Sounds and smells also deserve your attention. As you observe the scene where brain surgery is about to begin, do you hear the laughter of children

---

[*]The SCAM concept is taken from the author's previous work, *Newsgathering*, 1986.

playing across the street from the hospital? Life goes on outside the life-and-death setting of the operating room, and that eerie touch of symbolism will heighten the reader's experience.

Character

Static descriptions of scenes are dull; they come to life only when characters enter. Your observations of character can come on several levels, ranging from the superficial physical aspects all the way to deeper values and motivation. A good writer depicts character through action, in any event, so it is hard to discuss character without also discussing action.

Your observations will focus on activities, partly to understand character and partly to illustrate it. Often the understanding comes through interviews, including those with friends and colleagues, the people who can explain the phenomenon you are witnessing.

Imagine, for example, the successful but fiery-tempered play director. People who know him say he gets outstanding results from mediocre actors because he alternately loves them and hates them. He knows precisely how much love and how much hate to expend on each performer, and some need more of one or the other. So as you attend rehearsals and watch your director in action, you'll watch for examples—dramatic scenes perhaps—of that love-hate relationship. If it happens often enough, you will have confirmed and illustrated a significant character trait. Take complete notes so that you can re-create the best one of these scenes in your story.

Your observation of character should also focus on symbols. People are constantly telling the world about themselves and their opinions through possessions, mannerisms, clothes, even through such subtle signs as body posture and hair style. The observer who remains alert for symbols will not only learn a lot about the topic or person being observed, but will also use them as illustrations. Consider some examples: An advertising executive wears a button that says "It's not creative unless it sells." The apartment of a stunningly beautiful fashion model is a mess—abject chaos. The learned professor does *not* have a television set in the house. Why not? The question should be explored.

Action

As noted, action illustrates character, and your anecdotes come not from interviews, but from witnessing scenes that represent character traits.

But other kinds of action should be noted, too, depending on your purpose. Your story about traffic hazards on California freeways can benefit from observations of action. Drivers in Los Angeles are so frustrated that they've taken to shooting at one another, so what kinds of situations can you observe that provoke the frustration? As someone, a traffic officer perhaps, drives you along the freeway at rush hour, you tally instances. How many sudden, unannounced lane changes do you count? How many slow, careless, or possibly intoxicated drivers can you spot? You could have your police officer escort identify them for you as a means of showing the officer in action, commenting on the near accidents and foolish activities of the motorists under observation.

Don't neglect the emotional trifles that make people laugh or cry. A magazine writer, Ken Moore of *Sports Illustrated,* calls this one of the most important parts of interviewing and observation. Anytime you hear people laugh, he says, think back to whatever caused the laughter. Re-create the scene in your story to allow your readers to laugh along with the participants and thus respond emotionally as well as intellectually.

Meaning

Scene, character, and action can and should come together to produce the ultimate synthesis—the meaning. Details gained through observation—setting, character traits, and action scenes—will be arranged in an orderly manner to show the elements of the topic under discussion, whether it be a phenomenon such as traffic hazards or a personality such as a celebrity. In short, this is where the trifles gained through observation are arranged to illustrate major points.

Consider an example. A Denver writer, David Chamberlain, wrote an article for the *Los Angeles Times Magazine* about CBS-TV sports color reporter John Madden, who often appears in TV commercials for various products, including Miller Lite beer. ("John Madden, Mr. Big," January 25, 1987.)

The setting for the article is an Amtrak train en route from Chicago to Dallas. This has more than usual significance, for Madden, a former football coach, suffers from claustrophobia and never travels by plane. On this occasion, he is going from an assignment in Denver to one in Dallas—and doing it by way of Chicago because trains don't run direct from Denver to Dallas.

And so the writer has added touches of description of the setting, the phantom starts, the inexplicable delays, the crowded club car that lacks the elegance of early years but is more of a "rolling concession stand, where passengers wait in a long line at a window for microwaved food and drinks in plastic cups." Chamberlain soon brings character and action into the scene.

> As the line lengthens past Madden's seat and word of his presence spreads through the train, people begin to approach.
> "Boom!" a man ventures, borrowing Madden's favorite word for describing violent football collisions.
> "Whap!" Madden returns without hesitation.

The scene illustrates a point that comes out of the story, that Madden is gracious with autograph-seeking fans, a point riveted by still another scene illustrating Madden's rise from humble beginnings in Daly City, California, to become a sports celebrity.

What Madden has become is evident on the train as he signs autographs on napkins, menus, tickets and, inevitably, cans of Miller Lite. A middle-aged couple approaches with two of the latter.

"They better be Miller," he says in a friendly growl.

"We wouldn't have it any other way," the man assures him. "Make one out to Leon and one out to Shirley."*

Thus from the observations of the writer, accompanying Madden on the train, comes a sense of meaning, an illustration of celebrity status accompanied by a gracious manner with admiring fans. Madden is quoted explaining that manner: "It takes about three times as long to explain to someone why you won't give them an autograph as it does to actually give them an autograph."

Thus has an element of meaning emerged through the combination of character, action, and setting, along with quoted commentary gained through informal interviewing.

So *meaning* as part of SCAM really refers to the central theme of what you're trying to project through a piece of writing. Points work off the central theme, such as Madden's demeanor with fans, and they are illustrated by scenes the writer has witnessed.

To summarize, observing for meaning involves two elements. The first is observing to discover some kind of meaningful item—a point, a trend, a personality trait, a characteristic—or to confirm one obtained from another source. The second is to use one or more specific observations to illustrate the point, in Madden's case the two encounters with fans on the train.

If this seems vague and confusing, you are probably en route to becoming a splendid journalist. That remark is not intended in jest. It merely confirms that the world is complicated, and things happen that seem disorderly, totally meaningless, hopelessly chaotic. If any kind of central point exists, it will not announce itself in bold letters against a crimson sky. A central theme and the supporting points are what you, the journalist, decide upon, much as a reporter decides upon the most important element of a news event for the lead paragraph. It is never easy, and chances are that no two journalists would agree on what those points should be.

THE ETHICS OF PARTICIPANT OBSERVATION

In recent years, journalists have called into question the use of certain observation techniques. For media dedicated to exposing deception in government, it's not easy to justify their own deceptions merely for the sake of a sensational story.

One problem focuses on the use of fabricated scenes—the result of too little observation by writers too lazy or too incompetent to do the necessary

* "John Madden, Mr. Big," by David Chamberlain, *Los Angeles Times Magazine*, January 25, 1987. © 1986, The Times Mirror Company.

research. Exposes of this behavior—notably the Janet Cooke incident—have caused newspaper and magazine editors to delete such fakery whenever they spot it. Among the common offenders is the "composite," a technique used by fiction writers to develop a character made up of the traits of several real people. To present a composite in factual articles is misleading and therefore discouraged by most editors except when the fiction is clearly stated, as in a hypothetical example.

Editors also question certain participant observation techniques. The famous Mirage Tavern, set up to expose demands for payoffs by city inspectors in Chicago, was defended by the *Sun-Times* as the only way such a story could be done; traditional reporting methods simply were inadequate. Nonetheless, a Pulitzer Prize was not awarded because members of the selection committee complained of the deceptive techniques.

Participant observation is deceptive whenever the identity of the journalist is not made known to the other participants. Perhaps it makes little difference in the kinds of projects that are essentially journalistic pranks or benign features, such as spending a day on skid road begging for handouts. It's not so clear when an undercover reporter identifies speakers making comments that they would not have made if they'd known the reporter's identity.

Although one hesitates to apply hard rules, it does seem that any use of participant observation ought to undergo a fourfold test.

1. Who will be harmed? The benign slice-of-life project—the day on skid road—has few ethical problems.
2. Can the information be obtained by conventional journalistic research, including nonsecret participant observation?
3. Will the public good outweigh the reputation for deceit and trickery that will follow a journalist who uses such methods?
4. Can the journalist reasonably expect to convince a panel of citizens that public good outweighs the deceit?

Ethical considerations are not the only reason to avoid participant observation in journalism. It's time consuming, expensive, and often dirty and dangerous. The secret-identity participation is also inefficient. In the weeks required to gain acceptance as a participant in a secret society, another reporter could unearth more information simply by finding informants.

CHAPTER ELEVEN
Interviewing for Quotes and Anecdotes

> **Q.** Can you give me a funny story, a true story
> drawn from your experiences in life, that
> illustrates your point?
> **A.** No, nothing comes to mind.

When they've gained interviewing experience, journalism students tend to discover two new problems. One is obtaining anecdotes from their interviews. The other is obtaining quotes.

These problems beset writers more than they do broadcast interviewers. The latter have their own set of problems with quotes, described in Chapter 14. Meanwhile, consider the plight of the nonfiction writer.

Perhaps nothing more frustrates the serious writer than wresting out of an interview that touch of color—the humorous or poignant anecdote that illustrates a point. Ironically, people seem to delight in spinning stories about their daily experiences to anyone who will listen. Yet some mysterious element of the interview seems to freeze their minds just at that critical point where the interviewer desperately seeks an illustration in dramatic story form.

Are anecdotes all that important? To answer that question, think back to Chapter 1 and the stories about Ann Curry and Nora Villagran. Ann, you will recall, clumsily spilled her coffee at the luncheon counter and succeeded thereby in getting more candor from her source. Nora fell down the flight of stairs, showing up disheveled at Joan Baez's house, thereby achieving an unexpected level of personal candor: just two barefooted women talking.

Writers find stories like those particularly effective to illustrate the hard-to-believe little ironies of life. If someone tried to convince you that you can obtain more candor in an interview by falling down a flight of stairs, would you believe it? Of course not—how absurd. Yet to present it as a factual story involving real people makes it believable. People can compare it to similar events in their own lives, and they may decide that, under the circumstances, it's not so absurd after all.

So nonfiction writers who illustrate their points with interesting anecdotes accomplish three important goals.

1. Their writing is more believable.
2. Their writing is more fun to read; it entertains as well as informs.
3. Their writing is closer to people. Readers identify with characters and episodes in anecdotes, comparing them with their own life's experiences.

Compared to eliciting anecdotes, you'll find interviewing for quotation less a problem. After all, you can quote almost anything said in a conversation. Everything, in fact. A professor of education once joked that his students were so serious that when he said "Good morning" to his class, they'd write it down verbatim. So the problem with quotations centers on selection rather than availability of material.

Whatever the problems, the suggestions here may help you develop the ability to obtain more colorful quotes and anecdotes for your nonfiction articles. Some key elements cited in earlier chapters apply here, however. If people stiffen and talk artificially when you interview them, perhaps it's because conversational rapport has never been established. Often that means that you, the interviewer, must relax and assume the more informal demeanor under which anecdotes and quotable remarks flow more freely. If people don't tell stories or give personal examples, perhaps it's because you didn't state your need for them in your explanation of purpose. If they don't provide specifics, perhaps it's because you haven't probed for them.

LEARNING TO RECOGNIZE QUOTATIONS

Obtaining good quotes from an interview involves two tasks. The first is recognizing a good quote when you hear it in conversation. The second is carrying on the kind of conversation that encourages quotable remarks.

To illustrate the first problem, consider an example. As an exercise in a news-writing class, a teacher asked students to write a news story from a verbatim transcript of a hypothetical student council meeting. The transcript showed a lively debate on a controversial issue. One student's story characterized as follows the comment of a participant in the debate.

> She alluded to the fact that the People's Coalition was devoid of the feminine gender, and she chastised the chairman of the coalition for falsely claiming to represent the interests of all the people.

The transcript shows that the woman actually said this:

> Harry, there isn't a single woman in your People's Coalition. You don't represent the people at all—you represent only male chauvinist people. Power to the people—hell!

How much more simple, concrete—even more dramatic—is the quote. It not only captures personality but it's more specific. And it's six words shorter. It had never occurred to the student to use it to add color to the story.

Some novice writers tend toward a far-different problem—they put *everything* in quotes, even routine data. To quote a person saying "I was born in Sandusky, Ohio, in the summer of 1929" is to destroy the quotation's special ability to add zest to your story by careful selection of the conversational flowers from the ordinary weeds. To illustrate the character of the grizzled mule skinner at the Grand Canyon, you do not quote him reciting routine data such as his 1929 birth in Sandusky. Instead, you quote him cracking a wry joke with a group of tourists starting the precipitous trail to the bottom: "Be mighty careful, ladies—I can always get plenty of tourists, but a trained mule is hard to replace."

You might even picture a writer offering similar advice: "You can always get plenty of words, but a good quote is hard to find." You find good quotes by recognizing them as they whiz by in conversations. To do that, you must first consider some definitions.

By definition, a quotation simply means reporting what a person said. The *direct quotation* belongs in quotation marks and should run verbatim. *Paraphrased* quotations are what the person said but in somebody else's words, usually the writer's. *Fragmented* quotations are mere snippets of conversation. Thus when Jane Doe says, "Living in New York is like living in a cement mixer—it's tough and confusing," the direct quotation is what you see between the quote marks. A paraphrased quotation says *Jane Doe says living in New York is difficult and confusing.* The fragmented quote says Jane Doe finds living in New York confusing, *"like living in a cement mixer."*

How do you use such quotations in written material? Here are some common ways.

Use Quotes for Authority

Imagine yourself on an airplane and someone says, "This aircraft is not working properly." You'd pay closer attention if the comment came from the pilot than the small boy sitting next to you. An authority quote, then, gains currency by the stature of the person saying it. You use verbatim comments from people presumed to know what they're talking about. "Ours is a singularly violent community," says the police chief. "Our foreign policy lies in a parlous and desperate state," says the secretary of state.

Quote for Human Color

Keep an ear attuned to the way people talk. Stay particularly alert for personal asides offered in ways that differ distinctly from the way you write. Have you noticed in some newspaper stories that the quotes all sound alike? And that they sound just like the body of the story itself? Is that because sources talk the way reporters write? No, it's because reporters tend to use quotes that fit the way they write, or, worse, they don't listen keenly to the way people talk. Pity. It's fun to listen to different people saying the same thing.

The police officer says, "At approximately 0400 hours, I observed the subject vehicle traveling at a high rate of speed."

The college professor says, "Though I was bereft of any instrument to accurately ascertain the forward motion of the vehicle, I should tentatively suggest, in the absence of more systematic empirical data, that the motion was rather in an expeditious manner."

A bystander says, "Man, that puppy was flying like a bat outta hell."

In short, your story's quotations should show individual character stamps, each representing a style of expression distinctly different from the way you write. Do that and your writing becomes a rainbow of colorful expression, rather than a dull monotone.

Quote for Authenticity

A personality story that discusses its celebrity subject's shyness becomes more believable with a direct quote: "Yes," says Mr. Big, "I suffer agony in anticipation of meeting somebody for fear they won't like me."

In a similar vein, authenticity shows through quotes that reflect the jargon of the topic. You show the former hobo talking in the jargon of his past: "There we were, a couple of bindle stiffs just off the red ball express, diming up on the stem." It sounds authentic, though you may have to translate the meaning—hobos just off the fast fruit train, panhandling on Main Street.

Quote Figures of Speech

Some people normally talk in metaphorical ways. You can encourage others to do so by the way you ask questions. Some figures of speech have become cliches, *Bat outta hell*, for instance. Though you might not use them in your own writing, they do convey a reckless kind of street jargon that's colorfully appropriate when quoting witnesses.

INTERVIEWING FOR QUOTATIONS

How do you encourage people to talk more quotably? You might try talking more quotably yourself. You tend to get out of an interview what you put into it—dull questions, dull answers. Here are some suggestions for encouraging quotable material in the interview.

Fish for Figures of Speech

Certain questions stimulate imaginative answers, and one of the best is to ask for a simile or an analogy. The question is a simple one: "What's it like?"

"What's it like to be looking for your first job?" somebody asked a group of college seniors. "It's like sorority rush," one replied. "It's like asking your wife for money," said another.

Use Metaphorical Questions

If you want metaphorical answers, try asking metaphorical questions.

Q. Commissioner, a man in your precarious position, getting unmerciful criticism from all sides, must feel lonely, a man sitting on an iceberg in a storm-tossed sea.

A. No, it's more like lighting a cigar while sitting on a barrel of high-octane gasoline.

Depending on the seriousness of the predicament, that sounds like a headline-grabbing quote. True, you colored the question a little. Had the commissioner replied, "Yes, that's a good way of putting it—sitting on an iceberg," then you'd not use the quote. It's yours, not his. But if you prime the pump with metaphorical questions, you may eventually receive metaphorical replies. So if you want colorful answers, try asking colorful questions.

Quote the Classics

An evening spent with Mark Twain or a book of quotations will produce examples of quotable remarks. They can help you in two ways. First, they help you recognize a passing remark as something comparable to the classic quotations you've studied—and thus worthy of quotation in your article. Second, they allow you to salt your questions with classic comments that serve as the basis for quotable discussion. Thus:

Q. Senator, the news media controversies that focus on your work have a familiar ring. They bring to mind the quote from Oscar Wilde in *Dorian Gray*: "There's only one thing worse than being talked about, and that's not being talked about." What do you think?

A. Yes, the one great thing about being talked about is the opportunity to talk back. The chance to get your views across to the people can't be all bad.

Show Your Appreciation for a Quotable Remark

Show it dramatically! You'd think sources would tire of lavish praise, particularly those of high attainment that you normally interview for news articles. Not true. Noteworthy people often suffer from criticism, and they yearn for recognition. So when you make a fuss over how much you enjoy a quotable remark, you open the floodgates. "Ah, ha!" says your respondent. "So *that's* the kind of material she wants!" You'll probably get more of it as the conversation progresses.

Similarly, you must encourage people to use their normal manner of speaking. People often try to clean up their conversation for your benefit—the hobo doesn't talk about "diming up on the stem" for fear that you might not understand or appreciate the jargon. You must show your enthusiasm for such jargon, perhaps even explain why you'd like to use it in your story. The more enthusiasm you show, the more jargon you'll hear, and one way to show enthusiasm is to adopt examples of the jargon in your own conversation through the remainder of the interview. So henceforth you discard "panhandling" in favor of "diming up."

Silence

This has been cited before as the interviewer's friend, not the enemy as so many novices think. A pregnant kind of silence, in which you convey the idea that the respondent should continue, can bring forth a quotable remark. Imagine this scene. The source has talked for several minutes about a complex issue. She finishes. You wait expectantly. She's not sure she's made a convincing point, so her mind runs through a more effective way of saying the same thing. More effective usually means shorter and more pungent or poignant. "In other words," she begins—and then comes the succinct summary or the colorful metaphor.

Argumentation

The suggestion that interviewers maintain a low profile should not be carried to extremes lest a malignant dullness creep into your dialogue. To suggest argumentation as a means of eliciting quotable remarks does not belie the rule, but adds another dimension to the interview dialogue. Argumentation especially helps a broadcast interviewer bring excitement to the conversation. Some respondents enjoy a good scrap and feel cheated if one does not emerge. Broadcast interviews move more quickly into touchy or controversial areas than do print interviews. The viewing public demands it, and sources usually expect it.

This does not mean picking a fight with your respondent. Interviewers should remain neutral and open-minded. But they commonly use counterarguments, usually attributing them to someone else. "Senator, your political opponents disagree sharply with what you say.... Let me quote Congressman Claghorn from this morning's paper . . . ." Armed with such quotes, you can proceed as provocatively as you want with little or no adverse effect. The senator is angry with *them*, not with you. In politics and public affairs, the rhetoric becomes extreme sometimes: "Mr. Author, one critic has called your novel a crock of melodramatic shibboleth—how do you respond?"

"Can I quote you on that, Senator?"

ELICITING THE ELUSIVE ANECDOTE

As noted, students find eliciting anecdotes the most difficult aspect of interviewing. Perhaps the young journalists do not fully understand what an anecdote is or how it's used. Often they expect it to come ready-made from their sources, all polished and ready to drop into their magazine piece. That seldom happens. People talk about their experiences; storytellers spin anecdotes. Most people are not storytellers; writers are—or should be.

Thus the legendary story of Ann Curry's spilled cup of coffee did not emerge as a full-blown anecdote. She merely mentioned that the interview took a turn for the better shortly after she spilled her coffee. A storyteller asked for the details and shaped them into an anecdote that illustrates the role of human vulnerability to enhance conversational candor.

That story, in any event, stands as a prime example of an anecdote. By definition, an anecdote is a brief factual account of an incident that illustrates a point. The more interesting, amusing, or poignant, the better. In this example, the spilled-coffee story illustrates the point that a display of human vulnerability can improve interview candor.

Here are some suggestions for improving your ability to obtain anecdotes from interviews.

Prime the Pump by Telling Stories Yourself

Try this experiment sometime. Ask someone to tell you a humorous story from experience that illustrates how a foolish human blunder displays human vulnerability and thus opens candor in a conversation. Now sit back and wait for your story.

It probably won't come. In the first place, the level of abstraction obscures your meaning. Second, the request for "a humorous story" can intimidate people who are not accomplished storytellers. What if they tell a story and you don't find it "humorous"? Better not take a chance.

But suppose you illustrate with one of the stories you've picked up in this book, the spilled coffee or the stairway fall. Tell such a story and your respondent's mind will begin to search for similar experiences. The story seems so universal in its application to human affairs that it can precipitate tales of similar experiences in areas other than journalism. One student used it to land a story by a woman who grew up on a farm. She met her husband of forty years by just such a gaffe. She'd been trying to impress this certain boy, she explained, but he paid her scant attention until he happened to visit her house on an errand and encountered her just as she finished cleaning the stables and "smelled like horse manure." She was mortified. He was intrigued. The young man loved horses, and the chance encounter with the hopelessly smelly young woman started their lifelong relationship.

Obtaining anecdotes by telling them does not require you to be a good storyteller. Quite the opposite. If you're too good, you can intimidate sources. Start with a low-key story and stumble quite a bit in telling it. Your source will feel free to top your story, and then you can begin an escalation process. Where do you obtain such stories? Experienced journalists take them from previous interviews. Others can clip and file stories from published sources.

Seek Examples

When people talk in generalities, little but dull abstractions result. When you write your story, you need specific examples. So you ask for them directly in a scenario that typically runs like this interview with a fire chief:

Q. You talk so matter-of-factly about your work—I wonder, have you ever been frightened when on the scene of a fire?

A. Oh, lots of times. [Do you merely settle for that, perhaps as a direct quote? Not if you want a good story.]

Q. Well, as you think back over those times, which one stands out in your mind?

A. I think it must have been the time someone said a child was trapped on the third floor of an apartment building, and we went in looking for her.

Q. I'd like to hear the details . . . .

Probe for Details

The scenario above is the ideal—you ask for examples, find a particularly thrilling one, and out pour the details just for the asking. Often, however, it doesn't work that way. Often a respondent's mind grows hazy at a request for examples. This happens because of the peculiar way the human mind retrieves events from memory. The information is there, we know; it's just that we can't get at it immediately upon command. The mind needs "cues," such as key words that trigger memory. Often an interviewer who realizes this problem can provide the cues. Imagine the scenario where the fire chief's mind goes blank at your request for examples.

A. I know I've had frightening experiences, but right now I can't think of any worth mentioning.

Q. I suppose they would come in certain kinds of situations, such as a building about to collapse, or maybe someone being trapped, or maybe something involving imminent explosions—

A. Ah! Trapped! Yes, that reminds me of the time . . . .

Often experienced interviewers can draw from *their* memories or from preinterview research. Clips often yield accounts of scary episodes you can ask about. Colleagues, family, and friends often mention events that the chief might not think to bring up. Modesty, false or otherwise, sometimes intrudes on candor. "Be sure to ask the chief about the time . . . ." suggests a colleague, and such clues may provide your best anecdotal material.

Listen with the Third Ear

Catching half-articulated hints can provide a rich source of stories. We've talked earlier about how our strongest convictions are often born of dramatic experiences. Look for anecdotes in those experiences. Suppose you are interviewing a social worker about runaway children. "Sometimes," she says, "running away is the wisest and most mature thing a child can do." That's a startling and paradoxical observation. What basis does a social worker have for saying that? So you probe for the details. You learn that some children's home conditions—abusive parents, alcoholism, drugs, whatever—are so wretched that no right-thinking adult could reach any conclusion other than the one reached by the child. Now you begin to probe for the worst example the social worker can recall. You learn that a mother dies, a 10-year-old girl takes on the full responsibility for running the household only to suffer constant physical abuse from a drunken father. Given a detailed account of such a scenario (a true story, incidentally), the reader will likely arrive at the same decision the child did.

Assembling the details for an anecdote requires patient probing. You must pursue the subject relentlessly. "What happened next? . . . What did she say? . . . What did you say? . . . Where did all this take place? . . . What was the weather as you were talking on the sidewalk—hot, rainy, snowy, what? . . . How were you dressed?" Clearly, the more experienced you are as a writer, the more you'll know what to ask in these detail-seeking forays.

They are a little awkward, however. Respondents often tire of the work involved, comparing it unfavorably to housecleaning, but articles do benefit from such detail. Unfortunately, most people lack the keen observation powers of a good journalist. They are not pleased when questions arise that they can't answer. Sometimes they're tempted to stretch the truth. Try to be patient, and encourage them to be, too.

Witness the Incidents Yourself

As discussed in Chapter 10, personal observation provides a splendid way to discover anecdotes that illustrate points. Is the celebrated actor so insecure that he doesn't know what to order for lunch? If possible, take him to lunch and find out for yourself. Do the military cadets on bivouac make little jokes about their officers? Sit with them at chow time and listen for yourself.

CHAPTER TWELVE
Telephoning, Note Taking, and Taping

Q. Hello, I'm your friendly neighborhood computer conducting a survey of community attitudes. I would like to ask you some questions. Some questions will call for a yes-no answer and others will call for a more extended answer. Do you understand what I have just said?

A. Hello, this is your friendly answering machine substituting for Jim and Sally who can't come to the phone just now—if you'd like to leave a message, just wait for the tone . . . .

In my experience, the three most frequently asked questions among professional journalists attending workshops on interviewing techniques are on interviewing by telephone, taking notes, and using a tape recorder.

INTERVIEWING BY TELEPHONE

A Chicago radio station once called a bank to check on a rumored robbery. To the reporter's astonishment, the phone was answered by the robber himself. The dialogue that followed stands as a testimonial to the efficiency, even the drama, of the telephone as an interviewing tool. It also supports a remark by the late A. J. Liebling, *New Yorker* press critic: "There is almost no circumstance under which an American doesn't like to be interviewed . . . . We are an articulate people, covetous of being singled out."

Q. What's going on out there? I understand you got a robbery.
A. Yes, who's this speaking, please?
Q. WGN.
A. WGN?
Q. Yes, sir.
A. Well, this is the robber, the so-called robber, I guess.
Q. What are you doing in there?
A. Well, I just want to tell you honestly, WGN, I tried to make it the shortest way possible, and it's the wrong way.
Q. Well, what's going on there, sir?
A. Well, I'm surrounded and at this moment I would like to request that I have a minister because I'm going to take my life.
Q. Now don't do that, wait a second! Are the police outside or are they inside?
A. Yeah, just a second—
Q. What's going on there, sir?
A. Yeah, they've surrounded the bank here.
Q. Yes.
A. And— [The interview concludes with voices in the background: *Hold it right there! Freeze, man! . . .*]*

Newspaper reporters estimate that they spend fifty to eighty percent of their interviewing time on the phone. One infamous Chicago police reporter, the late Harry Romanoff, claimed to spend 100 percent of his time on phone interviews. He developed them to such an art that he earned the title, "Heifitz of the Telephone." He knew every corner drugstore in Chicago and could thereby reach the scene of a crime faster than any competitor. He simply called the store nearest the scene and cajoled the manager into fetching a police officer who would then provide the details (Moore, 1973).

Romanoff became a legend from the rough-and-tumble *Front Page* era of newspapers. He charmed and cajoled the timid, talked tough to officials and cops when necessary, and didn't hesitate to identify himself as the county coroner or a defense attorney to obtain information. Editors today would frown on many of his methods as unethical. Yet he showed dramatically what a reporter can accomplish via the telephone. Subsequent generations of reporters have used at least one of his techniques—calling people known to

*Walter Cronkite, *Eye on the World*. © 1971 by Cowles Communications. Reprinted by permission of the publisher.

be near the scenes of news events, though they do it today by using a special telephone directory organized by street numbers.

The procedure for telephone interviewing runs along the same lines suggested in earlier chapters. You formulate an interview purpose, such as following up on a news tip. You call up, identify yourself, state your business, and proceed with the interview. Perhaps something like this:

A. Hello?

Q. Good evening, I'm Mary Jones from KMTR-TV Channel 16 News. We've had a report that there's a big fire in your neighborhood and I'm writing a report for the six o'clock news which goes on the air a minute and a half from now. I'm curious—can you see anything from your house?

A. Yes, from where I'm standing right now I can look out my window and see flames shooting up from the house right across the street.

Q. Well, we have a camera crew en route, but meanwhile I wonder if you could describe for my story what you're seeing right now from your window . . . .

Chances are that the witness will be thrilled to speak for broadcast, just as the Chicago bank robber seemed to be. For routine news calls, nothing surpasses the telephone as an instrument of journalistic research. Radio reporters often use phone interviews for "actualities"—the radio term for sound bites.

Feature writers, too, find the telephone useful in instances where they want information from a wide variety of sources. Sometimes a decision to use the telephone involves a trade-off: Would you prefer to spend four hours fighting crosstown traffic to conduct one face-to-face interview, or would you rather interview a dozen different people by phone during the same hours? It depends on circumstances, but sometimes twelve phone interviews will yield more information than a single in-person conversation.

Busy public officials also prefer to work by phone, particularly after they've become acquainted with a journalist, such as one who covers a newsbeat regularly. For them it's quicker, more efficient, and more impersonal (no need for the social amenities of face-to-face contact). For the reporter, the phone allows you to work in casual clothes and to keep your notes, clippings, articles, and other reference materials spread out on your desk.

Reporters for national magazines and newspapers have developed long-distance phone interviewing to a fine art. The long-distance phone has a high priority in the minds of many busy executives. A reporter for the Washington-based national paper, *Chronicle of Higher Education,* finds it effective to announce his location over the phone: "This is Jack Magarrell, *calling from Washington, D. C.* . . ." That touch sends the call promptly through secretaries and assistants and directly into key executive offices, he explains.

For sensitive kinds of questions, the telephone works with surprising efficiency. People often feel less threatened talking into an impersonal instrument precisely because it helps *not* to see a human reaction. Thus the very weakness of the telephone, its impersonality, becomes a strength in some circumstances.

Support for that view comes from a strange source. In Honolulu a man telephoned dozens of women, identifying himself as a doctor engaged in research on sex patterns. He asked for and often received intimate details of their sexual experiences. Only in retrospect did some of them become suspicious enough to call the medical association where they learned that the caller was a fraud. The women were charmed, they explained, by the "warm telephone personality" of a "skilled interviewer."

Just as evil-minded persons can use the telephone to exploit, so can altruistic journalists use it for the common good. If you want to become a skilled telephone interviewer, the following courtesies will help.

1. Have a clear-cut, easily explained purpose and get to the point quickly. People seem increasingly wary of phone calls, probably the result of increasing numbers of unsolicited sales calls, not to mention crank calls. When calling a stranger, you have perhaps ten to twenty seconds to make clear your purpose.

2. Use those seconds to say at least one thing that will catch the respondent's fancy, perhaps something flattering. In short, have a hook. Thus: "Hello, Ms. Ganter, this is Mary Jones from Channel 16 news—I'm working on a story about women who have started small businesses, and your name was given to me as one of the most successful examples in our locality. Would you mind talking with me on the phone for a few minutes?"

3. Speak clearly and distinctly. And calmly. Try to put a brisk but amiable and friendly quality into your voice, which is the only means you have to establish rapport.

4. Unless the call will be brief, give your estimate of the interview's duration—"perhaps fifteen or twenty minutes." You don't know what you're interrupting, particularly if the call has gone directly to someone's home as opposed to office calls screened by receptionists. After stating your business—and setting your interest-capturing hook—ask, "Is this a good time to call?" Except in emergencies, you'll be better off postponing a conversation than risk having a source become anxious about abandoned houseguests or a pie in the oven.

5. Make your icebreaker comments brief: "How's the weather back in Boston—as snowy as our papers say?" Personal asides might come later after rapport is established. Easterners tend to be more brisk and formal than westerners, midwesterners, and southerners, in my experience; easterners seem to resent the conversational prelude, while the others seem to expect it.

6. Don't allow long, unexplained silences on the phone. Note taking, a common reason for silence, requires explanation: "Just give me a moment to get that last comment in my notes . . . ."

7. Provide verbal cues to your listening: "Uh-huh, Hmmmmm," and the like (unless you are interviewing for a radio actuality, where the "Uh-huhs" can prove troublesome).

8. When interviewing on sensitive topics, you may need to provide credentials and references, perhaps naming mutual acquaintances who will vouch for your authenticity. It helps when you can say, "Your former colleague, Jim Jones, sug-

gested I call you because you're the only one who knows the answers to the questions I want to ask." Similarly, when you're about to conclude an interview, ask your source to name others who can help. Your source's name will provide entry to the new sources.

9. Above all, be courteous and friendly. And listen. You may find, as I have repeatedly, that the major problem with phone interviews is not starting them but ending them. One time a U.S. congressman said in answer to my cross-country call that he could spare me only a minute or two—yet ended up talking for an hour (at my expense). Interesting questions and sympathetic listening— along with insightful follow-up questions prompted by the listening—seem to keep sources on the line. And it still takes less time than most face-to-face conversations.

It doesn't stop when you hang up, either. A reporter for the *Springfield* (Oregon) *News* interviewed a notorious woman suspected of murdering one of her children and injuring two others. The woman kept calling him at odd hours, much to the dismay of the reporter's girlfriend. But refuse the calls from a newsworthy source, the reporter reasoned, and you might miss a good newsbreak. Such is the price you pay for careful listening. The calls ceased when the woman was arrested and eventually convicted.

TAKING NOTES

One can explain the note taking problem easily enough. The human mind cannot do everything at once. You have to listen, think up new questions, keep the interview on track, and take notes, all at the same time. The person you're interviewing is so interesting you don't want to miss a word. She says she has three reasons for taking a certain action. You take notes as quickly as you can, but by the time you've finished getting down reason 1, you've missed reason 2 because your mind was focused on 1. Or you tried to listen to reason 2 and then forgot most of 1.

The solution? Decide what you want out of the interview. If you literally want *every word*, then use a tape recorder. Note taking works best for routine news stories and for multiple-interview projects in which you plan to use only a small portion of each conversation. Most inexperienced interviewers take too many notes, trying to write down everything said, and as a result don't listen carefully. An interesting experiment in listening once turned up an unexpected result. Two groups of students listened to a seven-minute statement. One group took notes; the other didn't. Students wrote reports on what they had heard. Those who didn't take notes wrote more accurate accounts (though less detailed) than those who did (Abel, 1969).

Journalists tend to develop over time their own solutions to the note problem. Some experienced journalists take lots of notes on big yellow tablets; some take few notes in the most casual manner, such as on the backs of old envelopes. Reporters using the telephone often take notes on the word processor. Some reporters carry lap-top computers for note taking.

Organize Your Note Taking.   Chapter 9 on listening suggests that you organize your listening to make a mental note of major points and then supporting evidence. Good notes reflect that. One way is to use one side of a steno pad to record the main points and the other side to record supporting data, including observation, quotations, anecdotes, facts, and figures.

Control Your Interview to Accommodate Note Taking.   If you're watching for main points and supporting evidence, you learn to ask for information in largely that same way. Imagine this dialogue with, say, a politician.

Q. What do you see as the major economic problems of this region?

A. The governor is our major problem.

Q. Why do you say that?

A. The governor has been stalling for three years now and hasn't come up with a single proposal for improving the economy of this or any other region in the state.

Q. Do *you* have some specific ideas for improvement?

A. You bet I do! Dozens of them!

Q. Splendid! Could I hear a half-dozen or so of them, starting with the most important ones?

The reporter has phrased the last question so that the notes based on the answers will not only contain the main point (the governor's inaction), but continue with the supporting points (the politician's solutions), listed in order of importance. You'll find it a lot easier to write a story based on notes organized this way.

Some journalists prefer to listen carefully, *then* make notes after they have the points clearly in mind. This, too, can be worked into the interview method so long as the respondent knows what you're doing. So you say, "Let me see if I have this correct," repeating your understanding of the point. If it's correct, then: "Okay, let me get this into my notes before we go on to the next point."

Develop a Shorthand.   When you must get material word for word, a shorthand system helps. Some have taken formal shorthand or speed-writing courses. Most have at least a system of abbreviations and symbols for frequently used words. *Gt7 qts w 4 w > ez wn u no hw* is one reporter's shorthand for "Getting quotes word for word is easy when you know how."

Train Your Memory.   Writer Ken Moore, who covers running for *Sports Illustrated*, can't take notes when he's interviewing athletes while accompanying them on training runs. Moore seldom uses a tape recorder—it gets in the way of conversation, he says—but he memorizes the most significant comments and writes them down later.

All of us can work on memory. One way is to fix a quotable remark in memory by rethinking it a time or two, even asking about it in the interview. One pioneer correspondent, Edward Price Bell, said in 1925 that, when he interviewed the world's great leaders, he took no notes at all. He wrote his notes later, as memory served. "A word or phrase now, a sentence then, perhaps a paragraph or two as one wakes at night. I consider a week or even a fortnight not too long a time to give to the complete reproduction of an interview of some five thousand words" (Bell, 1925).

Type Your Notes. In a long-established newsroom practice, many reporters take notes on the VDT, particularly when conducting telephone interviews from the office. A shoulder hook holds the phone to their ear, freeing both hands for typing. In recent years reporters have begun to use lap-top computers, such as the Radio Shack Model 100, for taking notes in the field. This computer is hardly bigger than a small-city telephone directory, and it operates on batteries or, with an adaptor, plugs into household current.

Such devices are by no means the perfect solution to the note-taking problem, however. They do interfere with conversational rapport, particularly with inexperienced sources. They work best in perfunctory interviews with experienced respondents, such as police desk sergeants. A school superintendent in Honolulu finds himself annoyed by the clacking noise in the background when speaking to a reporter on the phone.

"It isn't the typing that bothers me so much as what it symbolizes," he explained. "It means the fine nuances of conversation are lost. Listening becomes mechanical. It's a linear thing, rather than immersion in the conversation. If you so much as utter a burp, you activate that darned typewriter!"

Introduce Note Taking Slowly to Inexperienced Respondents. Occasionally you'll find a respondent bothered by any kind of note taking. They talk merrily along, but clam up the moment you pull out a notepad and start writing things down. Then those carefree remarks drop out as posturing clods of trivia. Three suggestions for occasions where you think this could be a problem:

1. Introduce your notes at a routine stage. After icebreaking conversation, ask for routine information, names, spellings, addresses, and write them down. This is no worse than providing information at the driver's license bureau, and people do that routinely. Eventually, they'll get used to your making notes on other comments as well.
2. Listen carefully, repeat your understanding, and *then* make notes, as suggested earlier.
3. Use gentle flattery; make an agreeable fuss over how much you enjoyed a particularly quotable remark.

USING TAPE RECORDERS

Thanks to the growth of broadcast journalism over the past several decades, most news sources have become used to tape recorders. By its nature, broadcast reporting calls for unremitting use of recording devices. Many sources—celebrities and public officials especially—say they prefer that re-porters use tape, believing that it leads to fewer misquotations.

So the question affects print journalists primarily: whether to utilize a tape recorder or simply to make notes on conversations. It remains a controversial question. A veteran newspaper man in Honolulu tried a recorder for the first time after some 30 years on the job and had two reactions.

First, he was enthralled. "I can really *listen* to the conversation," he exclaimed. Second, he was bothered by his interviewing style. "I talk too damn much. I'm too impatient. I'm always cutting off my source just as he starts to say something."

Tape recorders are not a solution to all interview recording problems. Here, based on the experiences of many print journalists interviewed for this book, are some pros and cons. First the pros:

1. It's a good backup for note taking, just in case you miss something important.
2. You get quotes verbatim.
3. Freed of note taking, you can listen more carefully, pick up hints and half-articulated points.
4. Things said early in the interview are preserved. With notes, reporters often don't recognize the importance of early commentary because they don't have a firm grasp on the topic at that point.
5. They're useful in legally touchy stories as a backstop against claims of misquotation.
6. In sensitive interviews—for personality profiles, for example—you can listen again and again to catch fine nuances of personality and character that you might have missed originally.
7. You learn a poignant lesson about interviewing technique by hearing yourself on tape.

Some reasons *not* to use a recorder.

1. They're inefficient for tight-deadline reporting—there's barely time to make the necessary phone calls, let alone listen to a tape of the conversations.
2. They're similarly inefficient when you don't expect to use much of an interview—maybe just a quote or two from each of a dozen interviews, let's say.
3. They're prone to mechanical breakdown.
4. They're said to intimidate respondents, thus hampering rapport.
5. Transcribing the tape is time consuming.
6. Given the routine nature of most news interviews, there simply exists no reason to listen to the conversation again. Most conversations, a cynic once observed, are hardly worth listening to once, let alone twice.

The negative side contains three myths that should be dispelled. In the hands of a good interviewer, tape recorders seldom intimidate anyone. As noted, experienced sources prefer tapes, and the inexperienced ones tend to take their cues from the interviewer. If *you* are intimidated by it, they probably will be, too. Your intimidation shows via excessive preoccupation with the recorder's mechanical well being—the constant checking to see if it's still running—and in a certain stiffness and formality in your voice. But if you relax and talk normally, chances are your respondent will, too. Studs Terkel, perhaps America's greatest interviewing artist with a tape recorder, sometimes gives his machine a little kick (not too hard) just to show that a mere mechanical contrivance shouldn't be taken too seriously.

The second myth is that tape recorders can't be used for tight-deadline reporting. Some reporters routinely tape interviews, particularly telephone interviews, still taking notes as they normally would. But whenever a complicated quote rolls by too fast to write down, they merely record the number on the digital counter and later roll the tape back to that point to type out the quote.

The third myth is that of mechanical breakdown. True, recorders do break down frequently. The myth comes in blaming the machine instead of yourself. Here's how to avoid it:

1. Get an excellent machine—expensive but worth it—and learn how to use it.
2. Keep extra batteries available. Keep a pocketful of the AA batteries normally used for pocket recorders. Rechargeable battery packs have a nasty habit of suddenly running out of power, not gradually as regular batteries do. Carry an extra pack or two.
3. Be careful with extra-thin tapes (C-120); they tangle in cheap recorders.
4. Carry extra cassettes.
5. Check new cassettes before use to see that they roll freely; sometimes they stick.
6. Check your machine before each use like a pilot's preflight check of instruments: (a) batteries okay, (b) cassettes okay, (c) spare batteries and cassettes on hand, (d) microphone switch on, (e) short preinterview trial shows record and playback working okay.
7. Avoid recording in noisy places: restaurants, cocktail bars, factories, cars, planes.
8. Don't loan your recorder to anyone else. Don't use newsroom pool recorders if you can avoid them: the person who used it before you unquestionably is an idiot who dropped the machine from a fifth-floor window.

What Kind of Recorder?

The machine most used for journalistic interviews is the pocket recorder, which is roughly the size of a paperback book. It ranges in price from $25 to $200. It uses standard cassette tapes that run from C-30 (meaning you get thirty minutes recording time, fifteen on each side of a two-sided tape) to C-120 (two hours). Most operate on AA batteries or a battery pack that can be plugged in for recharging using an AC adaptor. With the adaptor you can also plug most machines into household current, saving the batteries. The best machines have a battery condition indicator, a built-in microphone as well as plugs for a remote microphone, a socket for earphones, and an automatic shutoff when a side of the tape cassette has been completed. The best also have digital counters, which resemble an auto mileage odometer. All machines will play back the tape on a tiny speaker.

News reporters are growing increasingly fond of the micro-recorder, which is tiny: seldom bigger than a pack of cigarettes, often smaller. It uses a tiny cassette hardly bigger than a man's thumb (one by one and a half inches), good for as much as forty-five minutes on each side. Some machines record at half-speed, giving you twice your forty-five minutes—three hours total recording time for both sides of the tape. The playback quality may not be the highest, but the cost is reasonable ($30 to $150), and the small size makes it convenient to slip into a purse or pocket.

You may find the following devices useful auxiliary equipment: the AC adaptor and rechargeable battery pack, a telephone pickup for recording telephone calls, earphones for private listening to playbacks, and a footpedal for stopping the machine when taking notes from the playback.

Using Your Tape Recorder

Reporters often use recorders at speeches and news conferences as backstops for their note taking. Here's where the digital counter proves handy. If you miss a quote, you simply write down the number on the counter with an explanation on your notepad. Later you run the tape to that number to play back the comment. Recorders are particularly useful for those fast airport lobby interviews where you have no time to sit down. Your important person walks briskly toward an appointment or a connecting flight. You can't take notes, but the recorder preserves the conversation.

Taping a face-to-face interview usually involves a certain etiquette. You explain the need for taping the session, and you secure the respondent's approval. Given a choice between your taking notes and taping, most opt for taping, especially when you explain how, freed of note taking, you can speed up the conversation and listen more carefully. "This way, we can talk like real people" is an often used explanation.

Most people's concerns actually center on two areas: (1) What if they want to speak off the record—can they shut off the machine? (2) What happens to the tape afterward?

Off the record refers to comments not intended for publication. Reporters handle question 1 in different ways; some will actually turn the machine off. Others say an off-the-record remark will be honored whether it's on tape or not—turning off the tape is awkward because it calls attention to the mechanics of recording rather than the nuances of conversation. And some reporters decline to hear off-the-record commentary at all. This is discussed further in Chapter 13.

What happens to the tape? Usually it will be erased and reused once the story is written. Your recorder automatically erases a previous interview whenever you record a new one.

You'll encounter exceptions to that erasure policy, to be sure. You'll keep the tape in legally touchy stories or if you think the source will claim misquotation at some future date. In rare instances, an interview might contain enough historical significance that it may ultimately end up in some university's archives. But most times a respondent simply wants some reassurance that things confessed in great candor for your benefit won't be played on the radio or end up as entertainment at your next house party.

Tape recorders can hinder rapport if placed directly between the two participants to an interview. Place your recorder to one side, out of the line of sight between you. Turn it on and leave it alone to do its job; avoid the temptation to check its operation. Use your curiosity and charm to sweep your source into the conversation, and soon you'll both forget the tape, at least until it clicks to a stop.

Note Taking while Taping

Writing extensive notes while taping is not a good idea because it negates your claim that you can listen better when freed of note taking. However, some token notes can be useful, for several reasons. First, notes can provide nonverbal encouragement; you can show what you think is important by making a note of it, perhaps even calling attention to the fact that you're doing so. Second, you may wish to note briefly items already covered in the interview just to keep track. You'll also jot down points mentioned in the interview that you want to ask about later, points you might otherwise forget. Third, taped interviews tend to ramble more than those guided by note taking. In a typical taped interview, for instance, the governor says, "I have three reasons for vetoing this legislation." The discussion of reason 1 rambles so much that you both forget to cover reasons 2 and 3. Not so with notes. Write down "3 reasons for veto" and you'll remember.

Reporters do, however, take extensive notes from taped interviews—back at the office afterwards. Most reporters don't transcribe. They take notes from the playback. A fast typist can almost keep up with a normal conversation, skipping the questions and concentrating on only the worthwhile answers.

The Ethics and Legal Implications of Taping

A certain lack of clarity prevails in this area, perhaps because of confusion over the difference between wiretapping, as in bugging or spying, and professional taping of journalistic interviews. Laws vary from state to state. The closest things to clear-cut regulations governing such matters are the wiretap laws.

The federal wiretap law permits taping of telephone conversations so long as at least one party to the conversation is aware of the recording. This means that in interstate telephone calls, the fact that the reporter is aware of the taping is sufficient to be legal whether the other party is aware of the taping or not. Most states either have no regulations covering this question or have laws similar to the federal wiretap law. In thirteen states, however, according to one authority, laws prohibit taping without *all-party* consent: California, Delaware, Florida, Georgia, Illinois, Maryland, Massachusetts, Michigan, Montana, New Hampshire, Oregon, Pennsylvania, and Washington (Middleton, 1979). However, some of these states have special exceptions. In Oregon, for example, it's illegal to secretly tape face-to-face conversations without all-party consent, but it's all right to tape a telephone conversation so long as one party (the reporter in this instance) is aware of it.

As in most legal matters pertaining to ethics in publishing, matters are seldom black and white; journalists therefore would be well-advised to err on the side of caution, which means inform your respondent if you are taping a telephone conversation.

CHAPTER THIRTEEN
Special Problems

Q. Senator, about your yachting tours to Barbados
    with the Mafia dons and the dancing girls—
A. I remember nothing, nothing at all!

How do you even *get* an interview with a busy executive or celebrity? How do you know you're hearing the truth? How do you cope with boring or hostile sources? How do you ask sensitive questions?

These represent a second tier of questions asked by those attending interviewing workshops and classes, the ones posed after telephone interviews, taping, and note taking have been dealt with (Chapter 12). The answers, though they may seem didactic as presented here—are based on experience, my own along with perhaps 300 interviews I or my students have conducted with professional interviewers. Not all of them were journalists. Many were doctors, counselors, police officers, psychiatrists, anthropologists, social workers, and fiction writers. We also interviewed sources ranging from frequently interviewed officials to those for whom an interview is a rare experience.

HARD-TO-GET INTERVIEWS

The more you know about your intended respondent, the more effective you can be in presenting a convincing argument for granting an interview. Here are some techniques common to journalism.

1. Be enthusiastic. It's infectious.
2. Arrange an interview through an intermediary who is sympathetic to your purpose. John Doe, a counselor, agrees that your story portraying a reformed alcoholic is a good idea as a means of educating the public about alcoholism, and so he agrees to propose interviews with one or more persons undergoing treatment.
3. Write a letter; perhaps send clips of past interviews you believe will interest your respondent. This helps if the person is hard to reach by phone or you think will respond better to a thoughtful letter than to a phone call.
4. Pose an intriguing question—direct to the respondent if you can or with an assistant if you can't. Lisa McCormack used this method to ask celebrities about their secret Walter Mitty fantasies (Chapter 10). It may open the door to full-fledged interviews.
5. Call to verify information obtained from other sources. Busy people who won't be interviewed often appreciate a reporter's care in checking information. When Lisa McCormack called Washington realtor Marshall Coyne to verify a quote, the response came in a gruff voice: "I want to tell you something. You're the first damned reporter who ever called to verify a quote—I like you!"
6. Enlist the interest of aides, secretaries, assistants, and spouses. Such people typically surround important people, and they are the ones to be convinced, not the celebrity. One persuasive argument is a truthful explanation of how important this story will be to the boss: "Everybody else in the industry, including his competitors, is quoted in this one, and I'm sure he wouldn't want to be left out." Be courteous to the underlings, and thank them whenever they do help.
7. Seek opportunities to meet your source informally, perhaps after a public speech, press conference, or at a social occasion. Or maybe even on the jogging path. Celebrities are left unguarded surprisingly often at such events. A quiet chat that includes an intriguing question can lead to an interview.
8. Offer to drive your all-too-busy source to the airport or to the next appointment. In Rhode Island, *Providence Journal* reporter Greg Smith obtained his interview by driving a town council president to a penitentiary to begin serving a sentence on a federal fraud conviction (Scanlan, 1986).
9. Focus your interview on a topic you know the source will enjoy discussing. Sally Celebrity is fed up with media attention on her romantic entanglements but would willingly discuss other topics.
10. Use flattery unabashedly. "Yes, I know you're busy . . . busy people are always the most interesting and important . . . we wouldn't want to talk with you otherwise." (Words used to convince a balky respondent who replied amiably, "Stop! Stop! I'll *do* it!")

11. Wear red. This is more symbolic than real, but wearing red became something of a fad among women reporters in Washington during the Ronald Reagan administration; the president seemed to show a preference for women in red. Now it means take advantage of any "in" you have. Patricia O'Brien, Washington writer for the Knight-Ridder papers, grew up in Somerville, Massachusetts. She once approached Thomas (Tip) O'Neill, of Massachusetts, then speaker of the U.S. House of Representatives. "Mr. Speaker," she said, "can an Irish woman from Somerville get an interview with the speaker?" "You're from Somerville?" "Yes." He gave her a big hug and replied, "Honey, you can have an interview anytime you want!"

12. Be honest and candid, particularly with people caught in moments of crisis. If the crisis is a public one, the details will get out to the public sooner or later. When agencies try to cover up—"stonewall" the media in the jargon of the Nixon administration— they often succeed in extending a minor embarrassment into a prolonged scandal. Bureaucrats and business executives are sometimes their own worst enemies when they refuse to respond to inquiries about problems that have somehow come to public attention. Your rational, gentle explanation of this as a fact of public life can succeed where threats and deceitful tactics fail.

Deceitful tactics? Media do use several standard ploys for wheedling information out of reluctant respondents, particularly the belligerent types who basically tell you to go to hell.

Among the standard practices of deceit:

1. Pretending you have information that you don't: "I have most of the story but just need a few details." The source provides those few details, thinking you have the story anyway, then provides more and more, until realizing that you started with almost nothing. That source will be twice wary when the next reporter calls.

2. Making up false facts or quotes, sometimes outrageous ones, which the source hastens to correct, thereby providing the information sought.

3. False dilemmas—"are you for abortion or against it": simplistic kinds of questions that force respondents to choose one or the other with little time (especially in broadcast interviews) to think through an honest or realistic answer.

4. Threats. "You goddamn whorehouse pimp, come clean with me or I'll have you pounding pavements in Hegewich—where's the body?" That's a quote attributed to the late Harry Romanoff, "Heifitz of the telephone interview," talking with a police officer (Moore, 1973). It probably wouldn't work today, if, indeed, it worked during the *Front Page* era. Today's threats are more subtle; reporters hint at prolonged periods of bad publicity or the wrath of editorial writers.

In most instances, deceit and threats achieve momentary gains at the expense of long-range trust. A reputation for deceitful interviewing methods soon gets around, leading to more difficult interviews in the future, perhaps to still more subterfuges just to secure information that other reporters obtain routinely.

"Was it something I asked?!!"

COPING WITH HOSTILITY

What is the reason for the hostility? If you can answer that question, you probably will be able to settle matters and go on with your interview. Sometimes *you* are the problem—your own thinly disguised resentment of certain types of people (you've always hated FBI agents or scruffy beardniks). The more tolerant you are, the better interviewer you'll be.

If you are not the problem, then what is? Asking directly may help. Ron Bellamy, a sports reporter for the *Eugene Register-Guard* in Oregon, did that after a fruitless twenty-minute fiasco with baseball player Reggie Jackson. Finally, Bellamy, seeing that the interview was going nowhere, asked Jackson whether there was some problem with the interview. That released a string of invectives about the biased reporting of a previous interviewer. Bellamy merely listened. Then, remarkably, the interview began anew. Freed of his anger, Jackson talked with new-found candor.

The incident suggests that hostility shouldn't be taken personally, if you've approached the interview well prepared, with an open mind, and particularly if you listen carefully. Hostility may stem not only from past problems with media interviewers, but from a fight that morning with a spouse or colleague, from worry over the very crisis that has made the respondent newsworthy, or even from indigestion or ulcers. If you know the reason for the problem, you may be able to defuse it or set it aside. When a doctor complained bitterly about media treatment of medical news, a reporter who had won awards for his medical writing, replied, "I won't blame you for the sins of the medical profession if you won't blame me for the sins of the newspaper profession." The doctor agreed, and the interview turned out fine.

ARE THEY TELLING THE TRUTH?

Truth in this context simply means factual reality. Despite a few studies that have suggested certain nonverbal giveaways when one is lying, eyeblink rates or jiggling the foot, for example, you really can't tell for sure just by looking. The problem is complicated by some interviewing tactics that tend to put sources on the defensive. Adversarial interviewing—the grand chess or poker game where each party works to achieve an advantage—does not necessarily lead to truth. Truth emerges best through the patient, nonjudgmental listening recommended throughout this text. But it never hurts to utilize some of the truth-checking devices noted here.

1. Homework. Good preparation solves a lot of problems when sources realize they can't utilize the proverbial snow job. Respondents are not stupid. They quickly perceive your level of knowledge by the kinds of questions you ask. It never hurts to cite in your conversation the other sources you have consulted or will consult and the documents you've read. Show your preparation in your questions: "Your mother tells me your childhood was not an easy one." Hard for Mr. Big to deny what Mother said—or what *else* she might have mentioned. Sometimes you may ask about a questionable statement: "Oh-oh, what you just told me doesn't square with what I just read in the *Wall Street Journal*—is my memory playing tricks on me?" The latter phrase eases the harshness of the confrontation, but your respondent knows full well that you'll confirm your memory at the first opportunity. The source will also exercise more care in future comments. Clearly, the respondent caught in too many factual errors will prompt you to discredit the answers throughout.

2. Sources. "Who told you this?" you ask your respondent. "Where and how did you acquire this information?" Aggressive probing along this line is far from the perfect solution, but it does intimidate liars and persons with "selective memories." It often enhances rapport with those who are on the level.

3. Corroboration. Try to find (or ask for) other persons (or written evidence) to confirm any doubtful statements.

4. Plausibility. Common sense often suggests whether statements have a ring of truth to them, and you probe to learn more about the ones that don't.

5. *Credibility.* You place more trust in people who have a reputation for honesty. Just as reporters earn good or bad reputations over time, so do news sources.

6. *Authority.* You place more weight on comments of those in a position to know: The police chief has a better grasp of a community's crime problems than, say, the city engineer.

7. *Time line.* Police detectives know that liars who fabricate events have a difficult time keeping the sequence of events in correct order each time they go over them.

NUDGING HAZY MEMORIES

Psychological studies suggest that people remember first things, last things, and unusual things. That's why you remember your first airplane flight, your most recent, and perhaps the one where things went wrong. This helps to explain why people can respond easily to such questions as "What was your most frightening experience?" or "Tell me about the highlights of your trip to China." People can remember such episodes. Memory also operates by association—you remember a humorous anecdote upon hearing someone tell a similar one. Thus, to remember a past experience, people need cues.

So the interviewer seeking to discuss past events comes armed with cues. Some may be news topics of the era. "We're talking about 1987—that was the year of the Iran-Contra hearings and Ollie North—remember?—the year of mines in the Persian Gulf, the big forest fires out west." Or they may be personal cues: "That was the year you vacationed on the house boat on Lake Powell."

Careful preparation is essential when you've come to interview about past events. Come to the interview with clippings, letters, and other documents in hand, and give your respondent a chance to review them before you start. In some cases, time permitting, you may drop off a packet of documents days ahead of the interview. Recollection of long-ago events takes time, even for the most willing of respondents.

If it's specific detail you want, ask a woman. Novelist Arthur Hailey told a TV interviewer that he finds women better than men at recalling personal and anecdotal material. A study (Bahrick, 1975) confirms the notion, showing women superior to men in ability to recall years later the names and faces of high school classmates.

EVASIVE RESPONDENTS

If in a broadcast interview you ask the president of XYZ Corporation when the company plans to stop polluting the environment, you may receive an answer like this: "Industry all over America has been working on the problem, spending billions of dollars, and I'm glad you asked the question because it gives me an opportunity to cite some of the splendid things XYZ has done in recent years to work with environmental groups to bring about solutions ...." The president has evaded the question. Evasion has indeed become an art form that typically employs these devices.

1. Bridging. The president's response is an example. A subtle transition bridges the conversation to a safer topic. Often the transition is not so subtle: "You may ask about pollution, but the *real* issue of American industry is unemployment [or unionism or the federal deficit, whatever]."

2. Questioning the Interviewer's Motives. "Do you ask such a question because you have a statement you want to make? Why don't you go ahead and make your statement, and then let's discuss it."

3. Use of Humor. An anecdote or humorous remark can often derail a topic, particularly on TV.

4. Intimidation. Sources use a range of tactics, such as belittling the question ("American industry is engaged in a life and death struggle against inflation, the deficit, and foreign competition—how can you even *think* of asking about pollution at a time like this?"). Others are a blustery, arrogant demeanor, nonstop talking, and even sexual innuendoes with members of the opposite gender.

5. Becoming Abstract and Academic. Respondents often lead you down a semantic offramp—"How do you define pollution; what do you think it really means to the American public; what is an acceptable level of pollutants?"

6. Employing a Hazy Memory.

The solution to all but the last (how can you distinguish between convenient forgetting and actual forgetting?) is simple. Simple to say if not always to do. Do your homework. Keep the interview on track. Listen carefully to the answers. Ask again if not satisfied. And again if necessary. On TV especially, don't hesitate to cut in whenever a filibuster or a bridging comes up. Above all, don't assume that the other person is always to blame for problems. Examine your own interviewing procedure to see if your belligerence or tricky techniques aren't the basic cause of the evasive defensiveness you encounter.

OFF THE RECORD

A reporter asks an official, "What do you think of the governor's latest proposal for school support?"

"I'm certainly going to study it with keen interest in the weeks ahead," responds the official. But then she confides, "But off the record, I think the governor is a silly fool for so outrageous a suggestion." Assuming you have agreed to go "off the record," you'll quote the first statement but not the second. You've also obtained a valuable news tip. Perhaps other officials, equally opposed to the governor's proposal, will talk publicly about it.

Journalists soon learn the meaning of a certain protocol in talking with elected officials and bureaucrats, most of it emanating from the experiences of journalists in the nation's capital.

Off the Record

By bureaucratic definition, statements identified as "off the record" are not to be published. They are usually intended for background information, perhaps to enhance the reporter's understanding of events. Or they may want to avoid premature disclosure of forthcoming events. A police chief, answering questions about drug laws, takes the reporter off the record to tell of a forthcoming raid on a suspected drug factory. The reporter has asked too many perceptive questions, so the chief has little alternative but to announce the raid off the record and to trust the reporter to keep it secret.

A reporter is not required to agree to off-the-record requests. Some will do so only in exceptional cases (the drug bust being a good example). Some tell sources that if they know something they don't want published, don't say it.

Not for Attribution

Statements so identified—according to Washington protocol—may be used but not identified as coming from the person who said them. Washington bureaucrats often use the terms "on background" and "deep background" to mean roughly the same thing. Thus news columns often contain blind attributions: "sources said" or "according to sources in the White House." The so-called news leak often comes out of such arrangements. Although attribution has long been a hallmark of news reporting, certain compromises have emerged: a reporter either takes the material not for attribution, or doesn't get it at all.

The process can lead to manipulation. A source "close to the governor" announces a new proposal for school tax reform. The source is the governor herself. She is sending up a trial balloon, it seems, and if the reaction is harshly negative, she may drop the plan without ever having said she was going to do it.

Other examples include the "little guy speaks out" phenomenon. A minor bureaucrat, fed up with the problems of an agency, leaks damaging information to the media on condition of anonymity. Sometimes, too, journalists may initiate the procedure, seeking for example to interview a large number of AIDS victims or reformed alcoholics with the understanding that none of them will be identified.

On the Record

This term is not normally part of journalistic jargon. If you contact a source, identify yourself as a reporter researching a story, and then start asking questions, the answers are assumed to be on the record: publishable. Most experienced sources realize this. Occasionally, an inexperienced one will merrily spill out a string of answers and then say, "Of course, you realize this is all off the record—I don't want any of this in the paper." An awkward situation indeed—you try to pick up the pieces as best you can. It helps to explain early in the conversation that you plan to use the answers in your story, but even that's no guarantee that the problem won't arise later.

THE NEWS CONFERENCE

The news conference is a necessary means of transmitting information, particularly in large cities where officials and celebrities cannot afford the time to grant individual interviews to many reporters. It is not an effective arena for the skilled interviewer. No opportunity exists for establishing rapport. Hostility, tension, and gamesmanship usually reign at such sessions, leading to defensive posturing by the speaker. Follow-up questions, the essence of good interviews, are impossible to ask.

A skilled and well-prepared interviewer would be foolish to ask a perceptive question only to hear or read the answer first in a competing medium.

Michael Thoele, a prize-winning reporter in Oregon, says he has asked only one question at a press conference in twenty years of reporting. That came when another reporter asked a district attorney a question that skirted dangerously close to premature release of information Thoele had worked hard to obtain exclusively. Rather than let the entire news corps stumble unwittingly onto his private gold mine, Thoele quickly asked a "diversionary" question.

MEDIA FREAKS

You won't work in journalism long before encountering media freaks, people who calculate every utterance to gain attention in the news media. They have studied the media, and they know every weakness. They know that media love confrontation. Media prefer attackers to defenders, fighters to lovers, high profile to low, violence to peace, simple solutions to complex, hard action to soft philosophies.

Media freaks don't merely talk, they hurl challenges and verbal exclamation points. They use plain Anglo-Saxon words. They attack revered institutions, including the party in power, big business, even big-time publishers and broadcast executives. They talk slowly for pad-and-pencil reporters and in thirty-second staccato bursts for broadcast sound bites. They have well-oiled duplicating equipment for publicity handouts. They "hate" editors and "love" reporters because they know reporters get stories on the air or into print, not editors. Besides, it's fashionable to hate editors. Best of all, they're always good for a colorful quote. In Hawaii, I asked a self-admitted media freak if his activities didn't add up to manipulation.

> *Manipulation?* If I manipulate the press, that's like two lovers playing with each other for their mutual enjoyment. Editors don't like me very much. One editor likes to think of me as a character. He doesn't like to think of me as having substance. He once said, "Look at all the space we've given you," and I said, "Space, hell! I've given you *news*. Good, solid news." Well, that's an editor for you. With reporters, we have a hell of a fine time.

WHAT WILL YOU WRITE ABOUT ME?

Respondents sometimes want to know precisely what you plan to say about them, even asking to see your material before publication or broadcast. Usually, stations and newspapers resist such requests. For one thing, deadlines won't allow it; many news reports barely make the deadline for the six o'clock news or the home edition. Journalists also try to avoid hassles with hypersensitive respondents who want to quibble over the meaning of every word.

Sometimes for magazine articles and feature stories, where time permits a more deliberate effort, journalists will have one or more sources go over the material to check for *factual accuracy*, but probably not for overall tone and conclusions. The better magazines are sticklers for accuracy; they employ large research departments for that purpose. Researchers sometimes call up interview sources to verify quotations.

Clearly, no right-minded interviewer can tell at the outset of research precisely how an article will turn out. That's what some respondents want to know at the beginning of a conversation. The proper response is, "I don't know."

As the conversation goes on, however, good interviewers have a way of subtly telegraphing how the story will appear, largely by the questions they ask. Their respondents are seldom taken by surprise, perhaps because all comments and issues that seem worthy of note have been thoroughly discussed in the interview. Consider an example.

"I've always hated my mother; she's been such a creep," says Sally Celebrity midway through an interview. Did she really mean that, or was it something said in a moment of anger? Some interviewers might seem to ignore the remark at the time and then write it into the lead paragraph of a head-line-grabbing story, all to Sally's surprise and dismay. She didn't really mean it the way it sounded, she says later. It was a slip of the tongue. She didn't expect it to go into the story.

The good interviewer would not let the remark pass without exploring it more. Did she really mean it? Why the hatred? What brought it about? What experiences has she had? And so on. The questions clearly indicate the remark deserves inclusion in the article. If she has any second thoughts about the remark, this would be the time to bring them up. True, you might miss a fiery quote, but what good is a fiery quote if the speaker won't stand behind it?

THE BORING RESPONDENT

The respondent bores you. What now? Look within yourself for the cause of that problem—perhaps *you* are the bore. Michael Thoele, who has reported for newspapers in Indiana and Oregon, recalls a case in point. He was sent to interview a woman from the Red Cross. The interview was boring, and so was the story. He was twenty-four years old, inexperienced in both newswriting and in life, especially as it related to volunteer organizations. So he didn't know what to talk about. Twenty years later he wishes he could do the interview again. He believes it would be a fascinating conversation. He would ask about the Red Cross role in natural disasters, such as floods, because he's covered floods as a reporter. He would ask about volunteer work because he has talked to enough leaders to know the difficulty, often the trauma, of recruiting volunteer helpers and getting them to do what they're supposed to do. With the self-confidence of twenty years of professional experience, Thoele knows he would find a good story somewhere in the conversation.

Within the breast of every living human, an editor once said, lies at least one great story. What's missing is not the story but the skilled interviewer to draw it out. The person who cries "boring" too often is the person lacking in perception and storytelling skills.

WHEN YOU'RE UNPREPARED

Reporters often must conduct interviews for which they have little or no preparation. Some enjoy the challenge. "It's like playing twenty questions," says one. If you are truly unprepared, the solution is simpler than you might expect. You do what a good quarterback would do on fourth down and long yardage. You punt. That is, you encourage the source to carry the conversational ball. You play a waiting game. As you listen you (1) pick up cues to orient yourself and get a grasp on the kind of story you might produce, and (2) pick up cues for follow-up questions. To start the conversation, you say something calculated to get the other person talking. "What brings you to River City, Senator?" It doesn't have to be brilliant. Indeed, reporters often carry in mind a supply of punting questions.

How do you feel about [you fill in the blank]?
What are some of the major problems [trends, changes] *in your field nowadays?*
Where did your interest in [fill in the blank] *start?*
What concerns are occupying your working hours recently?
What changes would you like to see?
What does the future hold in [respondent's field of endeavor]?

Of course, you are seldom totally without advance clues. A typical newsroom crisis runs like this. The assignment editor hangs up the phone and calls you over. "They're having a conference in the public utilities office about uses of solar energy and they have this expert in from Washington, D.C., and he has a spare thirty minutes right now, so let's hustle on over to the P.U.D. and get an interview with him for the six o'clock broadcast. Sorry to spring this on you so suddenly . . . ."

No use protesting why this wasn't thought of two weeks ago or even two hours. If you keep up with general news, perhaps read a news magazine each week, you may have at least superficial knowledge sufficient to jot down a few questions. What are the prospects for solar energy as a large-scale replacement for atomic power or hydro dams? Where is solar energy being used? With what effect? What research is being conducted on the subject? Further questions can follow GOSS—what goals are envisioned by those who advocate more use of solar energy?

If you have even ten minutes to prepare, how about reading clips from the library or electronic morgue or calling an expert at a nearby university?

ACCURACY

Beginning interviewers are so anxious about the conduct of the interview—establishing rapport, avoiding foolish questions, and so on—that they often neglect the seemingly minor details. The result is inaccuracy, with names misspelled, titles wrong, points misunderstood, technical details garbled, quotes mishandled.

Worse yet is an attitude among some young people that such accuracy really isn't important. "It's the primary thrust of creativity that counts," they say, an attitude that will usher them right out the door of most professional journalistic organizations and onto the unemployment lines, and good riddance.

Most mistakes result from interviewing problems. As noted earlier, oral communication is fraught with peril. People often don't say what they mean or listeners don't catch meanings properly. Little details slip by unchecked or unchallenged. Here are some problem areas:

1. Names, Addresses, Ages, Titles. If you have no other source for these details, then you must ask. The sooner the better. Just say, "Excuse me, I need to check the spelling of your name." Don't apologize; veteran reporters do it all the time. In the eyes of most respondents, doing so enhances your professionalism. Be especially careful on the phone; ask for phonetic spelling if necessary: "b as in buffalo." It's too easy to confuse b's and d's or s's and f's so that Mr. Sadler comes out Mr. Fabler. You must also recognize the exotic spelling of some first names nowadays: Jon, not John; Janee, not Janie; Tari, not Terry.

2. Major Points. As suggested before, repeat back your understanding of main points as the interview progresses.

3. Quotes. Unless you are dead certain of a comment you plan to quote verbatim, read it back for confirmation.

4. Context. Mistakes often occur because the interviewer does not understand the context in which things are said. The meaning of violent rhetoric among members of the city council becomes clear only when you realize the political background. They represent the community's two major political factions, which have been feuding for at least half a century. In short, the rhetoric is not as serious as it sounds.

5. Corroboration. Mistakes happen because the *source* has the facts wrong. Seek a second opinion or viewpoint, especially if the original source seems unsure. You'd be amazed at how many different versions reporters can receive of a single event—often a different version from each witness.

6. The Other Side. Issues have at least two sides, and it's clearly a mistake to report one side without checking with the other, especially when political attacks are involved.

7. Unwarranted Assumptions. Novice journalists tend to make assumptions rather than ask questions. An airplane pilot who had escaped a crash landing told a group of college reporters that his engine had caught fire during an instrument landing approach "just as I reached the inner marker." The young journalists reported the inner marker as something to be sighted visually—"fire occurred just as he *saw* the inner marker." They *assumed* that it's some kind of visible runway marker when in fact it's a radio beacon. The problem is not always confined to novices. When Washington's Mount St. Helens erupted in 1980, an astonishing number of east coast media reported it as located in Oregon. A New York editor explained sheepishly, "It's one of those things everybody *knows*, so you don't bother to check."

SENSITIVE QUESTIONS

The term "sensitive question" has perhaps taken on new meaning since the infamous Senator Gary Hart episode in 1987 in which the senator was observed receiving a late-night visitor, a young woman, at his Washington townhouse while his wife was away. The report eventually led to Hart's temporary withdrawal as a presidential candidate.

"Senator, have you ever committed adultery?" a reporter asked Hart in a subsequent news conference.

"I don't have to answer that question," Hart said, after some hesitation and grimacing.

Good theater. If you want theater, then by all means ask your sensitive question by firing directly from the hip, the sooner the better. Truth—factual accuracy—doesn't often fall out of such encounters, however.

The term sensitive question, however, is generally taken to mean either of two things: (1) potentially embarrassing or critical questions relating to business or public affairs, and (2) personal questions often related to traumatic events in one's life.

Embarrassing Questions

This is easier and simpler than most novices suspect. Investigative reporters do not expect confessions out of wrong-doing politicians or crooked business executives just for the asking. Rather, they do their homework. They prepare a case against them, and then, in a "confrontation interview," go over the evidence they have assembled to secure confirmation, denial, explanations, and, if possible, new information. Experienced reporters avoid arguments, angry accusations, and unfriendly attitudes. To their surprise, some respondents freely confess their misdeeds, sometimes, it seems, with a certain quiet pride. The journalist thus finds reason to agree with psychoanalyst Theodor Reik about the compulsion to confess: "It is clear that in the criminal two mental forces are fighting for supremacy. One tries to wipe out all traces of the crime, the other proclaims the deed and the doer to the whole world" (Reik, 1959).

Personal Questions

These kinds of sensitive questions seem almost too personal to ask for media reports. They should be asked only if they are of legitimate concern, part of the story. Your article on AIDS will fall flat if you don't ask victims to talk in detail about the drug or homosexual activity that led to the fatal disease. Your article on Alzheimer's disease needs case histories—dramatic, detailed ones—in which families discuss the trauma of caring for an Alzheimer's victim. In these situations, you don't shoot from the hip if you want candid answers. Suggestions:

1. Have a good reason for asking, and explain it thoroughly. If you explain that through your article you hope others will profit from the respondent's experience—that you've come to educate the public, not to exploit the troubled—then people may tell you the private details you seek.

2. Avoid pressure tactics. Explain what you want, but let people decide what they want to tell you. Often they talk candidly because they find it good therapy to do so, particularly if they sense your altruistic purpose and your nonjudgmental attitude.

3. Move indirectly into sensitive areas. If you want to ask about a person's experience with drugs or homosexuality, try discussing similar activities involving other people. Respondents, engaged in such discussion, often volunteer their own experiences as illustrations of points they want to make.

4. Listen keenly for hints and half-articulated feelings. Sometimes people want to tell you things about themselves, even bad things, but they don't know if you really want to hear them. You, meanwhile, hesitate to ask. People often break the resulting impasse by dropping hints, the way couples do in the early stages of a romantic involvement when neither is sure of the other's feelings. They test the climate with little hints to see what happens. Your AIDS respondent may speak of a "little problem" in childhood, slipping it in so unobtrusively that you're not sure you heard it right. *What* little problem? Maybe it's a first experience with drugs that had a strong bearing on the person's subsequent behavior. The problem may represent a key element in your report, something you could easily miss by not listening or not realizing that your source has reached a point of trust where candid discussion is possible.

CHAPTER FOURTEEN
The Broadcast Interview

Q. Dr. Zeiss, how do you feel about the world?
A. Based on all available evidence, I'd say it's
   round, though perhaps not perfectly so.
Q. Sir, forgive me, but I must take issue with you.
   I disagree flatly.

In his *Work of the Television Journalist*, Robert Tyrrell (1972) describes a novice BBC journalist sent to interview a British politician, the minister of housing. The young reporter warned the minister that he planned to ask some critical questions once the camera was rolling. They talked amiably for a few minutes, and the camera started. The reporter asked his first critical question.

"The minister turned puce with rage," recounts Tyrrell. "For several minutes he flayed both reporter and political opponents, leaving the young tyro shattered and practically speechless. As soon as the camera was switched off, the politician beamed a friendly smile and asked whether that was all right."

Theatrics. Performance. That's the primary way the broadcast interview differs from the print interview. Although the basics of interviewing remain largely the same, differences do exist. The need to perform, for example, calls for an inverted pyramid style of interviewing: ask the most important or exciting items first so you won't bore your audience. Performance also calls for differences in the way you phrase questions. Often the questions must include an explanation to the audience of their context and significance. Performance even limits the selection of respondents. In the minds of broadcasters, theatrical personalities and politicians outperform medical doctors, scientists, and scholars.

It's clearly important for those planning to enter broadcasting as a profession to understand these differences. It's almost as important for print interviewers to understand them, too, because most of what the public knows of journalistic interviewing comes from broadcast examples. Print interviewers who model their techniques after Mike Wallace or Phil Donahue may wonder why they fail to gain candor from their sources. Many eventually discover that interviewer theatrics and arrogance—though they may represent splendid showmanship—tend to render sources defensive and uncommunicative.

Broadcast interviewing resembles living room conversation—formal, theatrical, artificial—but capable of lively discourse. Print interviewing, at its best, resembles kitchen-family room-bedroom discussion, often lengthy, intimate, and candid. That's true, at least, for interviews done for newspaper feature stories, magazine articles, and nonfiction books, if not routine news. Freed of the need to perform in front of a camera, people are more likely to be themselves. Skilled, sensitive broadcast interviewers, however, can reach that level of candor despite the camera. Given time and nonjudgmental listening, many people eventually forget or ignore the camera. Broadcast interviews of this caliber are the rare exceptions, however. Print interviewers speak of mining tons of raw conversational ore for each ounce of golden insight. Broadcast interviewers tend to dive quickly for what glitters.

The interviewing styles do have similarities. They both require a firm sense of purpose, preinterview preparation, conversational rapport, and sensitive, nonjudgmental listening.

Broadcast technology changes rapidly, however, and interviewing techniques change, too. The major change in recent years has been the replacement of film with video tape. Not only has tape proved less costly, but it has opened up many new avenues of information-gathering methods.

The term electronic news gathering (ENG) has been applied to these new methods. One advantage is that time formerly involved in film processing can now be used to obtain more complete and up-to-date information. Another is that reporters can gather information from a wide variety of sources, many at remote locations, even beaming back video images through microwave relays and satellite transmission. Interviewers feel free to experiment with techniques. Instead of merely showing two people talking, ENG allows broadcast interviews to show more pictures of what they are talking about. Finally, ENG technology puts greater emphasis on writing and editing, utilizing the best of many sources rather than relying on a single source. The politician who rants and raves for dramatic effect in a TV interview now finds that ENG reporters have subsequently located other sources to respond, perhaps to rant and rave themselves. Tapes of the several interviews have gone through an editorial synthesis, resulting in a better-balanced report.

THREE TYPES OF BROADCAST INTERVIEWS

Broadcast interviews come in three distinct packages. One is the routine news interview leading to the ninety-second report on the evening news, including a twenty- to thirty-second sound bite. Second is the studio interview, live or taped, that ranges from the brief sessions on *Today* or *Good Morning America*, to the lengthy discussions on William F. Buckley's *Firing Line*. Third is the documentary interview, usually one of many interviews woven together on a topic of community or national interest, such as poverty, drug addiction, or environmental pollution.

1. The News Interview

The ninety-second news item on the six o'clock news on the local television station comes largely from the work of local reporters working with camera operators. The typical TV news interview involves two stages, a precamera interview followed by a brief on-camera segment in which the interviewer attempts to elicit a succinct sound bite that summarizes or provides a colorful insight into the topic.

The precamera segment follows largely the same pattern as a newspaper reporter's interview. Broadcast reporters become adept at the inverted-pyramid style of interviewing to obtain a preliminary grasp of the situation and the story angle they wish to pursue. As the details fall into place, they remain alert for quotable remarks, either to be cited in their stories or for the sound bite.

The "performance" comes in that second, on-camera segment. The camera is rolling now, usually shooting over the reporter's shoulder, and at this point the reporter will ask the question calculated to elicit the appropriate sound bite. A novice respondent might wonder why the question covers a point already discussed, but the reporter tries not to call attention to the rolling camera if possible. Indeed, as reporter you try to serve as a security blanket for nervous respondents through eye contact and empathic listening, trying to make the "ordeal" as conversational as possible.

Electronic news gathering equipment has made it possible to shoot longer interviews so that editors can select the best segments. It also allows reshooting an interview gone awry. And it allows camera operators to shoot relevant scenes other than the interview itself. As a result, some interviews run *voice-over*—that is, the discussion proceeds verbally as the screen shows examples of the topic, such as the snow-clogged streets being discussed by the weather forecaster or the street engineer.

Sometimes, if a reporter foresees a Q-A dialogue running intact, the camera operator may reshoot the reporter asking the questions, something not possible in the original interview unless two cameras are available. The dialogue will be reassembled at the station. This normally is—or should be—done in the respondent's presence, and care must be taken to ensure that the questions are the same as the originals.

2. The Studio Interview

As seen on *Good Morning America, Today, Tonight,* and similar programs, respondents, or "guests" as they are often called, come to the studio for interviews that may last anywhere from a few minutes to an hour. The interview may be live or taped, and in some instances, thanks to electronic wizardry, the guest may be in another studio, half a world apart from the interviewer.

Here, perhaps, is the quintessential broadcast interview, the one that differs sharply from print interviews in several respects. One difference is studio equipment, often several cameras, and a certain amount of confusion as the interviewer not only copes with the conversation—maintaining eye contact, listening, and thinking up new questions—but with such exotic broadcast fixtures as time cues and glowing red lights that signal which camera is on. All the while you're trying to help a nervous guest through the ordeal.

The confusion bewilders many a beginner. One professional recalled her first television interview: "I was so worried about time cues and which camera to face that I forgot to listen to the answers to my questions. It's hard to ask follow-up questions when you have no idea what you're following up" (Laine, 1976).

Yet it looks so easy in the hands of broadcast professionals such as Ted Koppel of ABC's *Nightline*. He not only copes with the technical problems, but often has as guests people of violently differing viewpoints located in remote studios around the country. He not only manages to remain calm, but invariably picks up on people's comments for his follow-up questions. The key, Koppel told *Newsweek*, "is that I listen. Most people don't. Something interesting comes along and—whooosh!—it goes right past them" (June 12, 1987). Listening amid the chaos of the typical television studio is a rare talent, like juggling a piece of fine china along with the usual five or six balls.

It's no different in one variation of the studio interview—the radio interview. There the secret of the good interview "is not the quality of the questions you ask, but the quality of attention you pay to the answers." So says one of radio's prime interviewers, Susan Stamberg of National Public Radio's *All Things Considered*.

Radio interviews are often done in a studio, but increasingly they're using the telephone. Radio interviews via phone can tap into peoples lives wherever they are, allowing more intimate interviews away from the artificiality of the TV studio. In a special self-interview for station WGUC, Cincinnati, Stamberg suggested why she sometimes prefers to interview by phone. "The phone takes me to places I can't visit in person, helps me tap people with expertise anywhere in the country or the world. Also, the phone is everyone's natural medium. The microphone inside the receiver is familiar to everybody, and won't intimidate them the way a larger mic would." More important, she finds that "I can really concentrate on what's being said, and I don't get distracted by the dress or tie or nervous tic."

3. The Multiple-Interview Documentary

Years ago a group of students at the University of California at Berkeley conducted a study of television news content. When NBC's *Sixty Minutes* undertook to develop a documentary on the subject of TV news "Happy Talk"—an attempt by many local stations to enhance ratings by using softer, more entertaining news—the Berkeley study became a subject of a television interview. For almost two hours, Mike Wallace interviewed the students who'd done the study. This was only one of many interviews done for the project. For all that work, the segment lasted only about twelve minutes when aired on network television, and the references to the Berkeley study ran only thirty or forty seconds, including a twelve-second sound bite. Only twelve seconds from a two-hour interview.

At the time it seemed an expensive way to produce a documentary, and the students marveled at the amount of money expended on film alone, not to mention the expense of the camera crew. Few local news stations could afford such extravagance. Today it is more common, thanks to ENG. Today's documentary employs comprehensive research, including many interviews, some taped, others done merely for background research. Teams of editors and writers extract the essence from the many hours of tapes to produce a documentary that may run as long as an hour, sometimes several hours in hour-long segments on each of several days.

And so through the years local television stations have produced a variety of multi-interview documentaries ranging from farm problems to crime. WCCO-TV in Minneapolis won several awards for its 1986 documentary on a local man serving time in Texas for a rape he didn't commit. The station spent $100,000 in staff time and expenses in its successful effort to document his innocence. WTMJ-TV in Milwaukee broadcast a report on poor driving, "Who's Behind the Wheel?" which revealed that many school bus drivers had long histories of traffic violations. And in Houston, station KPRC-TV won an investigative reporting award for its documentary revealing that at least seven inmates in the county jail died for lack of medical attention. Radio, too, utilizes the multiinterview documentary, such as WHAS-AM in Louisville, Kentucky, which broadcast "A Disaster Called Schizophrenia," exploring the effects of mental illness on the victims and their families.

Not all documentaries call for months of research and $100,000, however. The television "minidocumentary" may involve only four or five minutes of broadcast time, but the principle remains the same. Numerous interviews from a variety of sources come together to form a comprehensive report. The basis of a report on, say, a community's drug problem, often ranges from officials to junkies. The fact that many sources contribute insights and drama gives the documentary a more solid, authoritative feel, although it also involves more staff time and expense.

ASKING QUESTIONS FOR BROADCAST

Tomorrow you will conduct a five-minute interview with a newsworthy guest for the noon news. What now? Most of the suggestions cited in earlier chapters remain valid. Having a firm purpose remains Number One, even more vital than in print interviews. You do not want early fumbling when you're performing on the air. So find a narrow and specific purpose, one that can be accomplished in five minutes. You want to interview the governor about her controversial stand against the death penalty. Sally Celebrity is in town to promote her new book. You want Senator Fogg to talk about his candidacy for president, and you hope he'll announce his decision on your show.

Here are some areas where broadcast techniques differ from the ideas discussed in earlier chapters.

Preparation

The studio interview, especially, suffers when the interviewer is obviously unprepared. Not only does the guest notice, but so do thousands, even millions, in the audience. Preparation allows the interviewer to put authority in the questions, to evaluate answers and devise on-the-spot follow-ups, and to educate the audience should some obscure reference emerge in the conversation that viewers might not understand. Rather than ignoring the reference, you clarify it for the viewers: "When you mention 'Clint,' you're speaking obviously of the actor, Clint Eastwood, who starred opposite you in . . . ."

Interviews often go better if the audience prepares for them, too. That is, as ABC's Barbara Walters' interview specials illustrate, you share some of your preparation—often including film clips and still photos—to introduce your guest. A newsmaker's previous statements, as shown on the film clips, will provide background for your questions. Thus you don't have to preface a question with the comment, "Senator, in 1987 you said you opposed providing aid to the Nicaraguan contras; now I'd like to ask . . . ." You don't have to say it because the film clip has shown it much more dramatically that you could say it.

By the same token, never ask routine questions on a broadcast interview: "Where were you born? Where did you go to college?" If you can't find out through preparation, you certainly must ask them before the broadcast and include them in your introduction: "Tonight's guest, Senator Fogg, grew up in Cincinnati and graduated cum laude from Princeton . . . ."

Icebreakers

The performance aspect of broadcast interviewing often calls for more than the customary icebreaking conversation. Seven years of experience have taught one Seattle TV reporter, KIRO's Barbara Matt, to cope with anxiety problems.

1. The Mike Wallace-Geraldo Rivera jitters. "Is this going to be like Mike Wallace on *Sixty Minutes?*" The question occurs frequently, and Matt's response is to chuckle amiably and reply, "No, we don't do interviews that way."

2. Body language. A good TV reporter can tell quickly how the respondent feels about the interview, the nervous ones obvious by their rigid posture, lack of eye contact, sweaty palms, and sometimes by their having overdressed for the occasion. Such people need more than icebreakers—they need immersion in tubs of warm, personalized reassurance: Try to forget the camera and let's just talk.

3. Celebrity status. On both national and local television, the interviewer is often more widely acclaimed than the respondent. When she perceives this to be a problem, Barbara Matt often drops mention of her impoverished college years into the preinterview conversation. When an official of a blood plasma center refused to be interviewed, Matt confessed that she'd once sold her blood to earn money for college. She got the interview.

Phrasing of Questions

Television sometimes shows the question rather than merely asking it, a variation of the pictorial introduction just noted. When Barbara Walters asked actress Debra Winger her feelings about a love scene in the film *An Officer and a Gentleman,* a film clip illustrated the question. As Winger explained, what most viewers took for intense passion ironically turned out to be intense dislike for the actor.

If it's important to keep questions short in all interviews, it's doubly so for broadcast interviews. Some of the world's worst questions come out of presidential news conferences. A reporter once asked Lyndon Johnson a question so long and convoluted that LBJ glared at him and said, "I'll bet you can't repeat that question." He couldn't.

The point is simple: let the guest do most of the talking. That's not easy for people with a gift of gab, particularly with less-than-articulate respondents. The simpler your questions and the sharper your listening, the more articulate your sources become. So keep questions short. Preface them with a statement of context if necessary. "Senator Fogg, next week the Senate will vote on whether to confirm the president's appointment of Judge Doe to the Supreme Court. Tell me how you plan to vote and why." The more you personalize it the better: Tell *me* how you'll vote.

The best questions work off the conversation itself, questions you didn't know you were going to ask. On broadcast, conversational immersion rates better than linear Q-A dialogue. As Ted Koppel suggests, the key is *listening* and showing that you're doing so. Sometimes the best question is "Why? . . . Why do you say that?" It's particularly effective when something startling comes up, such as Sally Celebrity's announcement that she hates her mother or is swearing off all men.

Opening questions should arrive like soft pitches: ego reinforcing, easy to answer. They help calm nervous guests. "Senator Fogg, your national campaign to create more national parks has gained wide support from the media and the public. Why do you think people like the idea?" Once the senator has relaxed into his role, you can ask about troublesome things. If a guest stumbles on a first question, the embarrassment may hamper the entire interview. Some interviewers prefer to give out the first question before air time. The opportunity to think through that first answer helps to calm the guest's preinterview anxiety. Beware of filibuster answers, though; tell the guest to keep brief the discussion of that first question.

Most interviewers prefer not to suggest the subsequent questions before air time, however, for fear of losing spontaneity. If they know the questions, guests tend to rehearse answers. Stilted conversation results. With articulate guests, surprise questions often bring lively dialogue.

Organization

Short broadcast interviews contain only three or four questions, and so they tend to get to the important points as quickly as possible. That often means a less-gentle approach to sensitive questions. If the senator is involved in a widely publicized real estate scandal, then that will probably be no later than second on your list of four questions. Maybe first. That's what the audience wants to hear about, and that's what the senator expects, so why delay? Delay leads to viewer frustration and even to the guest's anxiety. On a longer interview, the key questions might be delayed until number four or five on a list of twenty. Some interviewers like to build suspense by promising to ask certain key questions "later in the program."

CHAPTER FIFTEEN
Covering a Newsbeat

Q. Hi, sergeant, what's new?
A. Nothing. Same old routine.

The interviewing implications of a newspaper or broadcast station's coverage of a newsbeat deserve careful attention. You are no longer concerned about a single interview. Once you establish a news source, chances are you'll be calling on that source on a regular basis. It becomes a long-term relationship rather than a single interview. The rapport and trust established on initial contact will affect future interviews, not only with that source, but with many others. Word gets around. A newsbeat—the county building, let's say—is a small society in which people get together frequently to exchange ideas, experiences, and gossip, and you can bet that the "new reporter on the beat" will enter into the discussion.

For that reason, the interviewing tactics of individual reporters become magnified over time. "He's sneaky—you've got to watch him all the time." Or, "She seems open and sincere—quite a change from the last reporter we had!"

Some agencies even have ways of taking care of reporters whose motives are less than honest. In Honolulu, one police reporter persisted in surreptitiously reading unauthorized file material. Recalls a police official: "One day we put a lot of junk in that file, including a fictitious murder. He picked it up and got all excited. We let it go just as far as the news desk, and then we

152

called the editor and told him it was all a hoax. We also told the editor why we'd done it. We didn't have any more trouble."

And so, without your quite realizing it, those impressions are making the rounds in ways that will make your job harder or easier in the future. Word spreads particularly quickly among reception and secretarial personnel who get together at coffee or in the cafeteria. Even your relationship with them is an important part of the overall beat coverage picture. Many reporters realize this and work as hard to cultivate secretaries as major officials. They pause to talk informally with them. They ask about spouses and friends, they admire photos of children, and they join them for coffee breaks. They often get news tips that way, or the personal acquaintance helps when they have to reach Mr. Important in a moment of crisis—it's that secretary you've gotten to know at coffee breaks who lets your call go through, or the one you've ignored or mistreated who doesn't.

Such people can also help you understand the government bureaucracy that's been entrusted to your reportorial care. Nothing is so intimidating to the young reporter as facing for the first time a bureaucratic iceberg such as city hall or the county courthouse. You find it populated with people who speak an exotic jargon. Garbage dumps are called sanitary landfills, and the act of filling one is called solid waste disposal. Meetings and hearings are filled with such opaque phrases as *first and second reading . . . declaring an emergency . . . defendant then and there being did then and there unlawfully . . . against the peace and dignity of the state . . . against the statutes made and provided . . . .*
Now what does all *that* mean?

THE BASICS OF NEWSBEAT COVERAGE

The principle of beat coverage is one of keeping in touch with reality. It means seeking information from the people who are involved in matters of public affairs or who regularly monitor such activities. Such people are called news sources, and they can range from presidents and governors to police precinct desk sergeants. As John L. Given said in a classic book called *Making a Newspaper* (1907), newspapers do not keep a watch on all humanity. Rather they station watchers at "a comparatively small number of places where it is made known when the life of anyone in the city departs from ordinary pathways or when events worth talking about occur." Such watch points include police headquarters, the county clerk's office, the fire department, the courts, city hall, the state legislature, Congress, the White House.

The dual concept—departing from ordinary pathways and events worth talking about—tends to define news, the commodity being sought whenever one covers a newsbeat. A Honolulu newspaper writer, Bob Krauss, suggests this example: You pass ten houses on your way home, and everything is routine at nine of them. The tenth is on fire. Which one would *you* talk about when you arrived home?

One definition, then, suggests that news depicts something occurring in unmistakable form: a fire, an arrest, a death, a riot, a bill sent to the floor of Congress, a vote, a speech, the remarks of a famous person. Newsbeat watching requires that a reporter identify the points at which news can occur. Some are better at this than others. If a journalist sees a building at a dangerous list, suggests Walter Lippmann (1922), you do not have to wait until it falls into the street in order to recognize news. Less perceptive reporters may have to wait. A legendary story tells of a novice reporter sent to cover the launching of a ship. He returned empty handed. The story didn't pan out, he told his editor. "Something went wrong and the ship stuck on the ways. They hope to get her into the water tomorrow." The reporter had failed to perceive this ironic turn of events—the deviance from ordinary pathways—as news.

Most concepts of news remain the same in the years since Given's and Lippmann's insightful comments. Broadcast and newspaper reporters still keep in touch with the watch points, still develop news sources, still keep an eye open for those points at which happenings or trends can be fixed, objectified, named, or measured. Perhaps reporters are better educated today, more sophisticated, but the principles remain the same.

Q: *Anything new today, Chief?*
A: *Just the same old routine.*

Beat coverage is by no means confined to stations and newspapers. Magazines also cover beats in their specialized fields. Shelter magazines such as *Sunset* or *Better Homes and Gardens*, for example, keep in touch with such sources as architects, home builders, nutritionists, research agencies, and others who deal in the home-food-gardening specialties of the magazines.

Whatever the field, the beat reporter works to define points at which the flow of political, social, and economic events can be reported. GOSS—the acronym for goals, obstacles, solutions, start—proves useful here because all agencies within a reporter's beat have goals. The reporter looks for mileposts along the way to accomplishing those goals—or obstacles that block progress. Among the points at which one might report progress, or the lack of it, could be these: an annual report, a labor dispute, a speech by an official, the announcement of a new budget or a tax increase. Any of these can be the point that defines or objectifies a trend.

It is not always necessary to report progress. Your city establishes a new crime fighting unit of elite officers who are deployed nightly to areas with high crime rates for burglary and violence. Is progress being made—the burglary rate dropping in those high-crime-rate areas? If the answer is yes, you have a story. If it's no, you have a bigger story: Despite the employment of an elite crew of officers, burglary and violence remain as high as ever—a newsworthy twist of irony.

Just where are these watch stations, the news beats where reporters keep an eye on events? A typical newspaper serving a middle-sized U.S. city would split them up more or less like this.

1. *Emergency services.* Police and fire departments, hospitals, medical examiner, ambulance services, jails, Coast Guard.
2. *Courts.* State, federal, and local courts, also appellate courts, juvenile, probate, and bankruptcy courts.
3. *City services.* City hall, city council, municipal agencies such as engineering, zoning, civil service, and many others.
4. *County government.* Tax collection, boards of commissioners, welfare, health and sanitation, elections, environmental controls, housing. State courts are often housed in the county building.
5. *State government.* Governor, legislature, and state services if the city is also the state capital. Highways, state police, motor vehicles, and so on.
6. *Federal.* Post office, immigration service, internal revenue, agricultural agencies, law enforcement agencies—these and many more have branches in most major cities.
7. *Business.* Chamber of commerce, business and professional organizations, major local industries, public utilities, financial institutions.
8. *Sports.* Professional and interscholastic athletics, outdoor activities, participation sports (golf, tennis, mountain climbing, running, sailing, and so on).
9. *Politics.* Political organizations, political leaders and candidates, office holders.
10. *Education.* School boards, student activities, colleges and universities, administrative offices.

11. *Social welfare.* Altruistic organizations, youth agencies, social betterment groups, government welfare agencies.
12. *Agriculture.* Farm agencies, granges and other farm organizations, farm research agencies.
13. *Transportation.* Airports, railroads, waterfront, highways, tourist agencies, hotels, airlines.
14. *Entertainment.* Movies, theaters, concerts, books, civic events.
15. *Medicine, science, technology.* Research agencies, museums, archival agencies, medical societies, college science departments.

Variations exist from community to community. On large newspapers, a reporter's work may be confined to just one of these areas; small papers and broadcast stations have smaller staffs, so beats are combined and coverage is less systematic.

GETTING STARTED ON A NEWSBEAT

Let's assume for discussion that you have been placed on the county court-house beat: county government and the state trial courts. How do you begin? If you're lucky, an experienced reporter will take you around, show you where public documents such as court complaints and petitions are filed, and introduce you to important people such as bureaucrats and secretaries. But many reporters have had to learn a beat on their own, usually by just diving in. The water is seldom as icy as you imagine.

Plenty of sympathetic and helpful people will come forward to provide assistance once your motives are understood to be sincere and honorable. In a few cases, *their* motives may be less honorable than your own. Some are more publicity conscious than others. They seem constantly involved in schemes to get something onto the six o'clock news, or in rare instances to keep something out.

Most people in public life are guided by high principles, and about two-thirds of them are eager, or at least willing, to work with media representatives on news stories. They have their own set of needs, paramount among which is public acceptance of their program. Highway officials want the public to know about repair projects or new construction. Health officials want to warn about dangerous epidemics of influenza, hepatitis, or sexually transmitted diseases such as herpes or AIDS. A county administrator wants to secure voter approval of a budget. And elected officials sometimes will go to extremes to curry media attention, believing that their future depends on it, as well it might.

You may think that all this works as long as the news is favorable to the agency or the bureaucrat. Some enlightened agencies, however, have concluded that it's unrealistic to assume that all the news about their departments should be favorable. They've learned that it's folly to have their departments portrayed favorably, only to face angry voters at a budget election with a request for more tax dollars to "handle our problems." *What* problems? All along the media have been running favorable reports—how come this eleventh-hour crisis?

As new reporter on the beat, then, you may be surprised to learn the extent of your welcome. You're sought out as often as you seek out. You're constantly tested with ideas for publicity. You're bombarded with news releases, tips, suggestions. Pseudoevents—ceremonies, news conferences, demonstrations, inspection tours—are staged for your benefit and the accompanying publicity.

Basic Steps for a New Beat

Here is a sketch of how a new reporter typically gets started on a news beat.

1. Attain a good working definition of news—what it is and how to recognize it when you encounter it—all in accord with your station's or publication's policy.
2. Identify the departments, agencies, and informal sources from which you expect to collect ideas for news and feature stories. Put them and their phone numbers in your Rolodex and keep adding new names as time goes on. These will include all potential sources, from chief executive officers to informal sources such as secretaries and janitors.
3. Read. Prepare as you would an interview. Read clips of previously published articles from that beat. Read professional journals, such as *Chronicle of Higher Education* if you're covering the local colleges or *Law & Order* if you're covering police. Ask to see public documents from various offices: memos, annual reports, brochures, copies of speeches. Monitor bulletin boards.
4. Identify ongoing issues and goals—precisely what is the agency trying to accomplish? Identify points at which accomplishment, or the lack of it, can logically be reported—perhaps on the occasion of an anniversary, publication of an annual report, the retirement of an old administrator, or hiring of a new one.
5. Establish a "futures book"—an appointment book in which you list all forthcoming ideas and events that you learn of. Asking sources to help you fill out your calendar often turns up ideas for stories.
6. Meet your prospective sources, one by one. Leave your business card. Explain your mission. Define news: what you want and why it's important. Discuss plans for regular contact, daily, weekly, or whatever's appropriate. Discuss GOSS, goals, and so on. Together identify potential stories for now and in the future.
7. Make contact with sources on a regular basis.
8. As time progresses, discuss informally the ongoing issues and the points at which such issues can be fixed or objectified. Probe for specific trends, records, events, future plans, and so forth.
9. Inform potential sources on the realities of the news business. Not every story will be favorable to a source or agency, and times will no doubt arrive when events dictate a story that causes displeasure. Anticipating such events and discussing them before they happen can dispel hard feelings sometimes, particular-

ly if you promise to be open-minded and fair—and your subsequent actions demonstrate those qualities.

One observer of media performance, Leon Sigal, suggests in his study *Reporters and Officials* (1973) that much bargaining occurs between the two. Experienced reporters confirm this. Write a story favorable to a source and you stand a better chance of getting tips, leads, and exclusive interviews in return. But any experienced agency head knows that refusal to cooperate— even after being "burned" by an unfavorable story—incurs the risk of more unfavorable stories as reporters seek alternate news sources. Thus a delicate balance of power exists between reporters and officials.

Occasions certainly do exist when reporters must use leverage to secure public information from recalcitrant public officials. In general, they find it wise to use the power of the media in moderation and only when all else fails. The reporter who deals honestly and openly with sources seldom has to resort to power tactics. You'll find alternative sources of information, often from inside tipsters and leakers whose presentation of the facts often is harsh, even ruthless. Enlightened bureaucrats sometimes realize that fact, and so they cooperate with the media even when their heart isn't in it.

THREE SOURCES OF NEWS

Systematic beat coverage is a three-legged stool. First is news from press releases, news conferences, meetings, documents, informal suggestions—in short, *source-initiated* material. Second is *reporter-initiated* news: interviews, pursuit of tips and hunches, follow-ups on projects.

The third—and the one too often overlooked—is the news that comes from the *interaction of a reporter and a news source.* This third leg produces a kind of intelligence neither party could produce alone. It happens informally. Some reporters call it coffee cup reporting, and one reporter confesses he consumes ten to twenty cups of coffee a day in informal discussions with the sources on his newsbeat.

It works to the advantage of both parties. One source, a state legislator in Hawaii, explains: "We meet over coffee or in the hallways or during breaks in meetings. The reporters just come around and ask what's the scoop on this bill or that issue. I think this is good because the reporters can ferret out stories that would not always be appropriate in a press release because they might hurt somebody's feelings. This way the public gets a more candid and realistic story."

Thus do useful stories emerge, the kind that sources wouldn't volunteer and reporters don't know about. But informal contact allows them to emerge naturally.

The informal give and take also works on the phone, at least after reporters have become acquainted with sources. One newspaper reporter happened to call a woman in community relations at the county courthouse. The conversation, which the reporter characterized as a "fishing expedition," led to a couple of useful story ideas. The story ideas came so casually that the reporter decided to write down the entire conversation afterward as best he could remember it, just to show how informal conversation leads to news— also to give an idea of the casual manner that serves as catalyst.

Q. What's new?

A. What's new? Well, same old routine.

Q. Ha! That's what they all say. You've heard this story about a reporter who calls up the courthouse and asks what's going on? Well, the county judge answers and says, "There's nothing going on," and he quickly hangs up. For once he was right. Seems the courthouse was on fire. Everybody had evacuated the building. So they were all standing around doing nothing.

A. Right, right. I get the picture. Hey, I smell smoke!

Q. *What?*

A. No, I'm kidding. You reporters are so *jumpy!* Well, if you want to know what's *not* happening, there's no commissioner's meeting next week.

Q. How come?

A. They're all going to a conference out of town.

Q. Are you going, too? Are you going to give a speech?

A. Didn't anybody teach you not to ask two questions at once? Yes. No. I'm going but I'm not speaking. I'm going to attend a session about how to bridge the credibility gap.

Q. No need. We all know you're an honest woman.

A. Except I lie to my husband and my kids and my friends—

Q. But only because you have so many state secrets, stuff that would really blow the lid off if people knew—

A. Well, no, I don't really.

Q. So, anyhow, who *is* going to give a speech? Anybody? Or is that two questions?

A. Three. One of the fellows in the Solid Waste Department—he's talking on "Solid Waste and Energy Production." That means burning garbage for electrical energy in case you didn't know.

Q. I know. Is he for it or against it?

A. For it, I hope.

Q. Well, that's worth a story. I'll call him and find out what he intends to say. So who else is going with you on this boondoggle—er, trip?

A. [Gives details. Conversation turns to another department, the Juvenile Department.]

Q. I've just about given up on that department. I used to work years ago in another county and got lots of stories from juvenile. Here, nothing.

A. They're very protective here.

Q. Someday they'll find they'd like more public support—

A. Say, that reminds me, speaking of the courthouse burning—

Q. Oh, no—

A. Seems that the Juvenile Department *is* interested in the public, so they've started some kind of educational programs with juvenile officers going out and talking to parents' groups about juvenile problems—what youth is all about today, what to look for in the way of problems, drugs, alcohol. Maybe there's a story there.

Q. Right. Could be. I'll check into it.

Perhaps the dialogue seems almost too casual, almost too personal with its references to honest women and jumpy reporters, almost as though this were a personal conversation, not business. Don't overlook its importance. The pair clearly enjoy chatting informally, but as the conversation goes on, both are alert to hints and reminders that can lead to the business at hand: fishing for news.

BLIND QUESTIONS FOR BEAT COVERAGE

Once they get to know their beats, reporters don't often have to resort to "blind" questions for news coverage, the questions that are purely fishing expeditions. Tips and leads and follow-ups will keep you busy. Sometimes, though, having a set of universal questions can help keep you from overlooking possibilities. Here are some examples of questions that can be asked of a news source—preferably in an amiable, informal way—when nothing else is important at the moment.

1. What kinds of problems cause you the greatest concern right now?
2. What projects are you working on?
3. When members of the public talk with you, what kinds of concerns are on their minds? What do you tell them?
4. What kinds of stories could the paper or station run to help you meet your goals?
5. What new trends are evident in your field? What is your department doing to adjust to these trends?
6. Do you have a vision for what this department might be doing five or ten years from now?
7. If you had more money, what new projects would you start?
8. Do you ever ask yourself, what *should* the department be doing in the future? What stands in the way of doing it?
9. What research is going on?
10. What personnel changes are being made or contemplated?
11. What experts or consultants are being brought in, and for what purpose?
12. What new equipment is being purchased and for what purpose?

13. What significant statistical trends have been spotted?
14. How will outside forces (economic, political, legal) affect your department?
15. What publications, reports, or memoranda are being prepared, for whom and to what end?
16. Are you or members of your department planning any trips, conferences, speeches, or meetings in the weeks ahead?
17. Who are some people in your department who have the most interesting jobs, have the most unusual insights into human nature, or have achieved the most remarkable goals?
18. If, as you suggest, absolutely nothing noteworthy is going on in your department, could the organization (or taxpayers) save money by eliminating it?

Question 18 may strike you as harsh, so perhaps you should get to know your source before you try it. I used it several times, and got remarkable results. One agency director approached days later with no fewer than 20 ideas for stories, of which half struck me as pretty good, and several of which eventually appeared in print. "Your question stimulated our thinking," the director said, "and we got to wondering, just why *are* we in existence? So we came up with these ideas as part of the answer."

So the lesson is—don't be afraid to pose challenging questions.

CHAPTER SIXTEEN
Multiple-Interview Projects

Q. Tell me, Senator, who would be some other
   good sources of information to talk with about
   your proposed legislation?
A. *No one!* Talk to no one but me; *believe* no one
   but me!

In 1983, the *Seattle Times* published a seven-part series of articles that essentially dealt with what seemed a simple enough task: making one airplane fly. Business writer Peter Rinearson undertook to tell the story of the airplane manufacturer's development of the Boeing 757, a commercial jetliner. At first he thought the job would take three or four weeks. As it turned out, he spent six months of seventy-hour weeks, consulted 325 categories of sources, conducted extensive, taped interviews with seventy to eighty people involved in the development of the aircraft, and amassed some 2,000 pages of transcribed notes from taped interviews. Rinearson found the task so complex that he developed a computer data base just to keep track of the information. He seemed to thrive on detail, right down to the handshake that occurred in the back seat of a car on a sun-drenched day near the Miami International Airport—the handshake that led to the birth of a new, revolutionary type of commercial jet liner. Two men shook hands just as the car jiggled over a railroad track. No novelist would dare include that kind of symbolism in a work of fiction: Critics would call it too contrived. But, as we will see, that's the way it happened. Literary nonfiction tends to free writers to depict reality as they discover it.

Project interviewing, then—multiple-interview projects that produce articles and documentaries rich in detail and substance—is an act of discovery, not of imagination. Yet such interviewing can be an act of creativity equaling a work of fiction. It can, at least, in the hands of a perceptive and patient interviewer. Magazine writers have a rule: "interview, interview, interview— and keep interviewing until your sources tell you nothing you haven't already heard." Rinearson's project is an example of what a journalist can accomplish through exhaustive interviewing for detail. The series, titled, "Making It Fly," reads like a novel, and it won several writing awards, including the Pulitzer Prize for feature writing. Later Rinearson began expanding it into a book.

Journalism has become ever more sophisticated. Reporters don't stop with a single interview with a single source. Truth more likely emerges from a variety of sources, and certainly more detailed and vivid accounts inevitably come from a journalist's diligence in consulting many sources.

It also offers the journalist more freedom, more independence, less reliance on any particular source. If you interview everyone involved in a situation, you are beholden to no point of view except your own. And so it offers more freedom, yes, but requires more responsibility to be fair to all concerned.

No longer are you at the mercy of an uncooperative or manipulative source. What one person refuses to tell you, another will. Even lack of cooperation from the subject of a biographical profile need not kill a project, as writer Gay Talese demonstrated when he wrote an article for *Esquire* about Frank Sinatra. When Sinatra refused to cooperate, Talese interviewed others around him and spent time hanging around the edges when Sinatra and his entourage appeared in public. Years later, Kitty Kelley wrote an unauthorized biography of Sinatra using largely the same research techniques (*His Way*, Bantam, 1986).

THE NATURE OF MULTIPLE-INTERVIEW PROJECTS

The multiple-interview project is easily defined; it's simply a journalistic project that involves more than one interview. Most journalism does, indeed, come from multiple sources, even the simplest stories. The police reporter calls a few witnesses to the bank robbery, thereby bringing the readers a more vivid account. The court reporter, rather than merely citing the verdict at the end of the trial, interviews the participants: judge, members of the jury, lawyers, and the accused, if it's a criminal trial. From such sources, the reporter collects a better picture of why the trial came out the way it did. A journalist writing a comprehensive magazine article about AIDS or hepatitis may interview everyone from researchers to patients, sometimes a hundred or more. In the magazine field particularly, the rule is get ten times more information than you need. And from there you can range upward to nonfiction books that may require years of research and hundreds of interviews.

The journalistic result of such activities goes by various names—comprehensive reporting, depth reporting, saturation reporting, new journalism, literary journalism, literary reportage, to name a few. More than anything else, it leads to the kind of nonfiction wherein documentary research, observation, and multiple interviewing come together in a grand synthesis to produce the kinds of nonfiction that combine the drama and color of fiction with the realism and authority of fact.

Multiple-interview projects are not just lots of separate interviews. Rather they are intricately related. Clearly, from early interviews the journalist learns a good deal that can be applied to all the subsequent interviews. A fact learned in, say, interview number 47 will not only change the complexion of all subsequent interviews, but may cause you to reinterview earlier sources.

SPECIAL REQUIREMENTS OF THE PROJECT INTERVIEW

By whatever name, such interviewing eventually attains the stature of an anthropological field project, sometimes complete with participant observation. Let's examine key factors that make the project interviews different from other interviews, factors you need to consider as you embark on such projects.

Guard Your Reputation

In communities where people know each other, your presence as a journalist gives them something interesting to talk about. Floyd Miller interviewed at least 100 persons in the small community of Nyack, New York, for a dramatic *Reader's Digest* account of a train-school bus collision that killed five teenagers and injured many more.

"What they tell you they have to tell of their own volition," he said (*Quill*, June 1974). "Your reputation must go ahead of you— your reputation as one who is sympathetic and who can receive information without judging."

Clearly, the interviewer who believes in fairness, completeness, and good, nonjudgmental listening has little to fear from the kind of talk that gets around. The reverse is even more true—bad vibes seem to travel on express lanes—so that subsequent sources become more wary and guarded as the project progresses. Indeed, it may not progress at all if matters become too negative.

As a result, you should take great care to avoid gossip. Don't spill to subsequent respondents things said to you in confidence by sources who have come to trust you. If you talk glibly about Jane Doe's personal life to Suzie Roe—things Jane told you in confidence—Suzie may enjoy the gossip, but she'll also think to herself, "What's he going to tell the next one about *me*?"

Another pitfall is aligning yourself with one or another side among the many political factions inherent in communities. We are talking here not of formal politics but of the various power factions one encounters in any group, be it homosexuals, factory workers, or Rotary Club members. Each group will work hard to recruit you to its point of view.

Finally, you should make clear in every instance just how you plan to use the information people give you. Will you quote them? By name? If so, they may not speak as freely and candidly, especially if they have much to hide, such as members of Alcoholics Anonymous. Whatever rules you establish you must, of course, follow, treating all participants the same or making clear why you are not treating them all the same.

Work with Key People

Every group has its leaders, some of them recognized in the published lines of authority, some of them merely influential in informal ways. To illustrate, you may want to develop a story on police detectives: What are they *really* like compared to the film-television portrayals? You'll know to negotiate with the police chief and the head of detectives to get their approval for your project. What may not be so clear is the existence of a person we'll call "Big Jim." He's the informal leader, and the other detectives take their cues from him. If Big Jim says you're okay, then you're okay. If you're smart, you'll interview Big Jim first and hope that he will put his stamp of approval on you.

Just why people like Big Jim hold sway over the group's opinions is an interesting question. Intelligence, character, skill, courage, charisma, wisdom, communications ability—all these cause some people to emerge as informal leaders and to thus be the key to the success of many kinds of interview projects.

Physical size has little to do with this leadership status. When sociologist Elijah Anderson (1978) began his three-year observation at Jelly's, the South Chicago ghetto bar, he enjoyed acceptance only after he met Herman, a small, brown-skinned janitor who patronized Jelly's regularly. It was Herman, the street-wise former pimp, hustler, and junkie, who introduced Anderson to his friends as the "cat gettin' his doctor's degree." In short, Herman was the key person whose approval became necessary for the project.

Journalistic projects, to be sure, don't always require the sensitivity of a study seeking to examine social relationships, but they have similar requirements, and approval of key people, both official and unofficial, helps to ease the way.

Collect the Small Fragments

What one respondent doesn't tell you another will, a fact that enables you to relax and enjoy the conversations without putting too much pressure on yourself and your respondents. That, in turn, often produces relaxed conversational style that leads to more candor and thus more information. On such occasions, no or few notes need be taken because you are looking for colorful fragments that will ultimately build up a mosaic of information consistent with whatever theme emerges out of your research. As time goes on, an hour-long interview may yield only a few new pieces of information, and that is all you should expect.

Often what you want are the small things, the illustrations of the theme or character you are trying to describe. Consider, as an example, Peter Rinearson's article on development of the Boeing 757. It began with the handshake in the back seat of the car just as it jiggled over a set of railroad tracks, a fact mentioned early in the seven-part *Seattle Times* story. The handshakers were Frank Borman, president of Eastern Airlines, and E. H. (Tex) Boullioun, president of Boeing's commercial airplane division. Roy Peter Clark later interviewed Rinearson about how he obtained that remarkable bit of information, since he obviously was not there at the time. Rinearson replied:

> I asked Borman—this is a verbatim quote—"I'm really trying to re-create that car ride. Was it a car like this?" (I was in a car with him at the time.) "Was it a limo?" And he chuckles, "No we don't have limos at Eastern. It was a private car or rental car. I don't know. There were three of us in the back seat. I was sitting on that side and Tex was on this side. It was cramped and crowded and there were other people around, but I don't believe anyone else knew that we had shaken hands." I said, "Was it a short ride?" He said, "It was about a four-minute ride from my office to the terminal." It was Borman who remembered the railroad tracks. "On that trip where you and Boullioun shook hands, do you remember if it was a nice day?" "Beautiful sunny day. As I recall, as a matter of fact, we had just gone over the railroad tracks that separate the terminal side from the office side, just halfway between."
>
> I wasn't going to take literary license here. I went to as extreme a length as I could to pin things down. The specific dialogue is Boullioun's recollection of the conversation. In single-spaced typewritten pages of transcript, I have close to 200 pages with Tex Boullioun alone. [Clark, 1984]*

As the above comment by Rinearson suggests, interviewing for such detail involves a certain tedium. It is not easy to re-create scenes based on information from interviews, yet Rinearson got sufficient detail to dramatize the precise point at which a new airplane was conceived through the agreement of Eastern Airlines to purchase the new craft:

---

* From *Best Newspaper Writings 1984* by Roy Peter Clark. © 1984 by Poynter Institute for Media Studies.

Once together in the back seat of the car, Borman told Boullioun he liked the bigger airplane design and was willing to gamble on it.

"All at once Borman had a flash that a 175-passenger airplane was what Eastern wanted," Boullioun recalled. "He said, 'If you'll build that, we'll go.'"

Boullioun replied, "You've got it."

And so, with a handshake—just as the car jiggled over some railroad tracks—the Boeing 757 was born. [*Seattle Times*, June 19, 1983]

Use Informal Observation and Interviewing

Some writers conduct a large part of their research without formal interviews, believing that they receive more candid information. It's a little like participant observation, and magazine writers do it all the time. The author of a *Reader's Digest* article on "intuition" spent much research time simply bringing up the topic whenever he met people socially. Almost everybody he asked had had some experience with it and could relate interesting anecdotes. Often they didn't even know they were being interviewed.

But don't be afraid to state your identity. Some make it a practice to announce, usually to a person sure to talk with everyone at the party, a current project in which help is needed. The topic could be anything, divorce, children, widowhood, whatever. When word gets around, people will approach to volunteer information, experiences, and points of view. Often journalists obtain ideas for stories by listening to what people are talking about. One editor, Edward Kosner of *New York* magazine, recalls attending a party filled with elegantly dressed New York City residents. What were they talking about? "Cockroaches!" And that prompted the magazine to produce an article on cockroaches.

This grassroots level of interviewing for projects can help journalists to move close to their readers by dealing with the things people talk about, rather than with official announcements out of City Hall or the White House, which, many journalists would agree, are not close to the people.

Magazines, especially, tend to write about the everyday problems of life in whatever specialty they serve. They offer advice on such mundane but important matters as preparing meals, buying a new house or remodeling an old one, and raising children. Magazine writers know that and often draw on their own life's experiences for source material. That, too, is a multiple-interview project. I spent eight years, for example, researching an article on child care, simply by observing and talking with my own children. Through this observation, I felt I had gained a worthwhile insight: kids are psychologically and physically tougher than most parents think, a notion I gained watching my then nine-year-old son struggle with—and finally succeed, in climbing a 10,000-foot mountain. I wrote an article (*Parents*, April 1973) suggesting that parents shouldn't protect children from the kinds of hardships that will offer them a chance to mature.

Trading Information

As you learn more about the topic under discussion, you yourself become the expert, strange as that may sound. Eventually, you find people granting you interviews largely to find out what you know. Your candor encourages their candor. Short of violating confidences, this seems an equitable trade-off. An anthropologist, Clyde Kluckholn, once suggested that "many human beings consciously or unconsciously resent being 'pumped dry.' If the anthropologist will tell enough stories about his own personal life to at least give the illusion that a swapping of information is going on, the subject will frequently be freer and less guarded."

In such instances, the respondent's questions will prompt you to talk a good deal more than you ordinarily would. Although you should guard against dominating the conversation, you can use your talk to good advantage. By this time, you have enough information to develop hypotheses. That is, you test ideas that represent possible thematic thrusts of your material, perhaps through questions like this in a conversation with a detective:

Q. Mind if I try an idea on you?

A. Go ahead.

Q. I wondered what you think of some of the conclusions I've been working out in my mind after interviewing a dozen men and women in the Criminal Investigations Division. First, detective work is not at all like you see on television—no thrill-a-minute shootups or knockdown brawls—in fact it seems more like the work of a scholar, a professor, maybe, tracking down leads, conducting interviews . . . .

Thus you suggest a hypothetical framework to explain some of the facts and ideas you have uncovered. Such conceptual questions have a valid function, particularly when asked of sources who are reasonably well acquainted with the overall picture. They may not agree, so then you discuss it further. Perhaps one convinces the other, perhaps not.

By submitting your ideas to this kind of testing, you emerge with a stronger, more valid kind of result. If your theories are solid, fine. If not, if people can poke holes in them, perhaps you're not quite ready to pull everything together into a final synthesis at this point. As academics are fond of saying, more research is needed.

CHAPTER 17
The Personality Interview

Q. Ms. Celebrity—may I call you Sally?—just
   what is it that makes you tick?
A. [Laughter] Are you kidding? I haven't the
   faintest idea.

Jeff Goldblum, the actor, used to agonize over whether to wear the red tie or
the blue one. Eventually, he gained enough self-confidence so that "today, instead of making twelve phone calls before he decides, he just goes and puts
one on." So reports his younger sister, Pamela. She also recalls that as a child
Jeff "liked to finish the last of the cereal, just so he could throw the box away.
It gave him a sense of accomplishment." So we learn in a personality article
in *Cosmopolitan* (by Jack Curry, May 1987). From other personality articles, we
learn a range of tidbits, such as Donna Rice falling on her head in a tumbling
routine and therefore losing an opportunity to be Miss Teenage South
Carolina (James Grant, *Life*, July 1987) or Don Johnson wandering into a room
on a riverboat one evening and hearing someone yell, "Hey, it's the guy from
Vice!" People scrambled to throw their illegal drugs out the window—they
thought he was a vice detective, not the star of the TV series, *Miami Vice* (Kurt
Loder, *Rolling Stone*, September 25, 1986).

These represent personality interviews wherein the journalist endeavors
to discover and report an aspect of someone's personal character, not only

report it but illustrate it by the kind of trivia described here. Show biz celebrities like Goldblum and Johnson—and even erstwhile celebrities like Donna Rice, who became deliciously notorious in 1987 as the woman who unwittingly helped to derail Senator Gary Hart's quest for the presidency—are the objects of intense public curiosity. Magazines and television in particular thrive on celebrities and hasten to provide a never-ending stream of celebrity profiles and sketches that typically include noteworthy details of personal trivia that help to define and illustrate character.

A former *Newsweek* editor, J. T. W. Hubbard, defines the content of the typical American magazine as consisting of four elements represented by the acronym SHIP. The letters stand for service, human interest, information, and personality. Hubbard defines personality as "little things about big people" and human interest as "big things about little people."

The distinction between personality and human interest might be considered a shade artificial today—surely personality can be captured within the unknowns who have achieved some noteworthy status worthy of media attention. And human interest tends to permeate all echelons of humanity, from unknowns to celebrities.

"So...tell me something interesting about one of your personalities."

Still, the media and the public both recognize these two elements of personality journalism. We enjoy knowing that the celebrities among us have many of the same ordinary traits and problems as the rest of us, and we equally enjoy learning that the ordinary among us are capable of remarkable insights, feats, and accomplishments.

Sometimes the bigger they are, the more we enjoy learning the ordinary things they do. One wintry day a neighbor saw Katharine Hepburn, then aged 75, shoveling snow from the sidewalk in front of her Manhattan apartment. James Brady recounted the incident in a personality sketch (*Parade*, November 15, 1987): "Miss Hepburn," the neighbor asked, "why are *you* shoveling the snow?" "Because it's on the ground," she replied. Although the incident may seem trivial in the extreme, it does dramatically characterize the gritty, independent woman that Hepburn has been throughout her life.

News media find it equally important to discuss the ordinary people who achieve extraordinary accomplishments. Sometimes survival is enough. Witness the world attention paid in 1987 to eighteen-month-old Jessica McClure who fell down a well casing in Midland, Texas. A plucky child, Jessica toughed it out for fifty-eight hours while rescuers dug a parallel shaft to reach her, and she survived to become a tiny heroine.

Most magazines devote a major portion of their content to people, big or little. One magazine, *People Weekly*, devotes all its space to people, blending the celebrities with the unknowns. The editorial formula has made *People Weekly* one of the most successful magazine start-ups in the history of magazines. It became financially successful within eighteen months of its birth, and in 1987 it won a National Magazine Award for excellence. And newspapers, meanwhile, have developed "people" or "lifestyle" sections that work to accomplish similar features.

The journalistic interviews behind personality stories clearly vary between the two types. One veteran interviewer observes that the little people often offer bigger rewards. Author-interviewer Studs Terkel (1974) says his tape recorder "can be used to capture the voice of a celebrity, whose answers are ever ready and flow through all the expected straits. I have yet to be astonished by one. It can be used to capture the thoughts of the noncelebrated—on the steps of a public housing project, in a frame bungalow, in a furnished apartment, in a parked car. . . . I am constantly astonished."

Not all personality stories depict honorable people. If it's important to learn what makes Sally Celebrity tick, it's equally important to understand the villainous character, from shady politicians to murderers and child molesters.

Personality interviews, then, find their way into just about every medium, ranging from book-length biographies to short sketches. Often magazines, newspapers, and broadcast documentaries will illustrate a major topic by focusing on a person in much the same way a novel focuses on a protagonist. You show poverty more dramatically by focusing on a single impoverished family than by having it discussed abstractly by well-fed bureaucrats, social workers, and academics. Simply put, *personification* attracts larger audiences and thus has more social impact than abstraction.

USES FOR THE PERSONALITY INTERVIEW

As long as you are talking with real people, every interview is a personality interview. Television, in particular, turns every respondent into a personality, no matter what the topic under discussion. Personality cannot help but show through; the audience sees for itself the personality in action, absorbing a torrent of nonverbal messages. When you see the gloomy athletic coach after the team lost the pennant, you really don't need to hear the answer to the inevitable question, "How do you *feel* about. . . ? " These are but fleeting glimpses of personality, but in time the glimpses coalesce into our perceptions of personal characteristics. So it is that the American public forms impressions of the charismatic John F. Kennedy, the ingenuous Jimmy Carter, the smooth-talking Ronald Reagan. This is television's greatest strength in the interviewing arena, but it may also be its greatest weakness, because often the personality detracts from the issues. Or, worse, the personality *is* the issue. And, to be sure, television doesn't always explain why—that is, ferret out the circumstances and life's experiences that create the image you see on the screen.

In print the projection of personality is more difficult. It depends largely on the writer's ability to capture on paper the personality traits that come through so clearly on the screen. Yet print has the advantage of a wider variety of presentations, at greater length and detail, and, not least, it has the ability to focus sharply on the characteristics of greatest interest to specialty audiences. In the specialized magazine field, for example, your personality interview of a famous woman may focus only on feminist issues for *Ms.*, on management issues for *Savvy*, or on outdoor issues for *Sierra*. Only the book-length biography allows room for all of these.

Indeed, the range of print uses for the personality interview is broad. Here, briefly, are some typical types.

1. Q-A Dialogue. Examples can be found in magazines such as *U.S. News* or *Playboy*.

2. Sidebars and Sketches. Both magazines and newspapers often give glimpses of people involved in whatever topic is under discussion. If the topic is safety around busy airports, an interview with an air traffic controller—presented in a short article alongside the main one—makes the problem more personal and dramatic.

3. Thematic Interviews.   The interview and the resultant article focus on a single issue or theme rather than using the everything-you-wanted-to-know approach. The latter approach is too thin and amorphous—and dull. Interview in detail on a narrowly defined topic and you'll better serve your readers. So you interview Sally Celebrity on a single, narrow, deep topic, such as, "How the adversities and traumas in your life have made you a better, more resilient person." The answers, examples, and anecdotal illustrations show the personality even in this narrow context.

4. Case Histories.   Sometimes the interview becomes so narrow and thematic that it focuses on a single incident or series of incidents. The personality emerges through the dramatic illustration of the activities described. "Can This Marriage Be Saved?", a long-running feature in the *Ladies' Home Journal*, stands as a case in point. We learn much about the personal character of the couple through the detailed discussion of their marital discord.

5. The Profile.   The *New Yorker* pioneered the profile in the 1920s. Its writers, not content merely to record the words of a celebrity, elected to write personality portrayals based on extensive research, including wide-ranging interviews. The interviews include not only the celebrity, but also family members, friends, enemies, business associates, subordinates—anyone who could add insight or anecdotal detail. The result is more comprehensive and more believable. It includes the dark side of the person's character, thus delivering a more honest and believable portrait. With so many diverse views available, the writer will probably discover the hidden nuances of personality. You can therefore write more candidly under the guiding philosophy of Andre Malraux, who once said that the truth about a person lies first and foremost in what the person hides. Most profiles contain, overtly or implicitly, a thematic statement: a notion of a central characteristic about the person. She's spurred on by ruthless ambition . . . . He's so insecure that he must dominate the lives of those around him . . . . Publicly she's a happy-go-lucky clown, but privately she's a melancholy person—and so on. Admittedly, such themes can be simplistic, particularly in the hands of an inexperienced writer. Sometimes the writer simply shows the person in action, leaving conclusions to be drawn by the readers. Even so, the writer cannot help but make subjective judgments through the selection of material to be included or excluded.

PROBLEMS OF COPING WITH PERSONALITY

If the personality interview were seeking only the routine facts of a person's life—date of birth, college degrees, career history, habits and hobbies—it would be simple indeed. But for the full-blown personality story you are seeking two aspects beyond the routine.

First, you must try to understand what the person is like: the essential character. Where did Ms. Celebrity come from, where is she now, and where is she going? What factors have influenced her life? This aspect would be simple enough if concrete answers were available. They aren't. And you won't gain much by asking Sally. She just lives her life, a life composed of thousands of odd-shaped fragments like a gigantic jigsaw puzzle. They defy any artistic or journalistic endeavor to piece them together.

And Sally Celebrity is as confused as anyone. You may be the first person to inquire of such things. You then become involved in an exchange of ideas that may lead to some joint conclusions. Or they may lead nowhere in particular. Celebrities, particularly, have built such complex self-facades that one observer finds them almost hopeless. Explains Thomas B. Morgan (1965) in the introduction to his book, *Self–Creations: 13 Impersonalities*, "Most better-known people tend toward an elegant solution of what they, or their advisers, call 'the image problem.' Over time, deliberately, they create a public self for the likes of me to interview, observe, and double-check." Morgan describes the archetype as Brigitte Bardot. "The existential focus of her self-creation was the exercise of power over men." She demonstrated that power by inviting Morgan to come to France to interview her. She broke an appointment and kept him waiting for a week before she suddenly and precipitously agreed to the interview.

The complexities of writing about people are perhaps best summarized by the late French novelist and biographer, Andre Maurois: "Except in those rare cases in which [the biographer] is writing the history of a man whose life happens to have constructed itself, he is obliged to take over a shapeless mass, made up of unequal fragments and prolonged in every direction by isolated groups of events which lead nowhere" (Whitman, 1970).

The second problem with the personality interview is one of illustrating character once you have assembled that shapless mass and established some order. This has been discussed earlier, notably in Chapter 10 on observation. Your writing comes out flat and lifeless unless you can portray the personality in action, a living, breathing, thinking, doing kind of human being.

Keen observation of the person in action, together with careful interviewing to obtain anecdotes, action narratives, and instances, will bring your personality to life and thus closer to your readers.

In essence, then, you are seeking to portray a personality in much the same manner as an actor plays a role. Any acting, according to one concept, the Stanislavsky method, must rest on a foundation of understanding of three aspects of character.

1. Who am I, and why am I here?
2. Where did I come from, and how did I get here?
3. Where am I going?

Your interview should seek not only to answer these questions, but to illustrate the answers.

CONDUCTING THE PERSONALITY INTERVIEW

Virtually everything said in this book is a part of the technique of the personality interview. Preparation? Of course—prepare the way Richard Meryman suggested in Chapter 8; study everything you can about your subject. Sharpen your mental and physical faculties. Listening? Yes, listen with the third ear, the one Theodor Reik recommends for analysts, "hearing not only what the patient speaks but also his own inner voices, what emerges from his unconscious depths." Observation? Of course. Look for everything that could be significant, particularly in a symbolic way. One writer of personality articles makes it a point to look for what the person considers humorous; the writer takes particular note of cartoons tacked on the office bulletin board. Another writer believes fantasies reveal character and so turns the interviews in that direction.

Purpose? This can be the most important of all. Without a keen sense of purpose, many personality interviews become mere shots in the dark—a few random questions, a quick search for some (usually hastily contrived) unifying theme along which to unravel the miscellaneous information collected.

In short, all the principles involved in interviewing take place in this ultimate of interviews, the one used to describe and illustrate personal character.

Here are some additional principles that seem particularly important to interviews designed to ascertain and assess personal characteristics.

1. Heed the Advice of Biographers. Find the dark side of the most honorable of characters and the bright side of the most despicable of characters.

2. Take Time. A full personality profile can seldom be assembled in limited time. Do not try to hustle along the biographical interview. Catherine Drinker Bowen (1959), in her *Adventures of a Biographer,* suggests that an interviewer is like a woman invited to waltz—"she must follow easily, no matter how intricate the side steps. A little tactful steering can put the conversation back on track, but there is no room for forcing or impatience."

3. Use Observation. Spend time with your subjects in typical events, even the small ones, such daily events as lunch or coffee or committee meetings or telephone conversations. Author Tom Wolfe (*The Right Stuff*) suggests "saturation reporting" as the key to good personality writing. "You have to constantly be on the alert for chance remarks, odd details, curios, anything that may serve to bring a scene alive when you're writing." (*ANPA Bulletin,* September 1970.)

4. Interview for Beginnings. Use them to trace a case history. When did the famous round-the-world sailor first take an interest in sailboats? When did the politician first awaken to the world of public affairs, the criminal commit the first small crime? People often tell charming anecdotes in response to such questions. This has been suggested earlier (as part of the goals-obstacles-solutions-start pattern, for example), but it is doubly important in personality interviewing. Like a fine novel or biography that begins even a generation or two ahead of the main character, your account of personality will benefit from attention to origins. To understand the child is to understand the adult. To understand how something started—particularly a personal situation such as a romance, a crisis, a new interest—is to obtain a sense of historical perspective and thus an insight into character. And, to belabor the obvious, the best storytelling begins with beginnings.

5. Interviews for Crossroads. As life continues, we all make decisions, big or little. Some of the major ones represent dramatic changes in our lives. So you look for crossroads. Did the notorious criminal have to make a decision whether to rob that first bank or not? Did the business executive have a difficult time deciding on a risky course of action, one that might endanger the company's future? What were the steps, the counterarguments, the sleepless nights—whatever—that led to the decision? Such a decision recounted in narrative detail can provide both suspense and character. No doubt other, similar cross points occurred, leading to similar decisions: to take a new direction in one's life, to take on a new responsibility. All are worth exploring. Even simple decisions can reveal character whenever they come to your attention: a decision to decline an invitation for a night on the town and to go home and read a book (or do the laundry).

6. Interview for Epiphanies. Out of experience comes learning. It cannot be otherwise, and so the personality interviewer seeks to discover the lesson whenever possible. Questions like, "What did you learn from losing your job (or failing the exam—whatever)?" often bring worthwhile insights that can be shared with your audience.

TWENTY PERSONALITY QUESTIONS

Most interviewers have favorite methods, special questions, for encouraging their subjects to speak candidly about themselves. Studs Terkel likes to ask, "When did the window open?" as a means of starting respondents off on a philosophical discussion of how they came to hold a certain set of beliefs. "Was there any one time, was there one teacher, one influence, or was it an accretion of events?" (Brian, 1973).

The example illustrates a truism about human nature: how people come to hold opinions and beliefs that guide their actions. They're not born with them, surely, and so the interviewer's task is to trace the beliefs back to their source. As Terkel suggests, the beliefs usually come in one of two ways—a sudden discovery, often resulting from an explosive or traumatic experience, or an accretion of events composed of tiny incidents that tend to form one's thinking—a little like building an ocean beach a grain of sand at a time.

To judge the impact of these questions, imagine answering them yourself. If you think you could deliver an interesting answer to any or all of them, then you can anticipate how another person might give similar answers.

One student who at first criticized such a list of "stock questions" as these as simplistic and boring confessed later that his interview with a fire chief was getting nowhere until he plugged in his first stock question: "Were you ever frightened in a fire?" Of course he was, many times, the chief responded, and he told several dramatic tales to illustrate just how scared he was, all to the delight (and surprise) of the interviewer.

So imagine yourself being asked these questions. What kinds of answers could you give?

1. What were the best times of your life (or of your involvement with any topic under discussion) and the worst?
2. What things, circumstances, and so on, make you angry? Sad? Happy? Frightened?
3. What makes you laugh? What makes you cry?
4. What were the major events of your childhood? What childhood experiences can you cite to explain what you are today—your successes, failures, your beliefs, opinions, your personality, your character?
5. What are your best character traits?
6. What are your worst faults? Make a list. (I used to hesitate to ask that question, but have come to see it as an entry into the negative side of any person I'm interviewing. I'm astonished at how often it's answered with devastating candor. I learned that you should never apologize for such a question.)
7. What kinds of material goods do you surround yourself with? What meaning can you attach to them? If your house caught on fire, what would you try to save? (Questions we use to good effect in classrooms and workshops; the material possessions cited by respondents range from tattered sets of ancient love letters to expensive stereos and computers.)
8. What do you read? Books on your shelf, magazines. These can be observed or asked about in the interview, with particular attention to favorite authors, books, quotable writing, and so forth.
9. Who are your heroes, your "ten most admired people" and why?
10. What are your major goals and problems, both professionally and personally, and what are you doing about them?
11. What kinds of people do you surround yourself with—from your spouse or significant others to friends, colleagues, subordinates?
12. Where and how do you spend leisure time?
13. What issues, concepts, philosophies really matter to you, both personally and professionally? What would you fight for, die for? Why? What actions will you (or did you) take to support what you believe?

14. What's a typical day like for you?
15. What do you dream or fantasize about?
16. How do you react to common problems? If somebody insults you, do you fight back, ignore it, or what? How do you behave at a party where you know no one? What if somebody pushes ahead of you in the cafeteria line?
17. What have been significant mileposts in your life? (Often interesting happenings emerge from such a question, such as a casual conversation with someone whose remarks were so inspirational as to change your life. The usual response covers such events as marriage, divorce, changes of location and employment, following a new vocational or avocational interest, and so on.)
18. What do you regret in your life; what are you proudest of?
19. If you could erect a billboard to explain the essence of your character, what would it say?
20. How would you like to be remembered?

THE QUINTESSENTIAL INTERVIEWER

And that brings us to the final point of this work. How should the interviewer be remembered? If you erected a billboard to pinpoint the essential character of the good interviewer, what would it say?

Some research evidence suggests that the essential traits of the good interviewer are warm, supportive, nonjudgmental, understanding, tolerant. One study found the personality characteristics of the good interviewer to be similar to those of ministers and accountants—and least like those of doctors and managers. That makes a certain sense—ministers represent tolerance and understanding, accountants represent precision and detail, whereas doctors and managers represent authoritarian characteristics. Another study suggested that respondents sometimes had trouble even remembering the persons who had interviewed them weeks or months earlier. That study pertained to survey interviews, however; only the most jaded of respondents would forget the essential character of the journalistic interviewer, largely for the reasons described in an earlier chapter: being interviewed is a novel and worthy experience for most Americans. A good journalistic interview can be a memorable experience, indeed, from the perspective of both interviewer and respondent.

A reporter once secured an interview with a notoriously closed-mouthed police officer, a woman who—for this interview at least—spoke with unusual candor about herself and her job. The reporter's colleagues referred admiringly to the interview story in the Sunday paper.

"How did you get her to open up like that?" they asked.

The reporter couldn't explain. She had seemed quite open in the interview. Curious, he visited the officer and recounted what his colleagues had said. How come, he asked, you talked with me when you won't talk to others?

"That's not hard to explain," she replied. "I think I'm a pretty good judge of character. It took me approximately one minute into the conversation to decide that you were sincere. After that, it didn't matter what you asked; I'd try to answer whatever you wanted to know."

As for the others, she said, she detests reporters who pop their heads briefly into her office and ask, "What's new?" and, hearing nothing startling in response, exit promptly.

Having thus separated the sincere from the insincere, the listeners from the nonlisteners, she may well have captured the spirit of creative interviewing.

Appendix A: Interviewing Exercises

Any class or workshop group using this book will find that the best learning comes from interviewing experience. This appendix contains ten practice interviews designed for classroom or workshop use. They are the best of the many practice exercises we have tried in fifteen years of teaching interviewing classes at the University of Oregon and in workshops in many parts of the United States and Canada.

The best experience comes after a class or workshop has been separated into interview pairs, and the interviewers are given an assignment to interview the respondents on a particular topic that can be covered in a few minutes. Such an interview is a useful experience in itself, but the best comes after the group reassembles to discuss the experience. The discussion leader should pose certain questions. Did the respondents have an enjoyable experience? (Yes! Definitely. They got an opportunity to be listened to, and they usually felt free to talk about themselves.) Was the purpose of the interview made clear to the respondent? (Usually not.) What did the respondent like best about the interview? (Usually the chance to talk about oneself.) Worst? (Usually uncertainty about the concept or purpose of the session.) Did the respondents learn anything that they will incorporate into their own interviews—or did they at least have some advice for the interviewers? (Yes—and the suggestions often covered nonverbal points, such as frowning too much or slouched body posture, taking notes too excessively, absence of eye contact.)

The practice interviews in this chapter usually work best in groups of up to twenty persons. Half the class will perform as interviewers, the other half as respondents. The interviews are brief, usually not more than ten or fifteen minutes. They are among the most successful ones developed in our interviewing seminars— "successful" in that they often turn up common interviewing faults in dramatic ways that students can easily perceive.

The sessions seem to work best under these five principles:

1. Interviews must be "real"—role playing should be held to a minimum. Students should not assume the role of governor or county sheriff because most students have had few experiences that would qualify them to think and talk like governors or sheriffs. Participants in these exercises should portray no one but themselves, and the questions should elicit information that is real, not hypothetical. However, exercises that call for respondents to be evasive or taciturn or even a little hostile seem to contain the seeds of good learning experiences. If the respondents are asked to answer questions briefly and not volunteer any information (a hard thing for most people to do, by the way), then interviewers are forced to rely more on their interviewing skills, rather than having information handed to them with little effort.

2. Presentation of an interview assignment must be done out of earshot of the respondents to avoid adulterating the interview. Similarly, any classroom preparation for the interview should be done with the respondents out of the classroom.

3. The classroom or workshop atmosphere for postinterview discussion must be psychologically safe for even the most timid students; caustic criticism and sarcasm must be discouraged. I've found college students remarkably good at treading the fine line between empty platitudes of praise on the one hand and hurtful or mean-spirited criticism on the other. The best students will try sincerely to be helpful, quick to praise, but careful to make constructive suggestions for improvement.

4. Each participant should fill out a personal background questionnaire to be made available to interviewers for preinterview preparation. Among the points to be covered:

   a. Name, address, age, hometown, occupation [if not a student].
   b. List favorite sports, hobbies, foods, beverages.
   c. Cite one or two especially interesting places you've visited.
   d. Cite your plans for the future.
   e. List one or two of your favorite *publishable* "fantasies" [college students usually respond candidly to this question, but older professionals tend to be more guarded].
   f. List a favorite childhood activity.
   g. Cite a frightening or embarrassing experience in your life.

h. List one or two topics about which you have specialized knowledge [e.g., expert knowledge of antique cars or ghost stories or fly fishing or the writings of Samuel Johnson].

i. Cite an interesting fact about yourself that few people know about.

j. Cite the best thing that ever happened to you.

This tiny questionnaire has a remarkable ability to elicit character-revealing facets about persons—facets often unknown to their best friends. This is especially true when responding to items e through j. Participants filling out such a questionnaire must be warned that the answers are in the "public domain," subject even to possible class discussion. And yet they continue to cite extraordinary aspects of their dreams, fantasies, and good and bad experiences to an astonishing degree. It's almost as though most people's true inner character lies just beneath the surface, waiting to be discovered.

5. A postinterview questionnaire should be prepared to permit each respondent to comment on the following points and perhaps offer suggestions for improvement. Each respondent's completed questionnaire goes directly to the interviewer.

a. Was the purpose of the interview made clear?

b. Were questions clearly and succinctly stated?

c. Were the questions relevant to the stated purpose?

d. Was the interviewer a good listener?

e. Was rapport good? (Did you feel comfortable answering the questions? Did you feel free to be honest and candid, or were you guarded in your answers?)

f. Did any personal or nonverbal mannerisms please or annoy you (such as eye contact, body posture, too much talking, interrupting, note taking).

g. What constructive suggestions can you offer for improvement of the interviewer's technique?

CLASSROOM OR WORKSHOP INTERVIEW EXERCISES

Exercise 1

Interviewers ask their respondents to enumerate the specific material possessions they surround themselves with and which they prize the most—clothes, trinkets, jewelry, computers, cars, back issues of *Cosmopolitan*, anything that helps to define character.

Purpose. Encourage interviewers to seek concrete details that help to characterize or define a personality.

Suggestions. This is among the more successful exercises we've used over the years, provided the interviewers are well briefed on what's expected. I usually put it in the context of a personality feature in which a writer seeks to develop a "flashby" paragraph that characterizes a person through the possessions. The paragraph would cite a characteristic and then support it by flashing a list of possessions. Thus: "Jane Doe says she loves to read mystery stories, and so her most prized possessions include the complete works of Arthur Conan Doyle, creator of Sherlock Holmes, along with thirty other volumes ranging from a book of Sherlock Holmes party games to a well-thumbed *Sherlock Holmes Cookbook* that tends to fall open to the page containing a recipe for a meat pie dish called Colonel Warburton's Madness...." The exercise offers interesting challenges on how to approach and explain the topic. In this, as in all exercises, the interviewer takes notes and writes a paragraph based on the interview, while the respondent fills out the postinterview questionnaire.

Exercise 2

Same as Exercise 1, except interviewer asks for "heroes": the kinds of people the respondent most admires and why. The list can contain anyone, including celebrities, living or dead, or lesser known persons such as friends, teachers, or relatives. An alternative is to ask for "least-admired persons." Or try a Barbara Walters zinger, such as "If you woke up in a hospital, whom would you like to have in the bed next to you—and why?"

Exercise 3

Solicit the expression of an opinion on a topic about which the respondent feels strongly in order to obtain lively, character-revealing quotations.

Purpose. Encourage interviewer to find ways to bring out a personality through quotes.

Suggestions. Prepare by using the background questionnaire for clues. Interviewer may experiment with provocative questions—or possibly silence. See Chapter 11 for further suggestions.

Exercise 4

Same as Exercise 3, except interviewer also attempts to find a specific instance or anecdote that further illustrates the strong opinion.

Purpose. Encourage development of skills in obtaining anecdotes.

Suggestion. See Chapter 11.

Exercise 5

Explore a topic that holds some sensitivity to the respondent, such as a frightening or embarrassing experience or a private fantasy.

Purpose.   Learn to cope with people's feelings.

Suggestions.   You have to play it by ear when dealing with sensitive issues. Start by referring to the respondent's background card described earlier. Most student respondents freely discuss such things or they wouldn't have listed them on the card. Warm rapport helps. See Chapter 13 on "sensitive questions."

Exercise 6

Explore with the respondent the "specialized knowledge" listed in the personal background card.

Purpose.   Interviewers are usually thrust into an area about which they have little knowledge, which forces them to ask background and filter questions to gain understanding.

Suggestions.   It looks more intimidating than it really is. Most respondents enjoy playing the role of teacher on a favorite topic, especially if they have a good "student."

GENERAL INTERVIEW ASSIGNMENTS

The more extensive interviews done outside the classroom or workshop offer greater challenges. Such interviews work better, however, if they are more than hypothetical. Purely hypothetical interviews tend to gain less than serious attention from both interviewer and respondent. So most of the ones done by our interviewing classes have a practical purpose wherein members of the class take on a legwork assignment for a comprehensive editorial project. For example, members of a class interviewed graduating seniors for a writer preparing a story on the difficulties of college graduates finding employment during a period of economic recession. Another time they interviewed businesswomen in the community for a newspaper feature. They interviewed professors about topics ranging from students' excuses for late papers to teaching methods of prize-winning teachers. They've conducted personality interviews to be placed in the biography file of a daily newspaper.

Each student conducting such an interview prepares a "file": semiorganized notes similar to those provided by magazine correspondents that are combined with other files for a roundup story. The file is not a finished story, just notes on specific details, facts, figures, quotes, instances, anecdotes. For an example of a student-produced file, see Appendix B.

Here are some standard ideas for extended interviews.

Exercise 7

Interview a working journalist on the ways in which he or she utilizes the interview. (Alternative: Interview other persons who regularly use interviews, such as a social worker, doctor, nurse, counselor, employment recruiter, police detective.)

Purpose. Students gain ideas about interviewing by learning how the professionals do it. The best files can be duplicated for distribution to the class, thus giving the assignment a useful purpose, which in turn will make it easier to arrange and conduct.

Exercise 8

Interview someone who has been interviewed recently by the media.

Purpose. Learn how it feels to *be* interviewed.

Suggestions. Locate a respondent by watching interview programs on TV or obtaining clippings from a local newspaper. This project, like the interview with interviewers, has a practical purpose: information can be shared with the entire class. Useful insights often emerge about how respondents feel about their interviews. The best papers, or excerpts from them, can be duplicated for the class. The class should strive for a wide range of respondents— from officials who often speak to the media to private citizens for whom a media interview is a once-in-a-lifetime experience.

Exercise 9

Interview someone about a past event, such as a senior citizen who participated in some major event—fought in World War II or Vietnam, perhaps, or survived a great flood or tornado.

Purpose. Develop techniques of memory stimulation; gain interviewing experience.

Suggestions. Once stimulated, most people love to talk about the past. Examine Studs Terkel's books, such as *Hard Times* (recollections of the 1930s depression) or *The Good War* (recollections of World War II).

Exercise 10

A see-it-in-action interview. Find a respondent who's willing to have the interviewer observe as the respondent does a task involving action. Examples:

A coach or athlete during a game, a judge or attorney during a courtroom session, an airport control tower operator, a police officer or police dispatcher, a lively classroom teacher.

Purpose.   To sharpen observation powers and writing techniques in narration and description.

Suggestions.   Select a respondent engaged in the kind of action where your presence is unlikely to interfere or change anything. You have to work in your questions as best you can, because often you cannot interrupt the action. Review Chapter 10 on observation.

MISCELLANEOUS EXERCISES

Lots of other exercises are possible— asking about interesting places visited, plans for the future, childhood events, or the areas of expertise listed in the background questionnaire. News-writing classes offer other possibilities. One useful exercise calls for dividing the class into interviewer-respondent pairs. Each respondent receives a mock police report to study and digest. Each interviewer must obtain information for a news account not by inspecting the report, but by asking questions. If respondents are instructed to be closed-mouthed public information officers—"give answers only to specific questions; volunteer nothing"—then interviewers must work harder and thus gain more from the effort.

Another interesting exercise is to have four or five members of the class form a "legislative council" empowered to make a decision, such as whether the instructor should give a midterm exam in place of a difficult writing assignment. The council completes its brief (five minutes or less) deliberations in private, but with a tape recorder running. When it has made a decision, the remaining students are instructed to get the story by interviewing separately one or more of the participants, asking for details of how the council arrived at its decision and who said what. After the students have written news stories about the decision, they listen to the tape. The disparity between the witness accounts gained through the interviews and the actual discussion as revealed by the tape can be dramatic. Reporters often find that what they obtained through interviews was a mere fragment of the total story. They sometimes learn that witnesses do not recall specific details accurately. A useful lesson thus emerges for all concerned, including members of the council.

Appendix B: Sample Interview Report

The interview report or "file" is essentially a set of semiorganized notes from the conversation. It includes a brief biographical sketch of the respondent along with the comments, quotations, and anecdotes that are the heart of the interview. The following report is a condensed version of a report done by a student in an interviewing class at the University of Oregon presenting notes from an interview with a local newspaper columnist.

Respondent: Don Bishoff, columnist, *Eugene Register-Guard*, Eugene, Oregon.

Interviewer: Hedda Hoiland

Topic of Interview: "The real world of newspaper journalism—with emphasis on interviewing technique"

Background: Age 51, he obtained both bachelor's and master's in journalism from Northwestern University, Evanston, Illinois. He worked for his hometown newspaper in Richmond, Virginia. At *The Eugene Register-Guard* he has worked a total of 28 years, 15 as a regular reporter, seven years as an editorial writer, and six as a columnist. His column is noted for its light-hearted, featurish approach to community topics, and Bishoff has a rule he tries to follow as he produces his column: "Don't be dull!"

How the Feature Writing Started

In the early 1960s when Don Bishoff first worked for the paper, his editor, Donn Bonham, suggested that Bishoff dress as a rabbit the night before Halloween, go trick-or-treating, and then write a story about the experience. Bishoff rented a huge bunny suit, borrowed a potato sack from a supermarket and set out on the expedition. A photographer went along.

At one house an elderly man came to the door. "I said 'trick-or-treat,' and he just said 'Whoosh,' shut the door, and turned out the lights," Bishoff says. "I just stood there while he flipped the light on and off, and I heard him say to his wife, 'There is a full-grown man out there dressed up as a rabbit.'"

The pair went on to another house where the woman opening the door screamed and slammed the door. "We could see her through the window running through her house and grabbing the telephone."

Bishoff recalls that the photographer got cold feet and said, "Hey, let's get out of here; she's calling the cops."

Bishoff suggested that they stay on and see what happened. Five minutes later two police officers arrived and asked what's going on.

"I explained that we were from *The Register-Guard*, and we were doing this feature story on Halloween. He asked for ID, so I got down inside the rabbit suit, got my wallet out, and the photographer got this great picture of a cop checking a rabbit's ID." Recounting the event a quarter-century later, Bishoff says, "I did anything in those days." He says he'd never have thought of anything like the rabbit adventure on his own; his editor, Bonham, came up with those off-the-wall feature ideas. But he decided he liked feature writing, and, triggered by Bonham's wild ideas, he did a lot of it.

"It's a real cliche to say, but I've always liked people; people intrigue me. I've said to others that this is the greatest continuing education job in the world. Every time I interview somebody about whatever it is that he or she is interested in, I come away a little more educated."

And because of his esoteric information, he always wins Trivial Pursuit games at home.

He approaches feature writing from "the tree falling in the forest" theory. If a tree falls and there is no one to hear it, is there any sound?

"It seems to me that an unread story is a tree falling in the forest. If nobody bothers to read it, it's all for naught. It is as if it never happened. So I try to make every story as interesting as possible."

On Getting Ideas for Columns

Bishoff claims he has trouble finding ideas for his column; most of them ᴄᵣ   ᶳ suggestions from readers, other staff members, and editors. Humor   urce of ideas he considers important.

         ᵻble to see how essentially absurd life is, and look for the absurdities.   ᵌ to laugh at life."

His former editor, Bonham, once gave him a $500 bill with instructions to visit small stores, buy something trivial, and try to pay for it with the $500 bill.

Bishoff went to a tiny grocery store, found a 35-cent cantaloupe and gave the grocer the $500 bill.

"He looked at me, and I watched him getting furious. 'Do you really think a lousy little market like this has got change for a $500 bill?' he hissed. 'Why don't you take this to the bank?'"

"But the bank doesn't sell cantaloupes," Bishoff recalled replying, beating a retreat without the cantaloupe.

"Just think of what's the most absurd thing you can think of and then just test the human reaction. One thing I lament today is that we take ourselves too seriously, and we don't do enough stories for the fun of it."

Among the absurdities, Bishoff frequently writes about all the red tape bureaucracies produce.

"Bureaucracies get too caught up in themselves and forget why they are there in the first place."

Impact of His Writing

Bishoff doubts that his columns carry much influence around the community. In his seven years as an editorial writer, he wrote constant items of advice about what the City Council should or should not do, and only once did the council follow that advice, he says.

"My batting average as a columnist isn't much better than that."

But once he wrote about a tavern located in Noti, a rural community west of Eugene. Visiting the tavern he saw a variety of signs—NO SHOES, NO SHIRTS, NO SERVICE, and by one big NO was scrawled in the word "Niggers." Elsewhere was a sign, "Viva Apartheid."

Bishoff's column describing the place led to the state labor commissioner filing charges against the owner for violation of the state's civil rights laws. The owner was fined $5,000, but by that time he had sold the tavern and disappeared. No one has seen him since, says Bishoff, but occasionally Bishoff receives a postcard addressed to Don Bishit. One showed a photo of a dart board with Bishoff's picture in the center, nailed with darts.

The column also resulted in additional ordinances by the county and influenced new school programs in the local schools to educate students about civil rights.

But that's the exception, Bishoff says. Mostly his column is to entertain.

On Writing

A good column is organized around three elements: A lead to entice the reader. Then give the reader some meat, some substance, upfront. Finally, give the reader a kicker at the end.

Young people interested in feature writing should become good news reporters first, he says. Learn your trade. "Feature writing is nothing but news writing with a twist, but first you have to learn how to deal with the facts."

Even news stories could benefit from feature treatment, he says, such as a *Time* magazine type of lead that captures anecdotally a dramatic moment in the news event and then presents the hard facts starting with the second or third paragraph.

Interviewing

Good quotes brighten up a story. "I'm a believer in letting people tell their own story," he says. When he wants to interview someone for a column, he always tries to put himself in that person's situation.

"I think about how I would feel if somebody from the newspaper called me and said, 'I want to write about you' and started asking me a bunch of questions. I think I'd get real paranoid."

So he tries to put people at ease by saying, "Look, just start from the beginning, and I'll walk you through it and ask you questions as we go along."

He also tries to end the interview with a question such as, "Is there anything we haven't talked about that you think I ought to know?" or "Is there an angle we haven't looked at?"

"Frequently people will come to think about something and sometimes that will produce the best stuff of the interview." He also tells respondents that if they have second thoughts or want to talk to him some more or come back to say something in a better way, they are welcome to give him a call or send him a note. "Not everybody can come up with a brilliant statement right off the bat."

Sometimes he has to interview people he strongly disagrees with. In most cases he will tell them so in the interview. If there is an element of hostility there, he will try to say to them, "Look, if you don't talk to me it will look worse than if you do. I want your full and best shot of explaining why you do it this way. We may agree or disagree if that was the right way."

He explains, "I'd like people to think that I'm fair, that I may end up disagreeing with them, but that I at least give them their shot in print to tell their side of an issue."

Sometimes he gets a suspicion that the respondent is lying. He will then phrase the question in two or three different ways to crosscheck what the person is saying. Then afterward he will doublecheck the information independently. If it turns out that the respondent hasn't been telling the truth, he'll call the person and confront him or her.

Bishoff usually uses a tape recorder for interviews. He worries about becoming TRD (tape recorder dependent), but he also takes good notes to avoid the kind of situation he found himself in one time—interviewing a political candidate using a recorder, only to discover later that he'd put the batteries in backwards. Bishoff calls the tape recorder the luxury of a columnist; a reporter fighting a deadline will not be able to use it for interviews.

For telephone interviews, Bishoff takes notes directly on his computer as the conversation is progressing. Before conducting any interview by phone, he writes down every conceivable question on his computer. He also has the opportunity to scroll back over them at the end of the interview.

The list of questions also helps him remember such key questions as the respondents' age and how they spell their names. Bishoff admits he has a terrible time getting names spelled right. A former city editor devised a system for him.

"When I finish writing, I make a double-spaced printout of my column, and I go through and circle every proper name and indicate above where I have doublechecked." It seems to have solved the problem. He no longer gets nasty notes from the copydesk. He suggests it as a procedure that journalism students would find useful.

Bishoff says he feels comfortable using the telephone for interviews. This may be so because he worked for City News Bureau of Chicago in his graduate year at Northwestern University. The bureau was a small one, owned by the four Chicago papers published at the time. The bureau then handled only police news. Four reporters had to cover the entire city. They would go to the main police stations and use the phone to reach the precincts. They were given $1.50 worth of dimes at a time when phone calls were 10 cents.

"The first trick was to get the desk sergeant to let you use the extra phones there so that you didn't have to use this pitiful handful of dimes," Bishoff says.

Having to approach people on the phone doesn't come naturally to everyone, he says; "I was almost apologetic about being a reporter and having to bother the people I called." But because everything had to be done by phone, the inhibitions soon disappeared.

They disappeared to such an extent that Bishoff recounts a shady spot in his past. During his time at the City News Bureau, he said, it was strongly rumored that everybody hated reporters and that no one would talk to them. Therefore reporters would seldom identify themselves as such but would take on false identities such as officials or police officers.

"My standard identity was 'Officer Fischer from the 35th Precinct.'"

He would call up crime victims to get details for his "police report."

"One time I was calling this crime victim, talking to her on the phone and I heard the doorbell ring in the background. I heard some conversation, and then a man's voice came on the phone and said, 'Who is this?' I said, 'This is Officer Fischer from the 35th Precinct,' and he said, 'This is Officer Sloan from the 35th Precinct—and we don't *have* any Officer Fischer.' I quickly hung up the phone.

"I think we knew at the time that it was totally unethical, but we were convinced by the people who preceded us that this was the only way. It was sort of tacitly approved by our bosses. Their only concern was to get the story.

Today I'd never do anything like that, and I work for a newspaper that would instantly fire anyone who tried."

But Bishoff calls the Chicago experience "the greatest experience in the world, although I hated every minute of it at the time."

Bibliography

ABEL, FRIEDERICH E. "Note-Takers vs. Non-Note-Takers: Who Makes More Errors?" *Journalism Quarterly* 46 (1969): 811-14.

ADLER, RONALD B., LAWRENCE B. ROSENFELD, AND NEIL TOWNE. *Interplay: The Process of Interpersonal Communication.* New York: Holt, Rinehart and Winston, 1980.

ANDERSON, ELIJAH. *A Place on the Corner.* Chicago: University of Chicago Press, 1978.

ANDERSON, NELS. *The Hobo: The Society of the Homeless Man.* Chicago: University of Chicago Press, 1923.

BABBIE, EARL. *The Practice of Social Research.* 4th ed. Belmont, Calif.: Wadsworth, 1986.

BAHRICK, H. P., P. O. BAHRICK, AND R. P. WITTLINGER. "Fifty Years of Memory for Names and Faces: A Cross-Sectional Approach." *Journal of Experimental Psychology* 104 (1975): 54-75.

BEIER, ERNST G. "Nonverbal Communication: How We Send Emotional Messages," *Psychology Today,* October 1974.

BELKNAP, NUEL D., AND THOMAS B. STEEL. *The Logic of Questions and Answers.* New Haven, Conn.: Yale University, 1975.

BELL, EDWARD PRICE. "The Interview." *Journalism Bulletin* 1 (1925): 13-18.

BENJAMIN, ALFRED D. *The Helping Interview,* 4th ed. Boston: Houghton Mifflin, 1987.

BERNER, R. THOMAS. "Literary Newswriting: The Death of an Oxymoron." *Journalism Monographs,* No. 99, October 1986.

BIAGI, SHIRLEY. *Interviews that Work.* Belmont, Calif.: Wadsworth, 1985.

_____. *NewsTalk I.* Belmont, Calif.: Wadsworth, 1987.

_____. *NewsTalk II.* Belmont, Calif.: Wadsworth, 1987.

BOWEN, CATHERINE DRINKER. *Adventures of a Biographer.* Boston: Little, Brown, 1959.

BRADY, JOHN. *The Craft of Interviewing.* Cincinnati: Writer's Digest, 1976.

BRENNER, MICHAEL, JENNIFER BROWN, AND DAVID CARTER. *The Research Interview: Uses and Approaches.* London: Academic Press, 1985.

BRIAN, DENIS. *Murderers and Other Friendly People*. New York: McGraw-Hill, 1973.

BRIGGS, CHARLES L. *Learning How to Ask*. New York: Cambridge University Press, 1986.

BROUGHTON, IRV. *The Art of Interviewing for Television, Radio and Film*. Blue Ridge, Penn.: TAB Books, 1981.

BUCKWALTER, ART. *Interviews and Interrogations*. Stoneham, Mass.: Butterworth, 1983.

CANNELL, CHARLES F. AND ROBERT L. KAHN. "Interviewing." In *Handbook of Social Psychology*. Edited by Gardner Lindzey and Elliott Aronson. 2d ed., vol. 2. Reading, Mass.: Addison-Wesley, 1968.

CARNEGIE, DALE. *How to Win Friends and Influence People*. New York: Simon and Schuster, 1936.

CLARK, ROY PETER, ed. *Best Newspaper Writing 1984*. St. Petersburg, Fla.: Poynter Institute for Media Studies, 1984.

CORMIER, WILLIAM H. AND L. SHERILYN CORMIER. *Interviewing Strategies for Helpers*. 2d ed. Monterey, Calif.: Brooks-Cole, 1985.

DILLON, JAMES T. "Questioning." In Hargie, Owen, ed., *A Handbook of Communication Skills*. London: Croom Helm, 1986.

DONALDSON, SAM. *Hold On, Mr. President!* New York: Random House, 1987.

DORFMAN, RON, AND HARRY FULLER JR., eds. *Reporting/Writing/Editing*. Dubuque, Iowa: Kendall-Hunt, 1982.

DOWLING, COLETTE. *The Cinderella Complex: Women's Hidden Fear of Independence*. New York: Summit Books, 1981.

DOWNS, CAL W., G. PAUL SMEYAK, AND ERNEST MARTIN. *Professional Interviewing*. New York: Harper & Row, 1980.

EPSTEIN, LAURA. *Talking and Listening*. St. Louis: Times Mirror/Mosby College, 1985.

FRANKLIN, JON. *Writing for Story*. New York: Atheneum, 1986.

FRIEDMAN, HOWARD S. "The Modification of Word Meaning by Nonverbal Cues." In Key, Mary Ritchie, ed. *Nonverbal Communication Today: Current Research*. Berlin: Moulton, 1982.

GARRETT, ANNETTE. *Interviewing: Its Principles and Methods*. 3d ed. revised by Margaret M. Mangold and Elinor P. Zaki. New York: Family Service Association, 1982.

GETZELS, J.W., "The Question-Answer Process." *Public Opinion Quarterly*, 18 (1954), pp. 80-91.

GEYER, GEORGIE ANNE. "Securing the Elusive Interview—Geyer Tells How She Does It." *Editor & Publisher*, Feb. 12, 1979, p. 28.

GILLELAND, LARUE W. "Gilleland's GOSS Formula." *Journalism Educator* 26 (1971): 1920. See also *Editor & Publisher*, Sept. 18, 1971, p. 54.

GIVEN, JOHN L. *Making a Newspaper*. New York: Henry Holt, 1907.

GOLDSTEIN, TOM. *The News At Any Cost*. New York: Simon & Schuster, 1985.

GORDEN, RAYMOND L. *Interviewing Strategy: Techniques and Tactics*. 4th ed. Chicago: Dorsey, 1987.

GOTTLIEB, MARVIN. *Interview*. New York: Longman, 1986.

GRAESSER, ARTHUR, AND JOHN BLACK, eds. *The Psychology of Questions*. Hillsdale, N.J.: Erlbaum, 1985.

HALL, EDWARD T. *The Silent Language*. Garden City, N.Y.: Doubleday, 1959.

_____. *The Hidden Dimension*. Garden City, N.Y.: Doubleday, 1966.

HARGIE, OWEN, ed., *A Handbook of Comunication Skills*. London: Croom Helm, 1986.

HARPER, ROBERT G., ARTHUR N. WIENS, AND JOSEPH D. MATARAZZO. *Nonverbal Communication: The State of the Art*. New York: Wiley, 1978.

HARRAGAN, BETTY LEHAN. *Games Mother Never Taught You: Corporate Gamesmanship for Women*. New York: Rawson, 1977.

_____. *Knowing the Score: Play-by-Play Directions for Women on the Job*. New York: St. Martin's, 1983.

HARRISON, RANDALL P. *Beyond Words: An Introduction to Nonverbal Communication*. Englewood Cliffs, N.J.: Prentice-Hall, 1974.

HENNIG, MARGARET, AND ANNE JARDIM. *The Managerial Woman*. Garden City, N.Y.: Doubleday, 1977.

HENTOFF, NAT, ET AL. "The Art of the Interview." *(More)*, July 1975, p. 11.

HILTON, JACK, AND MARY KNOBLAUCH. *On Television! A Survival Guide for Media Interviews*. New York: Amacon, 1980.

HIRSCH, ROBERT O. *Listening: A Way to Process Information Aurally.* Dubuque, Iowa: Gorsuch Scarisbrick, 1979.

HOGARTH, ROBIN M., ed. *Question Framing and Response Consistency.* San Francisco, Jossey-Bass, 1982.

HOHENBERG, JOHN. *The Professional Journalist.* 4th ed. New York: Holt, Rinehart and Winston, 1978.

HUBBARD, J.T.W. *Magazine Editing.* Englewood Cliffs, N.J.: Prentice-Hall, 1982.

HUNT, GARY T., AND WILLIAM F. EADIE. *Interviewing.* New York: Holt, Rinehart and Winston, 1987.

INBAU, FRED E., AND JOHN E. REID. *Criminal Interrogation and Confessions.* 4th ed. Baltimore: Williams & Wilkins, 1986.

KAHN, ROBERT L., AND CHARLES F. CANNELL. *The Dynamics of Interviewing: Theory, Technique and Cases.* Malabor, Fla.: Krieger, 1979 (reprint from 1957).

KAISER, ARTUR. *Questioning Techniques.* San Bernardino, Calif.: Borge Press, 1985.

KEIR, GERRY, MAXWELL MCCOMBS, AND DONALD L. SHAW. *Advanced Reporting.* New York: Longman, 1986.

KESSLER, LAUREN, AND DUNCAN MCDONALD. *Uncovering the News: A Journalist's Search for Information.* Belmont, Calif.: Wadsworth, 1987.

KESTLER, JEFFREY L. *Questioning Techniques and Tactics.* Colorado Springs: Shepard/McGraw-Hill, 1983.

KINSEY, ALFRED C., WARDELL B. POMEROY, AND CLYDE E. MARTIN. *Sexual Behavior in the Human Male.* Philadelphia: W. B. Saunders, 1948. See Chapter 2, "Interviewing." Also see Kinsey, et al., *Sexual Behavior in the Human Female*, 1953, Chapter 3, "Sources of Data."

KLICK, R. E., AND W. NUESSEL. "Congruence Between the Indicative and Communicative Functions of Eye Contact in Interpersonal Relations." *British Journal of Social and Clinical Psychology* 7 (1968): 241-246.

KNAPP, MARK L. *Nonverbal Communication in Human Interaction.* 2d ed. New York: Holt, Rinehart and Winston, 1978.

_____. *Essentials of Nonverbal Communication.* New York: Holt, Rinehart and Winston, 1980.

_____. *Interpersonal Communication and Human Relations.* Boston: Allyn and Bacon, 1984.

KRIVONOS, P., AND MARK KNAPP. "Initiating Communication: What Do You Say When You Say Hello?" *Journal of Communication*, Vol. 25, 1975.

LAINE, MARGARET. "Broadcast Interviewing Handbook." Unpublished research paper, School of Journalism, University of Oregon, 1976.

LEE, IRVING J. *How to Talk with People.* New York: Harper & Brothers, 1952.

LIEBLING, A.J. "Goodbye M.B.I." *New Yorker*, 7 February 1948, p. 54.

_____. *The Most of A.J. Liebling.* New York: Simon & Schuster, 1963.

LIPPMANN, WALTER. *Public Opinion.* New York: Macmillan, 1922.

LOFTUS, ELIZABETH F., AND JAMES M. DOYLE. *Eyewitness Testimony.* New York: Kluwer Law Books, 1987.

LONG, LYNETTE, LOUIS PARIDISE, AND THOMAS LONG. *Questioning: Skills for the Helping Process.* Monterey, Calif.: Brooks-Cole, 1981.

LUNDEN, JOAN, AND ARDY FRIEDBERG. *Good Morning, I'm Joan Lunden.* New York: Putnam's, 1986.

MADGE, JOHN. *The Tools of Social Science.* New York: Garland, 1985 (reprint from 1953).

MAGEE, BRYAN. *The Television Interviewer.* London: MacDonald, 1966.

MALANDRO, LORETTA, AND LARRY BARKER. *Nonverbal Communication.* Reading, Mass.: Addison-Wesley, 1983.

MARCOSSON, ISAAC F.. *Adventures in Interviewing.* New York: AMS Press, 1971 (reprint from 1919).

MAYBERRY, D. L. *Tell Me About Yourself: How to Interview Anyone From Your Friends to Famous People.* Minneapolis: Lerner 1985.

MEAD, MARGARET. *Coming of Age in Samoa.* New York: Penguin (reprint from 1928).

MEDLEY, H. ANTHONY. *Sweaty Palms: The Neglected Art of Being Interviewed.* Berkeley: Ten Speed Press, 1984.

MEHRABIAN, ALBERT. *Nonverbal Communication.* Chicago: Aldine-Atherton, 1972.

_____. *Silent Messages.* 2d ed. Belmont, Calif.: Wadsworth, 1981.

METZLER, KEN. *Newsgathering.* 2d ed. Englewood Cliffs, N.J.: Prentice-Hall, 1986.

MIDDLETON, KENT R. "Journalists and Tape Recorders." 2 *COMM/ENT* 287 (1979).

MISCHLER, ELLIOT. *Research Interviewing*. Cambridge: Harvard University Press, 1986.

MORGAN, THOMAS B. *Self-Creations: 13 Impersonalities*. New York: Holt, Rinehart and Winston, 1965.

MOORE, WILLIAM T. *Dateline Chicago*. New York: Taplinger, 1973.

MORRISON, ANN M., RANDALL P. WHITE, AND ELLEN VAN VELSOR. *Breaking the Glass Ceiling: Can women reach the top of America's largest corporations?* Reading, Mass.: Addison, Wesley, 1987.

NICHOLS, RALPH G., AND LEONARD A. STEVENS. *Are You Listening?* New York: McGraw-Hill, 1957.

PATTEN, JIM. *The Journalistic Interview: A guide for the reporter*. Lincoln: University of Nebraska, 1976.

PAYNE, STANLEY L. *The Art of Asking Questions*. Princeton, N.J.: Princeton University Press, 1980 (reprint from 1951).

RANKIN, PAUL T. "The Measurement of the Ability to Understand Spoken Language." Unpublished Ph.D. dissertation, Univeristy of Michigan, 1926.

REIK, THEODOR. *The Compulsion to Confess*. New York: Farrar, Straus and Cudahy, 1959.

_____. *Listening With the Third Ear*. New York: Farrar, Straus, 1952.

RICE, STUART A. "Contagious Bias in the Interview." *American Journal of Sociology* 35 (1929): 420-23.

ROGERS, CARL R., AND F. J. ROETHLISBERGER. "Barriers and Gateways to Communication." *Harvard Business Review*, July-August 1952, p. 46.

ROGERS, CARL R. *Counseling and Psychotherapy*. Boston: Houghton Mifflin, 1942.

_____. *Client-Centered Therapy*. Boston: Houghton Mifflin, 1951.

_____. *A Way of Being*. Boston: Houghton Mifflin, 1980.

ROSHCO, BERNARD. *Newsmaking*. Chicago: University of Chicago Press, 1975.

ROYAL, ROBERT. F., AND STEVEN. R. SCHUTT. *The Gentle Art of Interviewing and Interrogation*. Englewood Cliffs, N.J.: Prentice-Hall, 1976.

SCANLAN, CHRISTOPHER, ed. *How I Wrote the Story*. 2d ed. Providence, R.I.: The Providence Journal, 1986.

SIGAL, LEON V. *Reporters and Officials: The Organization and Politics of Newsmaking*. Lexington, Mass.: Heath, 1973.

SINCOFF, MICHAEL Z., AND ROBERT S. GOYER. *Interviewing*. New York: Macmillan, 1984.

SLAVENS, THOMAS P. , ed. *Informational Interviews and Questions*. Metuchen, N.J.: Scarecrow Press, 1978.

SPRADLEY, JAMES P. *The Ethnographic Interview*. New York: Harper and Row, 1979.

_____. *Participant Observation*. New York: Holt, Rinehart and Winston, 1980.

STEIL, L., L. BARKER, AND K. WATSON. *Effective Listening*. Reading, Mass.: Addison-Wesley, 1983.

STEMPEL, GUIDO H. III, AND BRUCE H. WESTLEY, eds. *Research Methods in Mass Communications*. Englewood Cliffs, N.J.: Prentice-Hall, 1981.

STEWART, CHARLES J., AND WILLIAM B. CASH. *Interviewing Principles and Practices*. 3d ed. Dubuque, Iowa: Wm. C. Brown, 1982.

SUDMAN, SEYMOUR AND NORMAN M. BRADBURN. *Asking Questions*. San Francisco: Jossey-Bass, 1982.

TERKEL, STUDS. *Division Street: America*. New York: Pantheon, 1967.

_____. *Working*. New York: Pantheon, 1974.

TOLOR, ALEXANDER, ed. *Effective Interviewing*. Springfield, Ill.: Charles C. Thomas, 1985.

TYRRELL, ROBERT. *The Work of the Television Journalist*. New York: Hastings House, 1972.

VARGAS, MARJORIE FINK. *Louder Than Words: An introduction to nonverbal communication*. Ames: Iowa State University Press, 1986.

WALLACE, MIKE, AND GARY PAUL GATES. *Close Encounters*. New York, Morrow, 1984.

WAX, ROSALIE H. *Doing Fieldwork* Chicago: University of Chicago Press, 1971.

WEAVER, CARL H. *Human Listening: Process and Behavior*. Indianapolis: Bobbs-Merrill, 1972.

WEBB, EUGENE J., AND JERRY R. SALANCIK. *The Interview, or The Only Wheel in Town*. Journalism Monograph No. 2. Columbia, S.C.: Association for Education in Journalism and Mass Communication, 1966.

WEBB, EUGENE J., DONALD T. CAMPBELL, RICHARD D. SCHWARTZ, LEE SECHREST, AND JANET BELEW GROVE. *Unobtrusive Measures*. Boston: Houghton-Mifflin, 1981.

WEISER, A. "How Not to Answer a Question." In R. E. Grossman, L. J. San, and T. J. Vance, eds. *Papers From the 11th Regional Meeting of the Chicago Linguistic Society*. Chicago: Chicago Linguistic Society, 1975.

WERNER, ELYSE K. "A Study of Communication Time." Unpublished master's thesis, University of Maryland, 1975.

WHITMAN, ALDEN. *The Obituary Book*. New York: Stein and Day, 1970.

WHYTE, WILLIAM FOOTE. *Street Corner Society*. Chicago: University of Chicago, 1943.

_____. *Learning from the Field*. Beverly Hills: Sage, 1984.

WICKS, ROBERT J., AND ERNEST H. JOSEPHS JR. *Techniques of Interviewing for Law Enforcement and Corrections Personnel*. Springfield, Ill.: C. Thomas, 1972.

WIEMANN, JOHN, AND RANDALL HARRISON, eds. *Nonverbal Interaction*. Beverly Hills, Calif.: Sage, 1983.

WINEBERG, STEVE. *Trade Secrets of Washington Journalists*. Washington: Acropolis, 1981.

WOLVIN, ANDREW D., AND CAROLYN G. COAKLEY. *Listening*. 2d ed. Dubuque, Iowa: Wm. C. Brown, 1985.

YOAKAM, RICHARD D., AND CHARLES F. CREMER. *ENG: Television News and the New Technology*. New York: Random House, 1985.

ZUNIN, LEONARD, AND NATALIE B. ZUNIN. *Contact: The First Four Minutes*. Los Angeles: Nash, 1972.

Index